The Rise and Fall of Swedish Social Democracy

The Rise and Fall of
Swedish Social Democracy

Kjell Östberg

VERSO

London • New York

First published by Verso 2024
© Kjell Östberg 2024

1 3 5 7 9 10 8 6 4 2

Verso
UK: 6 Meard Street, London W1F 0EG
US: 388 Atlantic Avenue, Brooklyn, NY 11217
versobooks.com

Verso is the imprint of New Left Books

ISBN-13: 978-1-80429-465-9
ISBN-13: 978-1-80429-466-6 (UK EBK)
ISBN-13: 978-1-80429-467-3 (US EBK)

British Library Cataloguing in Publication Data
A catalogue record for this book is available from the British Library

Library of Congress Cataloging-in-Publication Data
A catalog record for this book is available
from the Library of Congress

Typeset in Minion by Biblichor Ltd, Scotland
Printed and bound by CPI Group (UK) Ltd, Croydon CR0 4YY

For my colleagues and comrades in the research project the Labour Movement in the Baltic Sea Region (with the poetic Swedish acronym Arioso): Håkan Blomqvist, Lars Ekdahl, and Werner Schmidt

For twenty-five years we have continuously analysed, discussed, and quarrelled about the development of the labour movement, the unfulfilled promises of communism, the potentials of trade unions, the possibilities and limitations of reformism, and not least the roads ahead.

Contents

Introduction

Swedish Social Democracy occupies a special place in the political history of the twentieth century. The Swedish model has long stood as a successful model between the communist planned economy and free-market capitalism. Sweden has had a Social Democratic prime minister for more than seventy-five years over the last century. Sweden would be a paradise if only there were a little more sunshine, the bourgeois French president Georges Pompidou is reputed to have said.

But above all it is socialists of various stripes who have turned to Sweden as the country that has gone the furthest in terms of welfare, equality, social consensus and gender equality. The focus has been on the Social Democratic Party, whose strong organisation, dominant political position, capacity for ideological innovation, and not least ability to implement a programme for the strong welfare state have attracted attention and often admiration. The ideologue and minister of finance Ernst Wigforss, the social engineers Alva and Gunnar Myrdal, the trade union economist Rudolf Meidner, and the politician Olof Palme all symbolised, each in their own way, a Social Democracy that appeared a little more radical than others.

Recently, a new generation of commentators has returned to the classic Swedish Social Democracy and its conquests. The reforms carried out in Sweden in the 1960s and '70s were more successful than one could have imagined, writes Bhaskar Sunkara in *The Socialist Manifesto*. Sweden was not only the most decent country ever; it was also the country in postwar Europe where the socialists undermined the power of capital the best.[1] Young people participating in Bernie Sanders's election campaigns or supporting Jeremy Corbyn's attempts to push the Labour Party to the left could see Swedish Social Democracy during its golden years as an example to be inspired by or to imitate.

---

1   Bhaskar Sunkara, *The Socialist Manifesto: The Case for Radical Politics in an Era of Extreme Inequality* (London: Verso, 2019).

This view has long been shared by leading scholars, too.

On the party's centenary in 1989, the anthology *Socialdemokratins samhälle. SAP och Sverige under 100 år (Creating Social Democracy: A Century of the Social Democratic Labour Party)* was published.[2] The book features several outstanding international and national scholars of the time – Gøsta Esping-Andersen, Tim Tilton, and Göran Therborn, to name just a few – and focuses on Swedish Social Democracy. The book can be said to represent a kind of culmination of the admiration that Swedish Social Democracy has inspired even among established scholars.

The introduction adopts an almost panegyrical tone: 'When industrial society was facing a profound crisis at the beginning of the 1930s, the Social Democratic Labor Party won political power and also demonstrated its ability to use it. Today, with the focus on structural change in the economy, adaptation to European integration, and ecological problems, the party is still a leading political force in the country.'[3] No one doubts that the message here is that the party will use power successfully to solve the problems of the day; few of the articles suggest otherwise. It is obvious that many of the descriptions put forward are close to the view produced by Swedish Social Democracy itself.[4]

The articles also provide an excellent overview of the explanatory models that are still dominant when discussing the reasons for the special position of Swedish Social Democracy. One such model is about ideological strength. Tim Tilton argues that the party shows a striking ideological continuity with roots back to the party's first leader, Hjalmar Branting, in the late nineteenth century. Tilton highlights the basic ideological lines that he argues have guided the party's political practice: an inclusive democracy that should permeate not only political but also social and economic life; the vision of society as a 'people's home'; the role of equality; the quest for control over the market economy; and the construction of the strong society as a precondition

---

2   Klaus Misgeld, Karl Molin, and Klas Åmark, eds, *Socialdemokratins samhälle. SAP och Sverige under 100 år* (Stockholm: Tiden, 1989). Published in English as *Creating Social Democracy: A Century of the Social Democratic Labor Party in Sweden* (University Park: Pennsylvania State University Press, 1992).

3   Misgeld, Molin, and Åmark, *Creating Social Democracy*, p. xii.

4   Åsa Linderborg, *Socialdemokraterna skriver historia: historieskrivning som ideologisk maktresurs 1892–2000* (Stockholm: Atlas, 2001).

for people's freedom of choice. Tilton's favourite thinkers, like most others', are Ernst Wigforss and Nils Karleby.[5]

The discussion of the role of ideologies was long coloured by Herbert Tingsten's magisterial *The Swedish Social Democrats: Their Ideological Development*.[6] His conclusion was that the party abandoned its Marxist-founded social transformation ambitions early on, adopted a markedly reformist line in the early twentieth century, and later gradually de-ideologised itself. Tingsten's interpretation fitted well into the social-liberal consensus that characterised postwar Western societies. Tingsten himself was one of the most ardent supporters of theories of the death of ideologies. That interpretation came to be challenged in the shadow of 1960s radicalisation. The greatest impact came from the political scientist Leif Lewin's *Planhushållningsdebatten* (The debate on economic planning) in 1967, which vigorously advanced the thesis that when the Social Democrats abandoned their Marxist fate in the 1920s, they managed to formulate an alternative and ideologically coherent programme with links to both Marx and Keynes.[7] The theory of socialisation mainly by nationalisation had to give way to theories such as the role of the planned economy developing in a socialist direction, Lewin argued.

Gøsta Esping-Andersen has highlighted the importance of a decommodifying and universal welfare state with the capacity to transform society. By building a welfare state that is increasingly free from the influence of the market, the Social Democrats have created a tool with the potential to drive development in a socialist direction. It has also been able to combine comprehensive social reforms with policies that have promoted growth and increased productivity. In addition, the party's ability to build alliances between the working and middle classes has contributed to the hegemonic power of the Social Democrats.[8]

---

5   Tim Tilton, 'The Role of Ideology in Social Democratic Politics', in Misgeld, Molin, and Åmark, *Creating Social Democracy*. See also Tim Tilton, *The Political Theory of Swedish Social Democracy: Through the Welfare State to Socialism* (Oxford: Clarendon, 1990).

6   Herbert Tingsten, *The Swedish Social Democrats: Their Ideological Development* (Totowa, NJ: Bedminster, 1973). Originally published as *Den svenska socialdemokratins idéutveckling*, 2 vols (Stockholm: Aldus/Bonnier, 1967 [1941]).

7   Leif Lewin, *Planhushållningsdebatten* (Stockholm: Almqvist & Wiksell, 1967).

8   Gøsta Esping-Andersen, 'The Making of a Social Democratic Welfare State', in Misgeld, Molin, and Åmark, *Creating Social Democracy*. See also Gøsta Esping-Andersen, *Politics against Markets: The Social Democratic Road to Power* (Princeton, NJ: Princeton University Press, 1985); and Gøsta Esping-Andersen, *The Three Worlds of Welfare Capitalism* (Cambridge: Polity, 1990).

Göran Therborn points to the party's organisational strength, but he also claims that the party has been lucky on several occasions, for example with economic cycles or the divisions within the bourgeois parties. His conclusion is nevertheless that the party has earned its power through its own skill.[9]

Another scholar of great influence should be mentioned in this context, namely Walter Korpi. He points to the decisive importance of the power resources that the labour movement has been able to mobilise for the emergence of the Social Democratic welfare state. He highlights the strong and well-organised Swedish trade union movement and its close links with the Social Democratic Party.

Rising living standards, increased economic security, longer leisure time, rising educational attainment, and a less personalised relationship with employers – all of these have significantly increased workers' resources and mobilisation capabilities, as have high employment and policy reforms such as pensions and other kinds of social insurance.[10]

It is remarkable how the book's authors not only celebrate the successful first hundred years of Swedish Social Democracy, but also take a positive view of the party's prospects. Therborn captures the general tone: 'What this past will lead to in the future is uncertain. However, it gives the SAP a good start into its second century.'[11]

Such an anthology would have been impossible just a few years later (as reflected by an interesting word change in Therborn's article in the English edition published in 1992, in which the word 'gives' has been sensitively changed to 'gave').[12] The sharp turn and adaptation to neo-liberal thinking that Swedish Social Democracy had already begun when the book was published is strangely absent. However, when Sweden went through a deep economic crisis in the early 1990s, it became clear that the new course initiated in the early 1980s was not just a temporary aberration. The Social Democrats now embraced a monetarist economic policy in which the fight against inflation took precedence over the fight against unemployment, while politics was increasingly

---

9 Göran Therborn, 'A Unique Chapter in the History of Democracy: The Social Democrats in Sweden', in Misgeld, Molin, and Åmark, *Creating Social Democracy*.

10 Walter Korpi, *The Working Class in Welfare Capitalism: Work, Unions and Politics in Sweden* (London: Routledge & Kegan Paul, 1978); and Walter Korpi, *The Democratic Class Struggle* (London: Routledge & Kegan Paul, 1983).

11 Göran Therborn, 'Nation och klass, tur och skicklighet. Vägar till ständig (?) makt', in Misgeld, Molin, and Åmark, *Creating Social Democracy*, p. 368.

12 Therborn, 'A Unique Chapter in the History of Democracy', p. 30.

subordinated to the market and austerity policies undermined key elements of solidarity-based welfare policy.[13]

International research on Swedish Social Democracy has continued. Today's analyses are reflected in titles such as *The Limits of Social Democracy* or *Il socialismo davanti alla realtà*.[14] Scholars such as Jenny Andersson, Jonas Pontusson, and Magnus Ryner are instead discussing the consequences of the party's neoliberal orientation and the shift of power from politics to the market.[15] The Swedish Social Democracy of today no longer appears as a source of inspiration for the debate on the future of the international left.

But when it comes to analyses of the reasons for the success and special role of Swedish Social Democracy in the political history of the twentieth century, it is still largely the explanations formulated when the party's reputation was at its zenith that dominate. There is every reason to return to this generation of scholars, both to draw inspiration from them and to subject their conclusions to critical scrutiny.

But there is a fundamental weakness that recurs in most of these contributions. They seek explanations essentially related to the strength of the Social Democratic movement itself. As a result, they often tend to reproduce Social Democracy's own self-image. Explanations based on the party's relations with – and dependence on – other actors are thus toned down, or disappear altogether.

This is true for the influence of bourgeois forces, not least Swedish capitalism. I share Gerassimos Moschonas's view that capitalism has changed Social Democracy more than the other way around.[16] A main thesis of this book is that for a hundred years, Swedish Social Democracy has linked its destiny to the development of capitalism – not as the result of any ideological degeneration or class betrayal, but as a strategic choice.

---

13 See below, Chapter 8.

14 Jonas Pontusson, *The Limits of Social Democracy: Investment Politics in Sweden* (Ithaca, NY: Cornell University Press, 1992); Monica Quirico, *Il socialismo davanti alla realtà: il modello svedese (1990–2006)* (Rome: Editori Riuniti, 2007).

15 Jenny Andersson, *Between Growth and Security: Swedish Social Democracy from a Strong Society to a Third Way* (Manchester: Manchester University Press, 2006); and Jenny Andersson, *The Library and the Workshop: Social Democracy and Capitalism in the Knowledge Age* (Stanford, CA: Stanford University Press, 2009); J. Magnus Ryner, *Capitalist Restructuring, Globalisation and the Third Way: Lessons from the Swedish Model* (London: Routledge, 2002).

16 Gerassimos Moschonas, *In the Name of Social Democracy: The Great Transformation, 1945 to the Present* (London: Verso, 2002).

When, after the democratic breakthrough, the party definitely chose the parliamentary road and deferred its socialist ambitions to an indefinite future, the main task instead became to create the economic conditions for the reforms necessary for the welfare of working class. The new generation of leaders, who were not unfamiliar with economic theory, including its Marxist variant, concluded that there was only one way forward: to make the existing capitalist economy as effective as possible, and then fight to ensure that part of the surplus could be used to combat unemployment and implement social reforms. Economic growth and a rational and efficient industrial sector became the Social Democrats' top priority. This meant that they lashed themselves to the same mast as Swedish capitalism. At times, there were substantial resources to allocate to social reforms, and the Social Democrats managed to use them successfully to lay the foundations of a welfare state that lay partly beyond the domain of market exploitation. But any hope that fundamental power relations might change was soon dashed. Time and again, Social Democracy tried to propose a trade-off: we will give further support to a more efficient capitalism if we gain a little more influence over production – industrial democracy, co-determination, wage-earner funds. But it was to no avail. The idea that the labour movement could seriously influence the power of capital over production lay beyond the limit of its pact with the latter.[17]

A one-sided focus on the endogenous forces of Social Democracy obscures the importance of the broader social struggles without which the social and political reforms attributed to Social Democracy would have been impossible to achieve. A second main thesis of this book, therefore, is that each such conquest has been won under the pressure of widespread social mobilisation involving movements far broader than those directly linked to Social Democracy. Indeed, not infrequently they have been achieved despite the hesitation or even resistance of Social Democracy.

There are several examples we will return to: the democratic reforms carried out at the end of the First World War, driven by mass movements beyond party control; the development of the 'people's home' policy of the 1930s, which took place under pressure from a widespread wave of strikes and a strong growth of new and old social movements, of which Social Democracy was only a part; and the welfare state that

---

17   This will be elaborated in detail below.

culminated in the 1970s – the result, in large measure, of the deep social radicalisation of the time, in which the new women's movement and a wave of wildcat strikes played decisive roles. Ultimately, the Swedish welfare state is a result of class struggle.[18]

The party and its members have played a prominent role in these mobilisations; but the struggle has had much broader social roots than that. More than once, the party leadership has intervened to curb them. It is possible to see a rhythm in these mobilisations. Just as economic development can be linked to a large extent with long- and short-term cycles, it is possible to discern waves of social radicalisation, periods of intensified social struggle, the revitalisation of existing social movements, and the emergence of new ones. Indeed, the vast majority of significant political and social conquests can be linked to such periods of radicalisation.[19]

For over a century, these waves of radicalisation were closely related to the different phases of industrial society. They can be described as intensified periods of class struggle; although much broader groups participated, the industrial working class was usually the leading social force. This base was widened during the radicalisation of the 1960s. The concept of 'new social movements' indicates that other, often younger groups were, at least initially, the bearers of radicalisation – and a pre-condition for the success of these movements was that they were based on broader alliances between class, gender, and ethnic groups. Nonetheless, the working class, broadly understood, played the decisive role in the outcome of the struggle.

This does not mean, of course, that it is possible simply to reduce the role of Social Democracy to one of carrying out the wishes of capital or the masses. The party is undoubtedly one of the most powerful political actors of the twentieth century, internationally as well as domestically. Its position within the working class was hegemonic for a hundred years. The Social Democratic–led trade unions organised 80–90 per cent of the workers, the vast majority of whom voted Social Democrat. Large sections of the middle classes also supported the party's policies.

18   Kjell Östberg, *Folk i rörelse: vår demokratis historia* (Stockholm: Ordfront, 2021).
19   Ibid., p. 12; Sidney G. Tarrow, *Struggle, Politics and Reform: Collective Action, Social Movements and Cycles of Protest* (Ithaca, NY: Center for International Studies, Cornell University, 1991).

The broad Social Democratic movement was extraordinarily well organised. It was, to use Gramsci's phrase, a party with a great capacity to produce and educate its intellectuals itself.[20] The leadership was recruited mainly from the working class, and it soon acquired extensive experience in leading struggles and movements. But it also gained experience of participating in policymaking and implementation. Increasingly, its focus shifted to the parliamentary arena. At the same time, participation in parliamentary work required a formalisation of decision-making structures in terms of centralisation and hierarchical development.

It is in this zone of tension between, on one hand, a movement with deep roots in the Swedish working class and, on the other, an efficient organisation, increasingly bureaucratised and integrated into a capitalist state apparatus, that the history of Swedish Social Democracy must be understood.

---

20 Antonio Gramsci, *Selections from the Prison Notebooks of Antonio Gramsci* (London: Lawrence & Wishart, 1971), pp. 12, 16.

1

Origins

*Far below him lay the noisy, reawakening town; the steam cranes
whirred in the harbour, the iron bars rattled in the iron weighing
machine, the whistles of the lock-keepers shrilled, the steamers at the
pontoon bridge smoked, the omnibuses rumbled over the uneven
paving-stones; noise and uproar in the fish market, sails and flags on the
water outside; the screams of the seagulls, bugle-calls from the dockyard,
the turning out of the guard, the clattering of the wooden shoes of the
workingmen – all this produced an impression of life and bustle, which
seemed to rouse the young man's energy.*

August Strindberg, *The Red Room*

In 1879, August Strindberg, considered by many to be Sweden's greatest
writer, published his breakthrough novel *Röda rummet* (*The Red Room*).[1]
It is often described as the first modern Swedish novel. One reason he
was able to write it is, of course, Strindberg's genius. But there was also a
new society to describe. The modern capitalists, the speculators, the
newspapermen, the new creative intellectuals, the socially committed
women – and, not least, the threatening workers – are depicted together
for the first time in Strindberg's powerful kaleidoscope.

The years around 1880 were a period of vast movements in Swedish
society. Together, they form a pattern that reflects the profound changes
in the social fabric and points towards a new society.

In 1879, Sweden suffered its first major banking crash, confirming
the country as an integral part of an international capitalist system.[2] In
response to the economic and social consequences of the economic

---

1   August Strindberg, *The Red Room* (London: Howard Latimer, 1913), available at
standardebooks.org. Originally published as *Röda rummet: skildringar ur artist- och
författarlifvet* (Stockholm: Seligmann, 1879), available at alvin-portal.org.
2   On economic and social development, see Lennart Schön, *An Economic History
of Modern Sweden* (London: Routledge, 2012), Chapter 2.

crisis, several thousand sawmill workers in Sundsvall, the economic centre of Swedish industrialism, went on the first major strike the country had ever seen.

The labour movement had arrived in Sweden.

Early Economic and Political Developments

In the mid-nineteenth century, Sweden was a backward country by European standards – economically, socially, and politically. The Industrial Revolution, which had been underway for a century in England, had barely reached the country, and the income of its citizens was among the lowest in Europe. Most of the population – just under 4 million – lived in the countryside. The capital, Stockholm, had fewer than 100,000 inhabitants and only a handful of towns had more than 10,000. Politically, power rested safely with a small layer of land-owners, noble bureaucrats, and military men in the king's shadow. The new constitution, adopted in 1809 in the wake of the French Revolu-tion, stated that the king alone was entitled to rule the country. Under the new monarch, Karl XIV Johan, one of Napoleon's marshals, this applied almost literally. Calls for democratic reform went unheeded for a long time. The old Parliament of the Four Estates (nobility, priests, burghers, and farmers), with its roots in the Middle Ages, still existed.[3]

As in many other countries, there is a nationalistic tendency in Sweden to present the democratic development of its own country in a particularly positive light. Even contemporary historians often tend to speak of a progressive Swedish *Sonderweg* ('special path'). They point to the position of Swedish farmers. Compared to many other countries, the proportion of landowning peasants had been high, and serfdom was abolished in the Middle Ages. Nor was the share of land owned by the nobility as crushingly dominant as in many other coun-tries. Emphasis has also been placed on the role of the local parish assemblies as meeting places for local farmers to discuss and decide on common affairs such as the care of the poor and education. This social arrangement, some historians argue, laid the foundations for a

---

3 On the political development of nineteenth-century Sweden, see Bo Stråth, *Sveriges historia. 1830–1920* (Stockholm: Norstedt, 2012).

tradition of democracy already in the old peasant society. It is also said that this is where the roots can be found of the culture of negotiation and trust in social institutions that is said to characterise the Swedish model right up to the present day. Similarly, some scholars argue that Swedish society has long been characterised by relatively small social differences.[4]

If you strip away the patriotic overtones, however, a different picture emerges. The group that wielded the power to influence local decisions constituted a very small minority of the population, mainly the wealthier landowners. State representatives, especially the priests, had a decisive influence, and closely monitored what was happening locally. In addition, there was increasing social stratification in rural areas. In the eighteenth century, 80 per cent of rural households owned their own land; by 1850, this was true of only one-half. This increased the number of crofters, farmworkers, and maids who had little influence on local politics. Meanwhile, there is no support for the notion that social disparities in Sweden were smaller than in other countries. Income inequality at the end of the nineteenth century was at least as great as in most large European countries.[5] And, as we shall see, relations between the social classes were not characterised by consensus.

Gradually, the capitalist mode of production began to take hold in Sweden.[6] In the 1850s, Sweden was seriously drawn into the international market economy for the first time. Agriculture in southern Sweden could now export oats, a commodity in demand at the time. The mines and ironworks of central Sweden supplied iron. Above all, Norrland could supply timber to forest-poor England. More than anything else, the emergence of a chain of sawmills along the Norrland coast, with the Sundsvall area at its centre, symbolises the first phase of Sweden's industrialisation.

The forests, previously largely unused, were turned into timber that was floated to the sawmills on the coast. The steam saw was the key

---

4   Henrik Berggren and Lars Trägårdh, *Är svensken människa? Gemenskap och oberoende i det moderna Sverige* (Stockholm: Norstedt, 2014).

5   Erik Bengtsson, 'The Swedish *Sonderweg* in Question: Democratization and Inequality in Comparative Perspective, c.1750–1920', *Past and Present* 244, no. 1 (August 2019), and Erik Bengtsson, *Världens jämlikaste land?* (Lund: Arkiv förlag, 2020).

6   For this development, see Schön, *Economic History of Modern Sweden*, Chapter 3.

technological innovation that made this dramatic expansion possible. A class of sawmill capitalists was soon established. The fact that they had names like Versteegh, Dickson, and Kempe suggests that the necessary capital often came initially from Holland, Scotland, or Germany. They were quickly able to amass large fortunes. From their sawmills arose a form of primitive accumulation. But also from the forests, they could buy cheaply from farmers who were unable to foresee the rapid rise in value. Resources that had previously been of low value became the basis for the development of large industrial capital.[7]

It was not only the capitalists who were formed into a class. A working class was also now emerging, most clearly seen around the sawmills. The need for new tools and machinery stimulated the emergence of mechanical workshops, often located in the bigger cities. This became a crucible of the new industrial working class.[8]

The economic liberalism that characterised Europe in the middle of the century also had an impact on Sweden. The guild system was abolished, as were export duties, and trade with more developed countries increased. Joint-stock companies made it easier to set up new businesses. New conditions for banks facilitated their role in financing new businesses, eventually delivering to banks control over large parts of Swedish industry. The symbol for this quickly became Stockholm's Enskilda Bank, founded by A. O. Wallenberg in 1856.

The state supported this development in several ways. The partial breakthrough of economic liberalism did not result in a night-watchman state, but one that actively contributed to the development of new infrastructure, railways and other forms of communications in particular. In sparsely populated Sweden, these things could not be left to market forces.

In 1866, the Estates were replaced by a bicameral parliament – though this development did not entail any profound democratisation of Swedish society. Just 10 per cent of the adult population could vote in the Second Chamber elections, and women were excluded.[9] For the

---

7   Ibid., pp. 102ff.
8   Ibid., pp. 111ff.
9   Torbjörn Nilsson, *Elitens svängrum: första kammaren, staten och moderniseringen 1867–1886* (Stockholm: Almqvist & Wiksell, 1994); and Stig Hadenius, *Swedish Politics during the 20th Century: Conflict and Consensus* (Stockholm: Svenska Institutet, 1997), pp. 12–14.

First Chamber, the requirements were even more exclusive, with only 6,100 people in the country eligible to take a seat.

At the local level, voting rules were tightened. Municipalities were likened to limited companies, and citizens were given a number of votes according to how much tax they had paid. Not only citizens but also companies were allowed to vote – and even women who paid taxes. A single company might wield several thousand votes, amounting to more than all the workers of the municipality combined.

There is, then, very little support for the view that democratic traditions in Sweden have been particularly strong. On the contrary, at the end of the nineteenth century the country was among those with the lowest percentage of voters. By 1896, in countries like Denmark, Norway, the UK, France, and Germany, between 65 and 85 per cent of adult males were able to vote in the equivalent of the Second Chamber. In Sweden, the figure was 24 per cent.[10]

Popular Movements

The reforms of the 1860s guaranteed political representation and influence for the upper classes and wealthy farmers. For all those still outside, the rapidly growing civil society of associations gradually became an important vehicle.

A variety of collective organisations were formed that exerted a growing influence over social development: temperance societies, women's associations, educational societies, gymnastic societies, savings banks, and insurance associations. The reason for this was the business community's need for networks and trade associations, and workers' need for health and unemployment insurance. The scope of education, when only rudimentary elementary schools and segregated higher education were available, was increasingly insufficient. Women organised to secure recognition of their civil rights, and to extend their access to education.[11]

Out of these myriad initiatives, three organisations emerged that gradually developed into mass organisations: the Free Church movement, the

10   Bengtsson, 'The Swedish *Sonderweg* in Question'.
11   Torkel Jansson, *Adertonhundratalets associationer: forskning och problem kring ett sprängfullt tomrum eller sammanslutningsprinciper och föreningsformer mellan två samhällsformationer ca 1800–1870* (Stockholm: Almqvist & Wiksell, 1985).

temperance movement, and the labour movement.[12] These movements have an almost mythical place in Swedish history, and are often assigned a crucial role in the democratisation of the country. What unites them is that they were mainly built from below, by the lower-middle class and workers. Politically, they belonged to liberal and socialist traditions.

The first to develop was the Free Church movement. Small pietistic groups had already emerged in the eighteenth century. Their gatherings challenged the Swedish feudal state, in which rigid church laws prevailed and the priest had a monopoly on preaching the word of God. New laws were quickly passed explicitly banning prayer meetings and other religious gatherings outside the control of the church. But the ideas lived on and there were repeated large-scale revivals around the country, and this revival movement became Sweden's first mass popular organisation.

Gradually, legislative obstacles were relaxed. In 1860, it was no longer forbidden to gather for religious meetings without a priest or to join another religious community. The Free Church movement thus took the lead in securing some fundamental democratic rights: freedom of assembly and freedom of religion.[13] The movement's members were often called Readers. A central idea was that everyone should be able to read, assimilate, and reflect on the Bible's message – not just cram the catechism into their heads uncritically. But this designation also indicates one of the great assets of the popular movements: literacy, which was greater in Sweden than in most other countries. By 1850, only 10 per cent of the population could not read.

In 1879, Baptist pastors introduced the American temperance movement – the Independent Order of Good Templars – and Sweden's second great popular movement had arrived. It grew at an unprecedented pace; by the turn of the twentieth century, it was the country's largest popular movement.[14] In the same year the Sundsvall strike broke out, and the labour movement was born.

---

12 Sven Lundkvist, *Folkrörelserna i det svenska samhället 1850–1920* (Stockholm: Sober, 1977); Kjell Östberg, *Folk i rörelse: vår demokratis historia* (Stockholm: Ordfront, 2021).
13 Gunnar Hallingberg, *Läsarna: 1800-talets folkväckelse och det moderna genombrottet* (Stockholm: Atlantis, 2010).
14 Lundkvist, *Folkrörelserna i det svenska samhället.*

The Formation of the Labour Movement

Social unrest and riots have been documented in Sweden since the Middle Ages. There are records of strikes among the workers who built Gustav Vasa's castle in the sixteenth century, and among workers in the important iron and copper mines of Bergslagen. In the first half of the nineteenth century, both hunger riots and violent street riots broke out in Stockholm.

When revolutionary winds swept across Europe during the spring of 1848, Sweden was no exception. Demands for extensive political and democratic reforms reverberated through the country. Radical artisans translated the *Communist Manifesto*, demanding universal suffrage and a republic; the very first translation of the *Manifesto* was in fact into Swedish. The battle was also fought in the streets. Mass riots broke out and barricades were built, as in Paris. Some thirty demonstrators were shot dead, most of them workers. But workers still lacked associations to represent them.[15]

The Sundsvall strike of 1879 and its aftermath fundamentally changed the balance of power. The strike broke out as a defence against wage pressures in the wake of the economic crisis. As the centre of the sawmill industry at the time, Sundsvall had played a decisive role in the development of Swedish capitalism. When the industry was hit by the international recession, wages were drastically reduced, and sawmill owners were granted a large state subsidy. As those owners celebrated with a lavish banquet, workers' minds must have been racing. In the absence of trade unions, class cohesion had to be expressed in a very tangible way. Workers, some of whose leaders had gained organisational experience from the Free Church movement, marched from sawmill to sawmill, dragging their fellow workers with them, and work was brought to a halt.

15 The main sources for the outline of the history of the Swedish labour movement include: Yvonne Hirdman, *Vi bygger landet: den svenska arbetarrörelsens historia från Per Götrek till Olof Palme* (Solna: Pogo Press, 1979); Lars Olsson and Lars Ekdahl, *Klass i rörelse: arbetarrörelsen i svensk samhällsutveckling* (Stockholm: Arbetarrörelsens Arkiv och Bibliotek, 2014); Seppo Hentilä, *Sveriges socialdemokratiska arbetareparti och reformismens genombrott: arbetarklassens ställning och ideologins förändring* (Helsingfors: Historiska föreningen, 1972).

Workers' unity continued to be manifested in a very concrete way, strikers camping out in central Sundsvall. A strike of this magnitude had never been seen before in Sweden. 'The International is here', wrote the conservative papers, terrified that the radical labour movement seemed to have arrived in Sweden.[16]

It was clear that the forces defending the status quo were prepared to go to great lengths to put down the strike. The governor requisitioned six gunboats and three elite companies from Svea Life Guards. Surrounded by the military, and without an organisation to represent them, the workers were unable to prevent representatives of the state from picking off workers one by one. Those who refused to return to work were arrested and evicted from their homes. Unsurprisingly, most chose to end their participation in the strike. In this way, the Sundsvall strike was delivered a decisive defeat. Many workers were not reinstated – and many chose to emigrate to the United States. Still, the importance of the strike cannot be overstated. The experience of the dramatic events it involved was discussed in all parts of society in the following years. Brochures and newspaper articles were distributed throughout the country, while new means of communication – the telegraph, newspapers, and railways – enabled rapid distribution of news.

A general conclusion was drawn that the workers had failed to resist the joint attack of employers and the state because their organisation was weak. The Sundsvall strike was followed the next year by a large-scale strike movement in Stockholm, representing the country's first significant wave of trade union organisation. In 1880 there were only a few unions in the country that we would recognise as such today. Five years later, there were over a hundred.

The new trade unions were built on a clear class basis. In the very well-written minute books of the highly literate workers, the topics that dominated the agenda in the first years are obvious: the level of wages; the forms of wages – monthly or piecework; the number of working hours; job security; and workers' power in the workplace. In short, the same issues that remain the focus of fighting trade unions to this day.[17] The workers showed great organisational skill and class cohesion. There were soon local trade union organisations in the major cities, and by the

---

16   Hirdman, *Vi bygger landet*, pp. 32–4.
17   Östberg, *Folk i rörelse*, pp. 35–40.

end of the 1880s, the first national trade union federations were formed. Federations of typographers, painters, and metalworkers were among the early ones. It is striking that both craftsmen and industrial workers played an important role in this process.

Trade union agendas were not limited narrowly to their own direct concerns. It soon became clear to workers that action had to be taken on several fronts. They took an active part in the broader social debate, carefully examining the political options on offer. In the early days it was mainly the Liberals who tried to reach the workers. But when the liberal workers' unions rejected universal suffrage and strikes, they repelled the young industrial working class.

Another current would soon prove much more attractive.[18] In the autumn of 1881, the tailor August Palm returned from working trips in Denmark and Germany, where he had come into contact with Social Democratic organisations. In Malmö, he gave a speech on the theme, 'What do the Social Democrats want?' Socialist ideas had come to Sweden, and they quickly found fertile ground. By Christmas of that year, Palm was in Stockholm. Over the next few years he made a series of agitational trips around Sweden, and started the first socialist newspaper, *Folkviljan* (People's will).

After a few years the results were evident. An important step was when the Central Trade Union Committee in Stockholm in 1885 adopted a clear socialist programme, and a Social Democratic leadership won control. In 1884, the first Social Democratic association was formed in Stockholm. Most of its members were workers, but now a small group of radical intellectuals had also joined. The first issue of *Social-Demokraten* was published in 1885: the young Social Democratic movement had gained a mouthpiece with national impact. That same year, the party's future leader Hjalmar Branting left the Liberals to join the socialist movement.

In the following years Social Democratic associations were founded in the large industrial cities of Malmö, Gothenburg, and Norrköping. Crucially, so were newspapers – *Arbetet* (Labour), *Ny Tid* (New times), and *Proletären* (The proletarian). From the very beginning, the trade unions formed the basis of the socialist movement. When the Social Democratic Party was constituted in April 1889, more than fifty of its sixty-nine delegates were appointed by trade unions.

---

18   Hirdman, *Vi bygger landet*, pp. 35–44.

What Was Social Democracy?

There have been many lengthy discussions about how to characterise early Swedish Social Democracy.[19] Was it originally revolutionary, or was it reformist-dominated from the start? The answer is that early Social Democracy was influenced by several different currents within the contemporary international labour movement.

August Palm had encountered German Social Democracy during his travels in Germany in the 1870s. He was particularly inspired by Ferdinand Lassalle's Allgemeiner Deutscher Arbeiterverein (General German Workers' Association) and schooled in the Gotha Programme of German Social Democracy. His first attempts to formulate his own programme included several Lasallean ideas, such as the call for state-supported worker-owned enterprises to compete with capitalist ones. But Palm was above all a skilled agitator, not a theoretician. For the trade unions attracted by socialist ideas, it was initially class organisation and the dream of a socialist future that appealed, not Social Democratic doctrines. The group of intellectuals who gathered around the Social Democratic Club in Stockholm also lacked a deeper socialist education. Gradually, they assimilated the thinking of the German Social Democrats.

The first congresses did not endorse a party programme, but they did adopt a series of resolutions. One of the most important was the demand for universal suffrage. Although 'class oppression may persist even in countries which have introduced universal suffrage and have no illusions about the immediate consequences, and suffrage is merely a means, the Congress nevertheless regards universal suffrage as the most important and educative political right in present-day society'.[20] This

---

19   Herbert Tingsten, *The Swedish Social Democrats: Their Ideological Development* (Totowa, NJ: Bedminster, 1973). Originally published as *Den svenska socialdemokratins idéutveckling*, 2 vols (Stockholm: Aldus/Bonnier, 1967 [1941]), pp. 127–69; Hentilä, *Sveriges socialdemokratiska arbetareparti*, pp. 101–21; Göran Therborn, 'Den svenska socialdemokratin träder fram', *Arkiv för studier i arbetarrörelsens historia* 27–28 (1984), pp. 3–71; Lars-Olof Ekdahl and Hans-Erik Hjelm, 'Reformismens framväxt inom svensk arbetarrörelse', in Klas Åmark, ed., *Teori- och metodproblem i modern svensk historieforskning: en antologi* (Stockholm: LiberFörlag, 1981).

20   Party Congress 1891, Jan Lindhagen, *Socialdemokratins program D. 1 I rörelsens tid 1890–1930* (Stockholm: Tiden, 1972).

wording reflected differences of opinion within the young party. While the Skåne district, whose leading representative was Axel Danielsson, was sceptical about how far the parliamentary path could lead, Branting was more hopeful. In a renowned speech in Gävle as early as 1886, he had said that universal suffrage was the price the bourgeoisie had to pay if it wanted to avoid a revolution.

On violence, the congress stated that the party was by no means seeking a bloody revolution, but intended only to use 'such means as correspond to the natural sense of justice of the people'. But the risk of violence was not completely dismissed. As Social Democracy was 'a revolutionary party which seeks a thorough transformation of the existing bourgeois society', it had to consider the possibility of resorting to violence in acute situations. As long as the peaceful means of universal suffrage had not yet been tried, the congress firmly declared its disapproval of all kinds of 'dynamite agitation', and strongly denounced the anarchist-influenced agitators 'who incite the masses to acts of violence against individuals'.[21]

It was not until the 1897 congress that the Social Democrats adopted their first formal party programme. This extract could be found in the Social Democratic programme for half a century: 'Social Democracy differs from other political parties in that it wants to completely transform the economic organisation of bourgeois society and bring about the social emancipation of the working class, the consolidation and development of spiritual and material culture.'[22] The rather short programme was written very quickly – legend claims overnight – by Axel Danielsson. This was possible because, not surprisingly, it closely followed the 1891 Erfurt Programme of the German Social Democratic Party. This means that Swedish Social Democracy at the turn of the century was programmatically lined up behind the Kautskyan orientation of the Second International. The programme contains a few immediate demands, mainly democratic and social, but no more far-reaching socialist ones. It has been characterised as strategy without tactics, and ends without means.[23]

21   Ibid., p. 10.
22   Ibid., pp. 13ff.
23   Seppo Hentilä, *Den svenska arbetarklassen och reformismens genombrott inom san före 1914: arbetarklassens ställning, strategi och ideologi* (Forssa: Forssan Kirjapaino Oy, 1979), p. 121.

The question of how to transform bourgeois society fundamentally remained open; discussion of the road to socialism had only just begun. At the same time, the labour movement was still far from being a mass movement. Nevertheless, the ruling class watched with concern the rapid growth of the socialist labour movement, and tried in various ways to curb its activities. Several democratic rights had been extended during the liberal period in the mid nineteenth century, including freedom of the press, freedom of religion, and freedom of assembly. The last decades of the nineteenth century, however, were a period of political reaction. To get to grips with the young labour movement, legislation on freedom of the press was tightened, and freedom of assembly was curtailed. Several leading Social Democrats were sentenced to prison, sometimes for a year or more, for provocative newspaper articles or illegal meetings.[24] There are many stories about the struggles between Social Democratic agitators and the local police. To evade the ban on meetings, August Palm sent out an invitation for a Sunday walk through Stockholm. Hundreds of workers showed up to hear Palm's impromptu socialist lectures.

The attacks on the democratic rights of the labour movement were inspired by what was happening in Germany at the same time, where Bismarck's socialist laws banned socialist agitation. The Conservative Swedish government also had plans to dissolve the Social Democratic Party, but they were never implemented. In general, repression of the young labour movement was milder than in many other countries at the time. For example, it was never made illegal to strike or to belong to a trade union – but, at the same time, it was not forbidden for employers to dismiss strikers or to use strike-breakers. Gradually, the labour movement managed to regain freedom of the press and freedom of assembly. At the same time, antagonisms in the workplace intensified.

Union Building

The 1890s were characterised by a growing number of industrial disputes. As trade union organisation expanded and membership grew, so did the number of successful strikes. Another important factor was the growing economic boom towards the end of the 1890s, which increased

---

24   Östberg, *Folk i rörelse*, pp. 51ff.

the demand for labour. The 1890s are full of stories of fierce union battles.

The use of strike-breakers also increased. Employers supported the formation of 'yellow' unions that were prepared to allow their members to act as scabs. Often, they were imported. The most famous example is that of the English strike-breakers who were housed on the ship *Amalthea* in Malmö harbour in 1908. A group of young socialists planted a bomb on the ship, killing one person and injuring around twenty more. Although such violent tactics were rare, this incident provides an idea of how the workers viewed the scabs.[25] It was no accident that Jack London's classic excoriation of the scab was constantly quoted in the trade union press: 'After God had finished the rattlesnake, the toad, and the vampire, He had some awful substance left with which He made a scab. A scab is a two-legged animal with a corkscrew soul, a waterlogged brain, and a combination backbone made of jelly and glue.'[26]

When the Social Democratic Workers' Party (Socialdemokratiska arbetarepartiet, or SAP) was founded in 1889, it had about 3,000 members; in its early years, it grew slowly. Activities were also decentralised, with the first party executive not elected until 1894. The workers' commune was now also established as a base for local activities.[27]

In general, the boundaries between party and trade union were fluid. Until the Swedish Trade Union Confederation (Landsorganisationen i Sverige, or LO) was formed in 1898, the party often had to take on coordinating tasks, such as supporting strikes. But in 1898, twenty-four national trade union federations formed the central organisation, the LO. A central question was how to formalise the relationship with the Social Democratic Party. Several unions feared that formally joining the party would make it more difficult to recruit members, making employers even more hostile to unions.

After intensive discussions, the decision was made that each local branch would decide for itself whether its members should be affiliated to the local workers' commune. No one questioned the close ties between the LO and the Social Democratic Party, however. Until collective membership was abolished in the 1990s, most party members were affiliated

25   Ibid., pp. 55–8.
26   'SCAB', People's History Archive, peopleshistoryarchive.org.
27   For this section: Hirdman, *Vi bygger landet*, pp. 61–5.

through their local trade unions. Up to the present, virtually all central union leaders, and most local ones, have been Social Democrats, and the LO has given substantial financial support to the party, not least during election campaigns.

Further key features of the LO's organisational structure should be mentioned here. LO unions organised blue-collar workers, at first mostly in the private sector. Civil servants, clerks, technicians, teachers, and academics were organised by other unions, which only formed their central trade union federations in the 1930s. This, of course, made it easier for the LO to maintain close links with Social Democracy. Moreover, LO mainly organised according to the industrial union principle, holding that all workers at a workplace should belong to the same union, regardless of their job. This facilitated concerted trade union action.

The position of women was given a subordinate role in the early labour movement, since it was largely based on the trade unions. Women were to a large extent part of the paid workforce, but were poorly represented in the unions. This does not mean that women did not participate in trade union struggles. Women matchmakers in Jönköping, spinners in Malmö, weavers in Norrköping, and bricklayers in Stockholm all went on strike, often successfully. But men's interest in letting women into their unions was often weak. Although the demand for women's suffrage was supported early on by the socialist movement, there was little willingness to pursue women's interests. The labour movement considered itself to be pursuing a class struggle, not a women's struggle.[28]

The Breakthrough of Industrial Society

Around the turn of the twentieth century, a new wave of radicalisation grew strong across Europe, driven primarily by the international labour movement. It had created powerful organisations based on trade unions, and was spearheaded by Social Democratic parties. Despite many restrictions, the parliamentary influence of the parties increased, and they continued to lead the fight for democracy.

---

28 Eva Schmitz, *Arbetarkvinnors mobiliseringar i arbetarrörelsens barndom: en studie av arbetarkvinnors strejkaktiviteter och dess inflytande på den svenska arbetar-rörelsen* (Lund: Lund University Publications, 1999), pp. 124–7.

In 1905, in the aftermath of the Russo-Japanese War, the first Russian Revolution erupted. This made clear that the socialist movement might not be content to take seats only in bourgeois parliaments. The workers' councils that emerged showed the possibility of alternative power structures. This development took place against the backdrop of a major international boom, in which both Europe and North America were industrialising at a rapid pace. Germany and the United States challenged Britain as the world economic leader, while new inventions such as the electric motor and petrol engine drove economic development. But it was also a time of increasing inter-imperialist struggle. Much of the conflict was over control of world trade and the wealth of the colonies. It exploded with the outbreak of the First World War in 1914.[29]

The international economic boom benefited Sweden's export-oriented industry. Manufacturing, as well as the pulp and paper industries, grew strongly. In general, the economy expanded faster than in most other countries. Several new companies were founded, particularly in the engineering sector – many of them based on inventions that were at the cutting edge of research. These companies were to form the backbone of Swedish industry for years to come: ASEA, LM Ericsson, Separator/Alfa Laval, and the Swedish Ball Bearing Factory (Svenska Kullagerfabriken). This was also true of companies in iron and steel production and of paper and pulp industries. The development of hydroelectric power provided abundant electricity for electric motors and the electrical engineering industry.[30]

Major banks played a crucial role in this development. For fast-growing companies, financing became a growing problem; especially given the recurrent crises, many companies fell under the control of the banks. Finance capital came to play a decisive role in the strong concentration of ownership that characterised Swedish industry. Since then, most leading Swedish industrial companies have had close relationships with banks such as Handelsbanken, Skandinaviska Banken – and, above all, Enskilda Banken.[31]

In the same period, social structures were also changing. Most Swedes still lived in the countryside. But the exodus from the countryside

---

29   E. J. Hobsbawm, *The Age of Empire, 1875–1914* (London: Weidenfeld & Nicolson, 1987).
30   Schön, *Economic History of Modern Sweden*, pp. 134–49.
31   Ibid., pp. 159–64.

increased, though this was a relatively slow process. Agriculture was still able to absorb some of the rapid population growth. During the recurring recessions, large numbers of Swedes emigrated to the United States; between 1850 and 1920, more than a million did so. By the turn of the century, Sweden had 5 million inhabitants.

New industries sprang up in mill towns, and even the big cities were increasingly dominated by such industries and their workers. The first significant growth in the Swedish industrial working class was taking place. Between 1890 and 1910, the number of industrial workers and craftsmen grew from 150,000 to 450,000.

A Workers' World

By this time, the labour movement was growing like wildfire. The trade union movement's membership more than trebled in the decade to 1907, when it surpassed 230,000. Sweden set a European record for union growth – and the workers soon used their resources of power. Swedish workers' strike activity was the most intense in Europe at the turn of the century, and would reach a new peak during the general strike ten years later. In addition, the number of victorious strikes increased as workers' organisations became stronger. The standard of living for the working class rose markedly at the beginning of the century.[32] The Social Democratic Party underwent a corresponding membership explosion – a direct result of the mass entry of trade union members into the party. Party membership trebled between 1900 and 1907, by which date there were 500 branches or workers' communes across the country.[33]

The Social Democratic Party was hardly a party in the modern sense. Rather, it was the political head of a much broader labour movement. In 1897, the first socialist youth league was formed. As it developed in an increasingly anarchist direction, another was formed in 1902. The Young Democrats, as the members of the new union were called, grew rapidly to a membership of 15,000. The leadership included a young generation who, a few decades later, would take up

32 Olsson and Ekdahl, *Klass i rörelse*, pp. 30–3.
33 Östberg, *Folk i rörelse*, pp. 66–9.

leading positions in the party – and, in many cases, also the state, including two prime ministers. These figures included, among others, Per Albin Hansson, Rickard Sandler, and Zeth Höglund. The new socialist youth league, Socialdemokratiska ungdomsförbundet, soon became the centre of the radical wing of Social Democracy, and the weekly *Stormklockan* (The alarm bell) became the main mouthpiece of the party left. Socialist Sunday schools were organised for the even younger generation.

The first women's clubs had already been formed in the 1880s. After the turn of the century the number grew rapidly, and by 1907 there were around sixty clubs. In the same year, a Social Democratic women's conference was convened for the first time. However, a women's federation was not formed at national level until after the implementation of women's suffrage in 1921. The male party representatives made it clear that, while they could accept local women's clubs, an independent women's federation would damage both men's and women's organisations.[34]

According to historian Christina Carlsson Wetterberg, the labour movement was never able to find a solution to the most important issue for working women: the conflict between work and motherhood. In practice, the movement accepted that women bore full responsibility for children and the family, and that men were considered sole bread-winners – even though many hundreds of thousands of women were their workmates. Instead of the patriarchal structures of the bourgeois family being challenged, they were simply reproduced.[35]

At the same time, the geographical landscape changed. The new working class and its organisations dominated in the working districts of cities, in mill towns, and in other industrial centres. Gradually, a proletarian public sphere emerged. An early problem was posed by the scarcity of meeting places. Public meeting halls were rare, and were lent to workers only reluctantly. Soon the initiative was taken to build the workers' own People's Houses. When, in Malmö in 1893, Axel Daniels-son inaugurated one of the first, he remarked: 'We have built ourselves a house of our own, where we can meet undisturbed and deliberate on our

---

34   Christina Carlsson Wetterberg, *Kvinnosyn och kvinnopolitik: en studie av svensk socialdemokrati 1880–1910* (Lund: Arkiv, 1986), pp. 189–203.
35   Ibid., pp. 276ff.

common affairs and provide a safe haven for persecuted thoughts.[36] By 1914, there were 350 People's Houses. In addition, there were a few hundred People's Parks, for festivities and leisure activities.

Equally important was the creation of tools to ensure that the socialist message reached the public. From the beginning, the party had been built around four district newspapers. In 1914, there were sixteen party newspapers from north to south, plus the Youth League's *Stormklockan* and the women's *Morgonbris* (Morning breeze). In addition, there were more than thirty trade union newspapers closely linked to Social Democracy.[37]

The labour movement was also an educational centre. Inspired by the temperance movement, thousands of 'study circles' were started around the country. The aim was to compensate the workers for a lack of schooling but also to give them knowledge as a tool to change the world and to train them to be politically active. In 1912 the Workers' Educational Association (Arbetarnas Bildningsförbund – ABF) was formed. By this time, the first full-time folk high school, Brunnsvik, had already been in existence for five years. An important part of the ABF's activities was running the workers' libraries. Literature played an important part in the educational efforts of the labour movement, and reading was widespread within the Swedish working class early on. At the top of the libraries' lending lists for a long time was the American labour writer Jack London, closely followed by August Strindberg. But the Swedish labour movement also produced its own writers. The movement's newspapers were filled with socialist poetry and short stories from the workers' world. Soon, a generation of professional writers appeared who had themselves emerged from the working class. A key figure was the woman knitter Maria Sandel.[38]

Consumer cooperation gradually came to be more firmly associated with the labour movement. Initially growing out of liberal currents that had germinated in the big cities, it soon became subject to the driving force of Social Democracy.

---

36 Östberg, *Folk i rörelse*, pp. 69ff.
37 Stig Hadenius, Jan-Olof Seveborg, and Lennart Weibull, *Socialdemokratisk press och presspolitik: 1899–1909* (Stockholm: Tiden, 1968).
38 Per-Olof Mattsson, *Maria Sandels litterära landskap* (Stockholm: Maria Sandelsällskapet, 2023).

The labour movement had considerable organisational and material resources at its disposal just before the First World War: newspapers, agitators, People's Houses, and trade unions with substantial strike funds. In addition, the movement began to acquire a whole apparatus of employed functionaries. The trade union movement already had a hundred, the newspapers nearly a hundred, and the party a dozen. After the electoral successes of 1914, there were over a hundred Social Democratic members of parliament. Although the party attracted a growing number of intellectuals from bourgeois backgrounds, the party was dominated at all levels, from the party leadership downwards, by people with working-class origins.[39]

Which Way to Democracy?

The labour movement was also radicalised politically. Increasingly, the struggle came to be dominated by the fight for suffrage.[40] In the late 1880s, progressive liberals and Social Democrats formed suffrage associations that gathered for national meetings. To press their demands, they convened a People's Parliament in 1893.[41]

The Social Democrats participated wholeheartedly, achieving a great impact. At the same time, the gathering was dominated by the more moderate views of the liberal forces on the extension of voting rights – rejecting women's suffrage, for example. The Social Democrats proposed a political general strike to put some force behind their words, but the Liberals condemned such a drastic measure. This did not prevent the Social Democrats from pursuing their line with great enthusiasm. Even the LO – which usually used the threat of a strike with considerable caution, so as not to drain strike funds unnecessarily – supported the proposal enthusiastically.

Preparations were carried out with great care. A major strike fund was set up, and a strike committee was appointed, comprising leading representatives of the party and the trade unions. The strike was a

39   Kjell Östberg, 'The Swedish Social Democracy: Civil Servants, Social Engineers and Welfare Bureaucrats', in Mathieu Fulla and Marc Lazar, eds, *European Socialists and the State in the Twentieth and Twenty-First Centuries* (Cham: Palgrave Macmillan, 2020).
40   Östberg, *Folk i rörelse*, pp. 58–63.
41   Hentilä, *Den svenska arbetarklassen*, pp. 123–33.

significant success. Hundreds of thousands of workers across the country went on strike. Newspapers failed to appear, and communications were paralysed. Even for the Conservatives, it was now clear that some resolution to the issue had to be found to maintain social peace.[42]

Several membership referenda were held within the party, and a clear majority came out in favour of another political strike; but the party leadership hesitated. One central argument was that it wanted to go down the parliamentary road first. The party had gradually been able to form its own parliamentary group. Hjalmar Branting had been elected in 1896, and in 1902 he was joined by three party comrades. It was hoped that the Liberals would push the issue in parliament, and Branting feared that using extra-parliamentary methods might make them more hesitant. Tactical considerations also led Branting to refrain from pursuing the issue of women's suffrage in parliament. This would only risk delaying men's suffrage and make cooperation with the Liberals more difficult. The women would have to wait. His 1901 suffrage motion only applied to men.[43]

The debate over which tactics the Social Democrats should use on the suffrage issue was a first sign of the disagreements that were to deepen within the party. Should the Social Democrats rely above all on their own forces, inside and outside parliament, or focus on pushing through reforms in cooperation with the Liberals? The relationship with the Liberals also had repercussions for the attitude of Social Democratic women to the women's suffrage movement. As in many other countries, it was led by liberal women. From the beginning, their central demand was that women should be able to vote on the same terms as men. As a large proportion of men still lacked the right to vote, this meant that most working-class women would not be covered by such a reform.[44]

'We can admire the work of the women's suffrage associations, and we should not be hostile to them', said Kata Dalström, the leading woman agitator, 'but cooperation with them is probably not possible.' Many of the ladies of the upper classes had a feeling of contempt for working-class women, while others argued that Social Democratic

---

42 Ibid., pp. 134ff.
43 Ibid., pp. 135ff.
44 Josefin Rönnbäck, *Politikens genusgränser: den kvinnliga rösträttsrörelsen och kampen för kvinnors politiska medborgarskap 1902–1921* (Stockholm: Atlas, 2004).

women should still be part of the women's suffrage movement. Opponents of this view received support at the International Socialist
Women's Conference in Copenhagen in 1910, which declared itself
against cooperation with the bourgeois-led international suffrage
movement.[45]

The labour movement played a decisive role during the political crisis
that erupted when the Norwegian parliament decided in 1905 to
denounce the union with Sweden, into which the country had been
forced in 1814. Conservative circles mobilised, and were prepared to
force Norway to stay – through war if necessary. The Social Democratic
Party Congress, which met in the spring of 1905, declared itself in
favour of the Norwegian people's right to decide 'freely and without
external interference on their own affairs'. At the height of the union
crisis, the Social Democrats, especially the Youth League, held large-
scale protest rallies around the country. Liberals also joined the
resistance. The strong popular support for Norwegian independence
probably played a decisive role in the government's failure to contest the
demands of the Norwegians.[46]

Popular Movements and Social Integration

But the labour movement was not the largest of the popular movements.
At the turn of the century, the temperance movement had by far the
most adherents.[47] It consisted mainly of organisations that had grown
out of the US-based temperance movement, chiefly the Independent
Order of Good Templars (IOGT). By 1910, the various orders had
more than 350,000 members. Since membership turnover was high,
perhaps a million Swedes received their first training in social movement work in the temperance movement during the first decades of the
twentieth century (at the turn of the century, the country had 5 million
inhabitants).

The temperance movement was initially supported mainly by
craftsmen, lower-class white-collar workers, teachers, and, after the

---

45   Ostberg, *Folk i rörelse*, p. 88.
46   Ibid., p. 66.
47   The main source for this chapter is Sven Lundkvist, *Politik, nykterhet och
reformer: en studie i folkrörelsernas politiska verksamhet 1900–1920* (Stockholm: Uppsala
University Press, 1974).

turn of the century, increasingly by workers. On a general ideological level, of course, the fight against alcohol was the most important issue of the temperance movement. Politically, it called for a total ban on the sale of alcohol. But the activities of the temperance movement went far beyond this narrow concern. The temperance societies offered opportunities for rich social interaction. There was much singing, and a theatre group might put on a play. Choirs, horn bands, and sports clubs also sprang up.

The temperance movement built thousands of halls for its meetings around the country.[48] It also played a key role in the expansion of popular education. Lending libraries became a magnet for young people from working-class and peasant homes who were hungry to read. Study circles – the heart of the educational activities of popular movements – were developed within the movement, studying everything from Swedish language and social history to astronomy. An important purpose of this broad educational activity was – to quote teetotaller Rickard Sandler, later Social Democratic prime minister – to turn the participants into citizens.[49]

Sobriety, community, and popular education were crucial. But there was another indispensable dimension to the temperance movement: the political. Participation in the day-to-day activities of the lodges has often been described as resembling a school of democracy, with members learning how to run meetings and study circles, take minutes, and keep a ledger. But the political activities of the temperance movement were far more assertive than that. It could be argued that the movement was Sweden's first modern political party.[50]

Political parties in the modern sense were only formed at the beginning of the twentieth century. Candidates for parliamentary and municipal elections were often appointed by ad hoc assemblies of politically interested people. This opened unprecedented opportunities for the association-minded teetotallers. Election meetings provided a venue for local temperance committees to bring together members of lodges, Free Church congregations, and workers' associations. As

---

48   Östberg, *Folk i rörelse*, pp. 74–84.

49   Ronny Ambjörnsson, *Den skötsamme arbetaren: idéer och ideal i ett norrländskt sågverkssamhälle 1880–1930* (Stockholm: Carlsson, 1988); Ronny Ambjörnsson, *The Honest and Diligent Worker* (Stockholm: HLS, 1991).

50   Lundkvist, *Politik, nykterhet och reformer*, Chapter 6.

incomes increased, more people had the opportunity to participate in the elections.

The IOGT built up its own electoral organisation at central and local levels in secret. It sent its members to nomination meetings to ensure that its own candidates would get onto the lists. Lodges organised election meetings, and printed posters and leaflets to support the non-drinking candidates.

Success came quickly. In 1911, more than 60 per cent of the members of the directly elected Second Chamber of parliament were temperance-minded. The influence of the movement was limited in the upper strata of society, but its influence was substantial among the Liberals (73 per cent) and Social Democrats (88 per cent). In the municipal assemblies, the picture was similar.[51]

It took some time before the political parties developed the political professionalism already demonstrated by the temperance movement. When they did, it was largely under the influence of members of the latter. Both the Liberals and the Social Democrats largely comprised those who had been educated in the temperance movement. Most of the Social Democratic Party's national board, and many union leaders, were members of it.

As the sociologist Gunnar Olofsson has noted, there were two defining aspects of the temperance movement. The first was its emphasis on the individual solution and personal abstinence. The second was its demand for state and local authorities to extend voting rights, in order to implement total prohibition. In this way, the temperance movement was caught between liberal individualism and the demands of the labour movement for collective solutions.[52]

The temperance movement came to play an active role in shaping the political culture in Sweden. In the lodges, liberals and socialists worked side by side and campaigned for common candidates. Until the 1910s, the Liberals dominated – often ensuring that the Social Democrats on the lists were not too radical. This meant that Social Democrats elected to political assemblies were less likely to be combative, and more likely to cooperate with liberals. It also had consequences for the political development of Social Democracy itself.

---

51 Ibid., Chapter 5.
52 Gunnar Olofsson, *Mellan klass och stat: om arbetarrörelse, reformism och socialdemokrati* (Lund: Arkiv, 1979), p. 140.

The political vision represented by liberalism sought to consolidate the notion that social conflicts could and should be resolved in harmony, without class conflict, through the political institutions of bourgeois society. Parliament was seen as a forum for rational deliberation for the common good. Parliamentarianism incorporated several of the main demands of the popular movements – in particular, the demand for political democracy. Modern bourgeois institutions came to coincide with the vision of democratic society held by the people's movements.[53]

At the same time, within the socialist movement at the beginning of the twentieth century, a series of hotly contested questions – both of principle and of tactics – were brought into the political foreground. At their core was the question of the political autonomy of the working class. The classical Marxist line was critical of class collaboration – not in the form of cooperation on concrete issues, such as universal suffrage; and not in the form of alliances in which the working class could participate on its own terms. But socialist transformation could only be achieved, the Marxists held, if the liberation of the working class became its own work.[54]

The Popular Movement's Parties

A central fact of the political development of Sweden was that the modern political parties that emerged in this period were chiefly outgrowths of the popular movements of the early twentieth century: the workers who built the Social Democratic Party, and eventually the Communist Party, emerged out of the labour and the temperance movements, while the Liberals grew out of the temperance movement and the Free Churches.[55] When the Farmers' Union was formed in the years around the First World War, this likewise reflected a political extension of farmers' movements. Only the Conservatives lay essentially outside the sphere of popular movements.

53   Kjell Östberg, *Byråkrati och reformism: en studie av svensk socialdemokratis politiska och sociala integrering fram till första världskriget* (Lund: Arkiv, 1990), pp. 85–8.
54   Geoff Eley, *Forging Democracy: The History of the Left in Europe, 1850–2000* (Oxford: Oxford University Press, 2002), pp. 86–93.
55   On this development, see Östberg, *Folk i rörelse*, pp. 85ff.

The foundations of the parties that emerged in this process were not confined narrow to the realm of formal politics and its auxiliary organisations, such as women's and youth associations. They were built on a much broader base of social movements which, depending on the party, might include trade unions, temperance organisations, religious communities, agricultural associations, cultural and educational organisations, sports clubs, and cooperative activities. This gave these parties deeper roots in society than parties created by parliamentary factions, political elites, or narrow social strata.

A political party derived from popular movement activity could hold a broadened democratic potential. Even if the parties were, in a sense, quickly absorbed into parliamentary work, a form of participatory democracy could continue to live on within them and in the movements on which they were based. In those movements, proposals could be formulated and decisions discussed, criticised, and challenged even between elections – and outside parliamentary institutions. Members were stimulated to broader social activity, and trained to think and act politically. They also participated in the practical implementation of policy at both the local and national levels.

Counter-offensive: The General Strike of 1909

It is easy to point to the great conquests made by the labour movement a few years into the new century. But not everything went smoothly.

Employers, of course, did not stand idly by as the unions moved their positions forward. They formed powerful organisations themselves. Immediately after the great political strike of 1902, they founded their own combat organisation, the Swedish Employers' Association (Svenska Arbetsgivareföreningen – SAF). The response to workers' strikes was an increasing number of lockouts, in which the frequent use of strike-breakers played an important role.[56]

In 1906, the SAF called a massive lockout to establish once and for all the unrestricted right of employers to determine working conditions

---

56 Hans de Geer, *The Rise and Fall of the Swedish Model: The Swedish Employers' Confederation, SAF, and Industrial Relations over Ten Decades* (Chichester: Carden, 1992).

and decisions on hiring and firing. All contracts had to contain a special clause, Section 23 – later Section 32 – to this effect. The employers were prepared to lock out 70,000 workers to enforce their demands. At that point, the LO retreated, lacking the financial resources to continue the resistance; the obvious risk was that the trade union movement could be torn to pieces. For seventy years, this controversial principle would apply to all contracts. But it was a compromise: at the same time, the employers' organisations in fact recognised the workers' right to join trade unions.[57]

The international situation deteriorated rapidly around 1910. A widespread recession swept across Europe, and hostility increased between the leading imperialist powers. The threat of a coming world war loomed ever larger.[58]

This period was also characterised by increasing social polarisation in Sweden as well, and in some of the biggest power struggles conservative social forces prevailed. The fighting culminated in the 1909 general strike, which soon developed into the greatest defeat of the labour movement up to that moment.[59] In the spring of 1909, a series of conflicts broke out across the country, and employers saw an opportunity to counterattack. They were now well organised and had built up substantial funds. The recession and rising unemployment weakened the workers' position, making employers less vulnerable to production stoppages. This was an excellent opportunity to try to stifle the growing trade union movement.

In the middle of the summer, the SAF demanded that all ongoing disputes be resolved on the employers' terms within two weeks, or they would gradually activate widespread lockouts. The unions had ducked many battles in recent years, but could do so no longer. Apart from anything else, there was great pressure from members to fight back: syndicalist-inspired propaganda for the general strike had been circulating for some time, and had won the support of many workers' groups. The LO responded by taking 300,000 workers out on general strike. Cohesion was high, but strike funds were low – estimated to last for only

57   Anders L. Johansson and Lars Magnusson, *LO: 1900-talet och ett nytt millennium* (Stockholm: Atlas, 2019).
58   E. J. Hobsbawm, *The Age of Extremes: The Short Twentieth Century, 1914–1991* (London: Joseph, 1994).
59   Bernt Schiller, *Storstrejken 1909: förhistoria och orsaker* (Gothenburg: Elander, 1967).

a week or so, while the employers were prepared for several months of conflict.

Strike committees were formed all over the country. The strike took place in an orderly fashion; pubs were closed, and there was talk of the 'revolution of the crossed arms', referring to the workers crossing their arms over their chests to demonstrate their peaceful action.[60]

After a month, however, the LO leadership began to prepare for retreat, albeit in the face of protest from many workers. One of the sharpest questions raised was whether the LO leadership really wanted to win. Why, for example, did they not take the railway workers out on strike to prevent employers from continuing exports from their well-stocked warehouses? Did the LO leadership want to show that the general strike was a dead end? Nonetheless, the leadership's decision stood. To continue would jeopardise the very existence of the unions, its representatives argued.

The price of defeat was high, as employers were generally able to dictate its terms. Large numbers of workers were never given their jobs back, and many of those were evicted from their homes. Blacklists of employees circulated among employers, and thousands chose, or were forced, to emigrate to find work. Fines or imprisonment were imposed upon 1,500 workers.

The trade union movement emerged greatly weakened. The year before the Swedish general strike, LO unions had 162,000 members; by 1912, membership had more than halved, to 79,000. The backlash had repercussions throughout the labour movement. The Social Democratic Party also lost half of its members. Dissatisfaction with what was perceived as the leadership's failure to act was a major reason why a few thousand of the most radical workers broke with the LO and formed the syndicalist Swedish Workers' Central Organisation.

This failure deepened the rift that had developed within Social Democracy over the strategic orientation of the labour movement. These contradictions were in close congruence with the debate within the Second International, and would lead ultimately to the rupture of the international labour movement.[61]

---

60 Hirdman, *Vi bygger landet*, pp. 89–95.
61 Hentilä, *Sveriges socialdemokratiska arbetareparti*, pp. 251–3.

Right and Left

For a long time the party's presence in political decision-making assemblies was very limited. Gradually, however, Social Democratic representation increased.

More and more workers earned SEK 800 a year, qualifying them to vote in the elections to the Second Chamber. In 1909 this restriction was removed for most men, though women continued to be excluded. At the same time, changes were introduced to the municipal voting system. This led to an increase in the number of Social Democrats elected to the Riksdag and municipal assemblies. In the parliamentary elections of autumn 1914, the party received 36 per cent of the vote, making it the largest party in the Second Chamber. This suddenly gave the party significant parliamentary influence. Demands for political and social reform were no longer mere aspirations enshrined in party programmes: some could now be translated into political decisions. This placed questions of party tactics high on the agenda.[62]

TABLE 1.1: SEAT TOTALS IN FIRST AND SECOND CHAMBERS

	1897	1903	1906	1909	1912	1914	1915
FC	–	–	–	–	12	13	14
SC	1	4	13	34	63	72	87
Total	1	4	13	34	75	85	101

The dominant theoretical figure within international Social Democracy gave little guidance. Karl Kautsky was convinced that socialism, including revolution, was both necessary and inevitable – so inevitable, in fact, that the transition to socialism became increasingly a matter of waiting for the right moment.[63] Social Democracy was not a force that *made* revolutions; revolutions instead *arose*, like irresistible social phenomena. Until that moment, the task of a Social Democratic party was to rally support and educate the public, so as to take over as a political

---

62   Östberg, *Byråkrati och reformism*, pp. 61ff.
63   Eley, *Forging Democracy*, pp. 86–98.

force wherever the revolution broke out. Given this wait-and-see approach, known as *attentisme*, discussion of the road to socialism also became a secondary issue.

At the same time, some weighty questions emerged that would dominate internal debates in the years leading up to the First World War. The factions that emerged around them had their counterparts in most of the parties affiliated to the Second International. In Sweden, they were generally called 'right' and 'left', but they could also be termed reformist and revolutionary', opportunist and class-struggle-oriented, or revisionist and Marxist.

It is of course an oversimplification to reduce the extensive and multifaceted discussion of the tasks of the socialist movement into a few labels.[64] The range of views on how the movement might realise its aims spanned a wide spectrum, from the left of Rosa Luxemburg and Lenin, which stressed the necessity of mass action and revolutionary uprisings, through Karl Kautsky's more or less official orthodoxy and the French leader Jean Jaurès's radical reformism, to Eduard Bernstein's more principled revisionism, in which reform and reliance on the state, combined with parliamentary cooperation across class boundaries, were key elements. Gradually, the state would be stripped of its oppressive character, as Branting put it.

It is possible to define these various tendencies in terms of how they grouped themselves around the concrete issues of struggle on which the international labour movement during this period was forced in practice to take a stand. The central goal – socialism – was agreed upon by all. Nor was there any disagreement about whether to fight for the right to vote or participate in parliamentary elections, whether to strive for social and economic improvements for the working class, or the importance of building trade unions and Social Democratic parties on a mass scale. Instead, as Social Democratic parties grew and gained social influence, debates about the link between reform and socialism, about the balance between parliamentary and extra-parliamentary work, and about attitudes to legal and extra-legal methods only became more highly charged. One central question related to the legitimate forms of cooperation with other

---

64   Donald Sassoon, *One Hundred Years of Socialism: The West European Left in the Twentieth Century* (London: I.B. Tauris, 1996), Chapter 1.

classes, in parliament and even in government; another concerned the correct attitude to war and armaments. Disagreement on these questions became so deep that it ultimately led to the rupture of the entire Second International, in a division between Social Democratic and communist parties.

In Sweden these conflicts crystallised around two poles in the years before the First World War. On one side stood a right-wing current, whose base was in the bureaucracy of the party, the parliamentary group, and the central trade union leaders; on the other was a left-wing tendency articulated above all in the Youth League.[65] The theoretical weight of the debate should not be exaggerated. Branting was aware of Bernstein's attempts to influence German Social Democracy in a more reformist direction. The left determinedly sought out the more ortho-dox mainstream of the Second International, and its main newspaper, *Stormklockan*, was also happy to publish articles by Luxemburg and Karl Liebknecht, as well as the Russian revolutionaries. When it came to the discussion of practical policy, however, the differences became increasingly apparent.

Tensions first became clear in the context of the political strike for suffrage in 1902.[66] The pressure from members to continue with new strikes was great; but Branting wanted to try the parliamentary route instead. 'We have two ways to go, the way of a general strike or the way of the elections', he remarked. 'These cannot be taken at the same time. If we call a general strike, we shall have no prospect of winning anything at the elections.'[67]

Branting was undoubtedly the leading figure of Swedish Social Democracy from the late 1880s until his death in 1925.[68] Born into a bourgeois Stockholm family, in his youth he belonged to the radical liberal student association Verdandi. But in 1885 he joined the Social Democratic Association in Stockholm. He soon held several leading positions within the party, often simultaneously: editor of the party

---

65   For this section, see Östberg, *Byråkrati och reformism*; and Hentilä, *Sveriges socialdemokratiska arbetareparti*, Chapter 3.3.

66   Hentilä, *Den svenska arbetarklassen*, pp. 134–6.

67   Birger Simonson, *Socialdemokratin och maktövertagandet: SAP:s politiska strategi 1889–1911* (Gothenburg: Historiska Institutionen, 1985), p. 137.

68   Olle Svenning, *Hövdingen – Hjalmar Branting: en biografi* (Stockholm: Bonnier, 2014).

Socialdemokraten and of the party's theoretical journal *Tiden* (Times).
He became the party's first member of parliament in 1896, and party
chairman and chairman of the party's parliamentary group until his
death. He became an ardent advocate for the party to focus its energies
primarily on social and political reform in parliament, in close cooperation with the Liberal Party. From his youth, he had enjoyed good
relations with Liberal representatives – especially with the party's chairman and first prime minister, Karl Staaff.

Ministerial Socialism and the Struggle against Militarism

The relationship between Liberals and Social Democrats was complex. In
the early period of the labour movement, the Liberals had made fruitless
attempts to gain influence over the trade unions.[69] But close parliamentary cooperation in parliamentary elections developed early on. Until
1910, Sweden had mainly the British type of majority elections, which
encouraged cooperation between Liberals and Social Democrats to
prevent right-wing candidates from being elected. It was the Liberals who
set the terms of this cooperation, and it was also they who made the
biggest gains.

These close relations, and the compromises they forced, were controversial within both parties. Many Social Democrats were opposed
to supporting Liberal candidates who had often occupied anti-labour
positions in parliament or as business leaders. But Liberal leader
Karl Staaff had further plans. When he formed his government in
1911 with the support of the Social Democrats, he remarked: 'Our
liberal policy is in fact among the more remarkable attempts in
modern times to turn the socialist paladins decisively to loyal parliamentary national work and to bring them into the responsibility
for what is done in state life.'[70] In two areas the Social Democrats
were to be made to come to terms with their history: they were to
fully accept the parliamentary rules of the game, and to give up
their anti-militarism and 'positively advocate effective military
defence'.

---

69 Östberg, *Byråkrati och reformism*, Chapter 5.
70 Ibid., p. 258.

The question of the participation of Social Democratic parties in bourgeois governments was a central and much-debated issue in international Social Democracy in the period before the First World War. It came to symbolise the movement's attitude to the political independence of the working class from the bourgeoisie. At its congresses, the Second International had repeatedly rejected Social Democratic participation on principle. The first Social Democrat to accept a seat in government, the Frenchman Alexandre Millerand, was also expelled from the Second International.[71]

The question of ministerial socialism was intimately connected with the attitude to military defence. Support for national defence was a condition for bourgeois parties even to consider closer cooperation of Social Democrats with government. The discussion of how to conduct the struggle against war and militarism was at the forefront of most of the congresses of the Second International. At the Paris Congress of 1900, it was decided that the socialist representatives in all parliaments were obliged to vote unconditionally against any expenditure on 'militarism, navalism or the colonial expeditions'.[72]

The famous Stuttgart Resolution of 1907 stated that it was the duty of the working classes and their representatives in parliament to do their utmost to prevent the outbreak of war by whatever means they considered most effective. But, at the same time, currents more favourable to national defence were growing strong in several sections of the Second International.[73] In Sweden, Branting was in favour of the introduction of compulsory military service in 1901, and believed that disarmament was out of the question. Swedish Social Democrats were to strive for '*a people in arms*, an army incapable of attack . . . but all the stronger for defence, an army, borne up by genuine civic spirit'.[74]

At the beginning of the twentieth century, there was a radicalisation within the party, in which young people played a leading role. Anti-militarism was a central part of their practice and propaganda. In 1908, the wording of the party programme was tightened to: 'Fight against militarism. Gradual reduction of military burdens, towards disarmament.' The phrase 'gradual reduction' naturally invited questions of interpretation as to how quickly this reduction

71   Eley, *Forging Democracy*, p. 87.
72   Ibid., pp. 86–93.
73   Ibid., p. 92.
74   For the following section, see Östberg, *Byråkrati och reformism*, Chapter 6.

might take place. In 1911, against the wishes of the party board, the congress therefore stressed that disarmament 'must be pursued with all possible vigour'. At the 1914 congress, the party executive tried unsuccessfully to have this formulation repealed. But the amendment stood.

This battle reflected above all the shift that had taken place within the party leadership. At the same time as anti-militarism had gained influence within the party, the party's policy in parliament had become increasingly pro-defence. But a dramatic change took place in the period 1911–14. When liberal leader Staaff was appointed prime minister in 1911, one of his promises was to reduce defence costs. He set up four committees to investigate how defence should be organised in the future, with one Social Democrat on each committee.

The next few years were characterised by strong domestic polarisation. The approach of world war was in the air, and conservative forces mobilised for increased defence spending. The right's mobilisation culminated in the Farmers' March of 1914. Around 30,000 people, mainly conservative farmers, gathered from all over the country to demonstrate in Stockholm. The sizeable demonstration marched to the palace and presented demands for increased defence funding to King Gustav V. The king willingly received the demonstrators and, in the infamous Courtyard Speech, railed against his government and sided with the demonstrators. Staaff was forced to resign and, in a move resembling a coup d'état, the king appointed his own conservative government.[75]

The conservative mobilisation had already affected the Staaff government's defence policy. The defence committees had quickly abandoned any ambition to reduce defence funding, instead proposing significant rearmament. The Social Democratic members went along with this, accepting virtually the entire proposed programme. They were later supported by the Social Democratic parliamentary group. The fractious atmosphere of the summer of 1914 led the parliamentary group to accept even higher defence costs.[76]

In 1911, a parallel development had unfolded in the discussion on ministerial socialism. In a resolution proposed by the party's left wing, it was decided almost unanimously that, 'In connection with

---

75 Hadenius, *Swedish Politics*, pp. 25ff; Hirdman, *Vi bygger landet*, p. 136.
76 Östberg, *Byråkrati och reformism*, pp. 244–6.

the decisions of the International Congresses of Paris and Amsterdam, the Congress declares that the entry of Social Democrats into a bourgeois ministry is not to be recommended . . . The party member who nevertheless enters a bourgeois government without such a mandate is thus deemed to have left the party.'[77] For Branting, however, ministerial socialism was a clear alternative: 'It then seems obvious that Social Democracy cannot say no to participation in the government in the long run. When we have accepted parliamentarism in all other respects, we must not shrink from the consequence of assuming governmental responsibility. It is therefore not possible to oppose in principle the participation of Social Democrats in a Liberal government.'[78]

Branting was not prepared to respect the decision of the Party Congress. In 1914, he began discussions with the Liberals about forming a joint government. When the Party Congress met in the autumn of 1914, the party leadership threatened to resign if it was not given the go-ahead to continue negotiations. Under this pressure, the congress agreed to participate in a Liberal government by a vote of 90 to 58 – though it was not until 1917 that such a government became a reality.[79]

Why the Turn?

How should we understand why the Social Democratic Party so clearly oriented itself towards the right of the Second International on central issues such as ministerial socialism and the attitude to military armament – even though the opinion of the membership as expressed at the Party Congresses pointed in a different direction?

The American political scientist Adam Przeworski has discussed in more detail the conditions for the participation of the labour movement in parliamentary work in a couple of books, *Capitalism and Social*

---

77 Sveriges socialdemokratiska arbetareparti Kongress, *Förhandlingarna vid Sverges socialdemokratiska arbetarepartis åttonde ordinarie kongress i Stockholm den 9–16 April 1911* (Stockholm: Partiet, 1911), p. 34.

78 Östberg, *Byråkrati och reformism*, p. 305.

79 Ibid., Chapter 9.

Democracy (1985) and *Paper Stones* (1986).[80] He argues that the labour movement was initially faced with a choice as to whether to participate in this form of political work at all. Once the decision was made, it set the limits for the development of the socialist parties. The problem was that once the organised labour movement decided to participate in political work, and was given the opportunity to do so, the main features of the bourgeois democratic structures, as expressed mainly in parliamentarianism, were already formulated. The function of the party therefore went beyond organising the working class in the struggle for socialism by all available means – it would also have to adapt to function in the parliamentary environment.[81]

Once universal suffrage was won, parties had to choose between 'legal' and 'extra-legal', parliamentary and extra-parliamentary tactics. To win the votes of non-workers, especially petty-bourgeois groups, in order to build coalitions and alliances, the party had to demonstrate wholeheartedly its commitment to abide by the rules and limitations of the parliamentary game. It also sometimes had to persuade its supporters to refrain from actions that could jeopardise electoral success.

The organisation of workers into mass organisations for parliamentary elections therefore risked confusing two different processes: on the one hand, the organisation of workers on a class basis; on the other, the organisation of as many people as possible to vote for the Social Democratic programme, which soon also included layers outside the working class. The movement also had to build, or strengthen, its apparatus – which produced a bureaucracy that was to a significant extent based in parliament. It is here that we find the social base of the Social Democratic Right.

A Workers' Bureaucracy

Ever since Robert Michels's *Zur Soziologie des Parteiwesens* coined the thesis of the iron law of oligarchy over a hundred years ago, the problem of bureaucratisation has been a recurring theme in research on the

---

80   Adam Przeworski, *Capitalism and Social Democracy* (Cambridge: Cambridge University Press, 1985); Adam Przeworski and John Sprague, *Paper Stones: A History of Electoral Socialism* (Chicago: University of Chicago Press, 1986).

81   Przeworski, *Capitalism and Social Democracy*, pp. 7–41.

development of Social Democracy, and so it will be in this book.[82] Michels argued that the gap between the cultural superiority and formal education of the leaders and the masses inevitably created a divide that was reinforced by the leaders' economic dependence. He also pointed to the importance of parliamentary work. It gave leaders greater prestige, but also allowed them to carry out their work without being subject to direct control by their members, or constantly visible to them.

Although Michels's theses were quickly challenged, several of his themes recurred in contemporary debate. Rosa Luxemburg made direct links between bureaucracy and the growing influence of the reformist movement.[83] Parliamentary work became a springboard for political careerists, as did the vast material resources of organisations. Leon Trotsky later pointed out how the material and political privileges of the workers' bureaucracy were rapidly alienating them from those they were supposed to represent.[84]

The social base of Swedish Social Democracy was originally mainly industrial workers organised in their trade unions. The trade union movement's rapid membership growth soon reached such a scale that some form of full-time management was necessary. It was, of course, a great success when the Metalworkers' Union chairperson Ernst Blomberg could be employed full-time in 1895. He no longer had to manage the business of a union of tens of thousands of members in the evenings and nights after ten hours of work as a copper smith. Soon, the other unions followed suit. By 1914, twenty-eight unions had sixty-eight central full-time officials.[85]

The Social Democratic Party had a minimal full-time cadre. As late as 1914, there were only three staff members: a party secretary, a treasurer, and a female assistant. But large numbers of Social Democratic functionaries were to be found in two other places: in the party press and in the parliamentary group. The number of Social

---

82 Robert Michels, *Zur Soziologie des Parteiwesens in der modernen Demokratie: Untersuchungen über die oligarchischen Tendenzen des Gruppenlebens* (Stuttgart: Kröner, 1970 [1911]).

83 Rosa Luxemburg, *Reform or Revolution* (New York: Pathfinder, 1970 [1900]).

84 Leon Trotsky, *The Revolution Betrayed: What Is the Soviet Union and Where Is It Going?* (London: Faber & Faber, 1937).

85 For the following section, see Östberg, *Byråkrati och reformism*, Chapter 2.

Democratic newspapers increased rapidly in the years after the turn of the twentieth century, and several of the journalists held prominent positions in the party. But the great rallying point for Social Democratic functionaries was the Social Democratic parliamentary group, which in 1914 included over a hundred members. It brought together the leading trade unionists, newspapermen, and prominent local representatives.

Most officials had originally been workers. Certainly, early central leaders also came from bourgeois or petty-bourgeois backgrounds. After the turn of the century, a new layer was recruited from there, not least to meet the needs of newspaper editors and members of parliament in the First Chamber. Even among journalists, however, the vast majority were of working-class background.

The officials of the movement were not paid large salaries. From the beginning, the benchmark was the salary of a well-educated worker. Slowly, however, their economic distance from fellow-workers began to increase. They were soon receiving other benefits that their members lacked, such as paid holidays and pensions. Above all, there was a great deal of continuity within the layer of officials. It was extremely rare for one of them not to be re-elected.

In 1915, the functionaries of the labour movement formed their own trade union. From the beginning, two issues were priorities. First, it demanded the abolition of congress elections for officials and the introduction of permanent positions; second, it demanded that the question of officials' pensions be resolved. The officials now considered themselves to be a separate profession with common interests. Not surprisingly, their union by one of its leading members was called the 'union of the satisfied'.[86]

In the struggles between the right and left of the party, the bureaucrats came to support the right in most cases. There were several reasons for this. The leaders of the trade union movement, not least after defeat in the Swedish general strike of 1909, took a cautious line so as not to jeopardise the gains that had been made or threaten the unions' coffers. The central party leadership, with Branting as its unifying figure, had a decisive influence on recruitment to newspapers and parliamentary groups, and was careful to appoint figures on the right of the party as

---

86   Ibid., pp. 73–6.

newspaper editors and parliamentary candidates. In the many parliamentary committees, MPs were trained to work in confidence with representatives of other classes. But the party's right wing did not rest on a 'labour aristocracy'. The representatives of the right and the left inside the party had remarkably similar social backgrounds.

The bureaucracy, centred in the parliamentary group, was the driving force in the political development of the party. It was the central carrier and transmitter of reformist ideas within the Swedish labour movement.[87] This development reflects a wider phenomenon. The labour movement did not exist in a vacuum, but was deeply influenced by the values that dominated the society around it.

The party's patriarchal features were prominent; its decision-makers were exclusively men. In the Riksdag, women were excluded by prevailing election regulations, and there was still none elected to the party board. Leading female agitator Kata Dalström had occupied a seat for a few years, but was not re-elected. The situation was the same within the trade union movement.

Another contentious issue related to nationalism and racism. It culminated in the campaign against the use of Polish seasonal workers, 'galiziers', in agriculture in southern Sweden. They were perceived as a threat to the attempts to organise Swedish farm workers into a union, and some of them were used as strike-breakers. The campaign organised against the 'Galician danger' was plagued by arguments steeped in racism. 'Shamefully dressed, lethargic and willingly living like a herd of cattle, representing the lowest stage of the commodity – labour power', wrote *Arbetet i Malmö*. The anti-Semitic currents that were a routine part of bourgeois thinking at this time also had an impact on some leading Social Democrats.[88]

In 1914, the Social Democratic Party celebrated its twenty-fifth anniversary. It was now able to look back on an impressive journey. In close cooperation with the trade union movement, it had shaped the Swedish working class into a politically cohesive class, ideologically, organisationally, and programmatically. The labour movement was the current that most consistently fought to democratise society. Social Democracy

---

87   Ibid., pp. 327–9.
88   Håkan Blomqvist, *Nation, ras och civilisation i svensk arbetarrörelse före nazismen* (Stockholm: Carlssons, 2006).

was in favour of the right to vote for both men and women without financial barriers or other restrictions. It was also the movement that best represented the broad majority of the country's population; both locally and nationally, its leaders mostly had backgrounds in occupations such as bricklaying, carpentry, or ironwork. But the women were missing. It was not yet clear what consequences the social and political divisions that were already clearly visible would have as Social Democracy started out on its march towards building a socialist society.

2

The Revolutionary Years

Social Democracy and the War

The First World War was a disaster for humanity. Tens of millions died. A generation of young men was slaughtered in senseless trench warfare. The proud declarations of the labour movement never to point guns at brothers in other countries proved worthless when the nationalist war drums began to beat. 'Humanity survived. Nevertheless, the great edifice of nineteenth-century civilisation crumpled in the flames of world war, as its pillars collapsed', as historian Eric Hobsbawm put it.[1]

Sweden remained outside the war, and the king's government declared Sweden neutral. At the same time, the government's sympathies, as well as those of most of the conservative bourgeoisie, obviously lay with Germany. Economic and cultural ties remained strong, and the German leaders soon learned that the government's neutrality towards Germany was 'benevolent'.[2]

Formal neutrality meant that the fateful question for the Social Democratic parties in the warring countries – whether to support their own nation's wars and armaments – was of no immediate relevance to the Swedish party. Nevertheless, the war had significant consequences for the Social Democrats. Already during the summer, the parliamentary group had actively contributed to the Riksdag's decision on a sharp increase in defence spending. At the outbreak of war, Branting declared: 'in the face of the pressure of war, the internal struggles of every people,

---

1 E. J. Hobsbawm, *The Age of Extremes: The Short Twentieth Century, 1914–1991* (London: Joseph, 1994), p. 22.

2 Stig Hadenius, *Swedish Politics during the 20th Century: Conflict and Consensus* (Stockholm: Svenska Institutet, 1997), pp. 27ff; Bo Stråth, *Sveriges historia. 1830–1920* (Stockholm: Norstedt, 2012), pp. 122ff.

however sharp they might be as a result of class antagonisms, must for the moment recede.'[3] The Social Democrats thus accepted the party truce that prevailed between the political parties, setting aside wider social struggles.

The war had helped Branting to win battles over the two crucial issues concerning the party's future strategy: support for military defence and ministerial socialism. He was now prepared to take the decisive battle with the party's left, even if it meant splitting the party: 'Once the majority of the Congress has taken its stand, however, it should go forward without being intimidated by any threats, not even by threats to blow up the party. There is no need to show reluctance or to stop halfway.'[4]

In the years to come, the left became isolated within the party. In the new party leadership elected in 1914, the left was excluded, despite having had between one-third and half of the delegates at the congress. Left-wing candidates also had great difficulty winning seats in parliament, with only seven out of over a hundred MPs being declared left-wing sympathisers. And their freedom of action was curtailed. When the leader of the left, Zeth Höglund, demonstratively voted against appropriations to the Royal House – in protest at the coup carried out by the king shortly beforehand – the parliamentary group introduced the so-called 'muzzle' statute. No motions could be submitted without the approval of the leaders of the parliamentary faction.[5]

The Left up to the Party Split

The party leadership's attempt to isolate the opposition led to a strengthening of left-wing cohesion.[6] The Youth League and its newspaper *Stormklockan* continued to be a focal point in this development. For the left, international contacts became important, and it participated in attempts to unite those parts of the Social Democratic movement that

---

3 Kjell Östberg, *Byråkrati och reformism: en studie av svensk socialdemokratis politiska och sociala integrering fram till första världskriget* (Lund: Arkiv, 1990), p. 244.

4 Ibid., p. 319.

5 Yvonne Hirdman, *Vi bygger landet: den svenska arbetarrörelsens historia från Per Götrek till Olof Palme* (Solna: Pogo, 1979), p. 148.

6 Werner Schmidt, *Kommunismens rötter i första världskrigets historiska rum: en studie kring arbetarrörelsens historiska misslyckande* (Stockholm: Symposion, 1996), pp. 103–9.

still opposed support for the war. Most important was the Zimmerwald Conference of 1915, which brought together participants from a dozen countries.[7]

The Zimmerwald Manifesto, essentially formulated by Trotsky, called for an immediate end to the war and a peace without land conquests or reparations. For the Russian Bolsheviks under Lenin's leadership, this was not enough. The so-called Zimmerwald Left wanted clearer demarcations from the non-revolutionary part of the Social Democratic left.

In the history of the Swedish communist movement, it has often been pointed out that the Swedes joined the Zimmerwald Left during the conference. This should probably not be assigned much importance. After the conference, the Swedish left continued without reservation to work in the spirit of the broad Zimmerwald movement for an immediate end to the war.[8] In the spring of 1916, the Youth League organised a workers' peace conference. The background was a concern that the Swedish government was wavering in its policy of neutrality, and it was feared that this might drag Sweden into the conflagration. If the Riksdag could not prevent such a development, the labour movement should also be prepared to arrange extra-parliamentary mass actions – and should the government throw the country into a war, 'all obligations to such a government would cease', said a statement from the conference. For these formulations, some of the organisers of the congress were sentenced to prison for incitement to treason. Zeth Höglund was sentenced to one year.

The conference contributed to increasing tensions between the Social Democratic Party leadership and the left, whose initiative was portrayed as disloyal and undisciplined. When the authorities intervened, Branting argued that the organisers had only themselves to blame by threatening a riot. But when the harsh sentences were passed, Branting also took part in the widespread protests against them.[9]

In the spring of 1916, the left started its own daily newspaper, *Folkets Dagblad Politiken* (The people's daily politics). In the process, the Social Democratic parliamentary group was effectively split in two. The formal break-up of the party was now only a matter of time. As the end of the war approached, the question of forming a government with the

---

7   Geoff Eley, *Forging Democracy: The History of the Left in Europe, 1850–2000* (Oxford: Oxford University Press, 2002), pp. 128–31.

8   Werner Schmidt, *Kommunismens rötter*, pp. 136–8.

9   Hirdman, *Vi bygger landet*, pp. 147ff.

Liberals also became relevant. Before then, Branting had already wanted to get rid of his left wing.

The formal split took place at the Party Congress in February 1917.[10] The party leadership targeted the Youth League – the centre of the left opposition. A resolution demanded that the Youth League withdraw its claim that the parliamentary group had 'substantially departed from the party programme', and that the League commit itself to complying with the decisions taken within the party organisation. They would also not be allowed to field their own lists in the upcoming parliamentary elections. If they did not comply, this would automatically result in their expulsion from the party.[11]

The position of the left within the party remained strong. In the election of delegates, it received 42 per cent of the vote, but under a new electoral system it won just over 20 per cent of delegates. Branting's ultimatum was impossible for the left to accept. It was accepted by a vote of 134 to 42, which in effect meant the splitting of the Social Democratic Party.[12]

The Swedish Hunger Riots, 1917–18: Women Light the Spark

The years between 1917 and 1921 probably represent the deepest, most dramatic and violent period of radicalisation we have witnessed. The world was shaken by revolutions and counter-revolutions, by strikes and demonstrations. The battles were primarily about who would hold power in the new world that was emerging from the ruins of war. It was clear to most that democratic reforms were inevitable. But what would they look like? And in what forms would they be implemented?[13] Some of those who had paid the highest price in the war, women and soldiers, were the first to strike out.

St Petersburg, now Petrograd, had been a powder keg for months. In the winter of 1917 the war entered its third year. With 2 million soldiers dead, hunger, strikes, and lockouts afflicted the civilian population. It

---

10 Werner Schmidt, *Kommunismens rötter*, pp. 142ff.
11 Sveriges socialdemokratiska arbetareparti: Kongress, *Protokoll från Sveriges socialdemokratiska arbetarepartis tionde kongress i Stockholm: den 12–20 februari, 1917* (Stockholm, 1917).
12 Ibid.
13 Eley, *Forging Democracy*, Chapter 9.

was the women textile workers of the radical Viborg (Vyborgsky) district who lit the spark on the morning of 8 March, International Women's Day. They no longer wanted to submit to queuing for food for hours after work, with no guarantee of finding something to eat. Under the slogan 'Bread and Peace', they marched through working-class neighbourhoods, bringing with them fellow workers and women they had come to know in the bread lines. Along the way, they made inventories of bakeries and grocery stores in search of black-market goods.

The men in factories and workshops soon followed. Towards evening, 100,000 were participating, and many more joined them in the following days. Workplaces were transformed into political meetings; the demands were articulated for the immediate implementation of eight-hour days and democratic reforms. A few days later, soldiers began to mutiny. Workers' and soldiers' councils sprang up in factories, housing estates, and trenches all over the country. After a week, the tsar abdicated. The Russian Revolution, one of the most momentous events of the twentieth century, had begun.[14]

A month later, residents of the small Swedish northern town of Söderhamn were met by an unusual demonstration. A couple of hundred women had spontaneously decided to go to the town to protest the unbearable food shortages. In Sweden, too, it was women who triggered the dramatic events of spring 1917 – the 'Swedish Potato Revolution'.[15] The poor harvests of grain and potatoes in the autumn of 1916 led to harsh rationing in the spring of 1917. Much of the meat production was exported to Germany, partly in exchange for coke and other scarce products. Britain's tightening blockade of Germany also affected Swedish grain imports.

The demonstrations spread quickly. The first weeks of action were usually led by women. After a while, the men followed. At first, the demands raised were almost exclusively linked to the food situation. It was therefore natural to address these demands to local politicians. Demonstrators marched to town halls, where they were met by politicians who mostly just complained that they could do nothing. But the workers, dissatisfied with this response, pressed the municipal

---

14 Ibid., pp. 139ff.
15 For this section, see Carl Göran Andræ, *Revolt eller reform: Sverige inför revolutionerna i Europa 1917–1918* (Stockholm: Carlsson, 1998); Håkan Blomqvist, *Potatisrevolutionen och kvinnoupploppet på Södermalm 1917: ett historiskt reportage om hunger och demokrati* (Stockholm: Hjalmarson & Högberg, 2017).

authorities to take extraordinary measures. Financial aid was distributed to the needy, and municipalities set up dairies, slaughterhouses, and wood yards in an attempt to secure cheaper supplies.

Gradually, the struggle became radicalised. Shops were looted and stocks destined to be sold on the black market were confiscated by the workers. In many places, demonstrators raided the countryside to take stock of farmers' supplies. In the big cities, open confrontations broke out between police and demonstrators, among whom women were particularly prominent. In Seskarö, in northern Sweden, workers disarmed soldiers sent out to restore order; in Stockholm, soldiers took part in the protest meetings. Council-like structures developed in several places. Workers took over parts of local administration, and references began to appear to the more resolute action of the Russian workers against the ruling class, such as dethroning the tsar.

What can be seen here is the emergence of embryonic independent workers' organisations. They were characterised by a broad representation of different workers' groups and political tendencies. Unlike in the organised labour movement, women were prominent.[16] Soon, the differences between the various currents in the labour movement became more pronounced. In February, the left had been thrown out of the Social Democratic Party, and in mid-May the new Social Democratic Left Party was formed. The syndicalists, who had already broken with the LO in 1910, also received a boost as the local struggles intensified.

The idea of workers' councils as an essential part of the transition to socialism, or as alternative democratic structures, had not been part of the political or ideological arsenal of the Swedish left before 1917. The criticism of the strong orientation of the right wing of the party towards parliamentary work had been a key element in the internal struggles. But, in the demands for democratisation of society, the emphasis was on reforming the existing structures in a first step towards universal and equal suffrage, a republic, and the abolition of the First Chamber of parliament.

The Social Democratic left played no central role in the emergence of the 'hunger wars', but it soon tried to use its local influence to develop the forms of struggle. The Socialdemokratiska Vänsterpartiet, SSV (Social Democratic Left Party), was formed in mid-May, during ongoing

---

16   Kjell Östberg, *Efter rösträtten: kvinnors utrymme efter det demokratiska genombrottet* (Eslöv: Symposion, 1997), pp. 19–25.

mass movements. At its Constituent Congress it adopted a Manifesto to the Workers of Sweden. Along with demands for wage increases, the eight-hour day, and universal suffrage, it also called on workers to 'immediately form local workers' councils in each place . . . with the full representation of the democratic elements of that place, in order to manage the local leadership of the mass action'. For the first time, the idea of councils appeared in a political programme.[17] A few weeks later, the SSV and the syndicalists jointly took the initiative to form the National Workers' Council. The National Council was an attempt to solidify the council-like structures that had emerged and, above all, to create a body to propagate the idea of workers' councils.[18]

The open protests culminated in a large demonstration outside Parliament House in early June. By then, however, the Social Democrats had strenuously intervened to try to take control of the movement.

The Social Democrats and 1917

The majority tendency within the Social Democratic Party was also taken by surprise by the demonstrations and riots of spring 1917. Unlike in the parties further to the left, enthusiasm was not undivided on the part of the party leadership. It did not mind using the demonstrations to put pressure on the Conservatives to win universal suffrage. But, with the parliamentary orientation that now completely dominated the Social Democratic leadership, the question would be decided in parliament, not in the streets and squares.

The consequences of the split in the labour movement were now becoming increasingly clear. The Left Party and the syndicalists wanted to maintain the economic struggle, stress questions of food supply, and stimulate further demonstrations and the emergence of independent workers' councils. The Social Democrats, meanwhile, wanted to bring the struggle into the parliamentary structures.

As the demonstrations spread – and in some cases became more violent – the Social Democrats became increasingly concerned about developments. It was feared that groups to the left of the party would not

---

17   Sveriges socialdemokratiska vänsterparti: Kongress, *Protokoll fört vid social-demokratiska vänsterns konstituerande kongress i Stockholm 13–16 maj 1917* (Stockholm: Fram, 1917).

18   Andræ, *Revolt eller reform*, pp. 96–107.

only take control of the movement, but would also eventually challenge the old party's leading position within the working class. Therefore, the formation of a new left party in mid-May could not have come at a more inopportune time. For one thing, there was already a negative view of spontaneous uprisings outside the party's control. Here the women's demonstrations were a particular problem, because women were largely unorganised, and thus beyond the disciplinary functions of organisations, especially trade unions.[19]

Criticism of what the Social Democrats saw as undisciplined demonstrations was also increasingly prevalent. The denunciations of women's 'excesses' and 'fanaticism' were harsh and unequivocal. A special statement from the Malmö workers' commune reasoned:

> Demonstrating at random, without having aimed at any definite point against which pressure is directed, is like fencing in the air; one dissipates forces and one dissipates weapons, but one achieves no result. We wanted to make these points seriously clear to our working women, who at the moment seem to be living under the delusion that everything can be achieved by demonstrations.[20]

This was addressed to women who, for the first time, were organising their own demonstrations, and whose initiatives planted the seeds of the whole mass movement of the spring of 1917.

In early May, when the demonstrations seemed to be reaching a peak, and gaining a foothold among workers in the big cities, the party leadership intensified its attempts to take control. Some of the younger leaders with roots in the Youth League, such as Per Albin Hansson and Gustav Möller, proposed that the party should join with the LO in calling a general strike to demand the right to vote. The proposal was rejected out of hand by the union representatives, as well as by Branting.

Instead, a '1917 Workers' Committee' was formed. Despite borrowing its name from the ongoing mass popular movement, the initiative was very much a top-down affair. The organisation was led by the central leaders of the party and the LO, with Branting as chairman. It

---

19   For this section, see Kjell Östberg, *Kommunerna och den svenska modellen: socialdemokratin och kommunalpolitiken fram till andra världskriget* (Eslöv: Symposion, 1996), Chapter 2.

20   Östberg, *Efter rösträtten*, p. 30.

formulated its basic strategy in two memoranda.[21] The first stated unequivocally: 'Our first solution is therefore: *a thorough revision of the Constitution*.' This was an attempt to shift the focus of the struggle to demands for parliamentary reform. The second memorandum indicated the same direction at the local level. It firmly denounced the violent workers' demonstrations, and established the Social Democratic alternative: the food shortage had to be solved by the political authorities, and the main orientation of the Social Democrats would thus be to demand representation in the municipal bodies.

At the national level, this is what happened. The bourgeois politicians in charge of the municipalities saw the advantage of having the workers' own representatives elected to the municipal bodies, and thus taking responsibility for crisis policy themselves. As a result, it was now often one of their own party comrades against whom the demonstrating workers had to direct their protests when they demanded better food rations and cheaper food.

Another component of the effort to disarm the mass movements was an attempt to dissolve the directly elected workers' committees, and instead let the workers' communes and trade unions – controlled by the Social Democrats – represent the demonstrators. Although the successes of the Social Democratic–led workers' committees were limited, they helped to split the mass movement.

On 5 June, the demonstrations flared up one last time before the summer recess, when the Riksdag was to discuss the issue of voting rights. The left mobilised outside parliament, and the government, fearing riots, called in military reinforcements. Branting had promised the conservative prime minister to try to quell the unrest. He fulfilled his promise by getting the demonstrators to move on to the People's House. However, his calls for calm were drowned out by the demonstrators' cries of 'General Strike, General Strike, General Strike!'[22]

No decisive victory had been won by the Social Democrats' attempts to pacify the mass movements. This was confirmed the following day, when the left gathered some 20,000 people for a large meeting just outside Stockholm, proclaiming the formation of the Workers' National Council. But the mass movement died out during the summer. One of the main reasons for this was that the acute food shortage had been

21   Östberg, *Kommunerna och den svenska modellen*, pp. 57ff.
22   Hirdman, *Vi bygger landet*, pp. 177–81.

relieved. Also, with the approach of autumn, political interest turned to the parliamentary elections to the Second Chamber.

They showed that the widespread radicalisation of the spring had had a clear impact. The elections were a major defeat for the conservative Right, while the Social Democrats lost one seat – seen as a success after the breakaway of the SSV. The new party received eleven seats.[23] The defeat of the Right ushered in a coalition government with the Liberal Nils Edén as prime minister and Hjalmar Branting as finance minister. This has been seen as the final breakthrough of parliamentarianism in Sweden. From then on, the king could not prevent the parliamentary majority from forming a government.

The government immediately declared that electoral reform was its priority, but gave no answers as to how it might win over the right-wing-dominated First Chamber, which could continue to use its veto with the support of the graduated municipal vote. The Social Democrats never took the initiative of reviving the extra-parliamentary movement to put pressure on their opponents. On the other hand, the Social Democrats in government actively participated in the modernisation of the state apparatus. The conservative state bureaucracy was seen as too closely associated with the right-wing government's failed trade policies, and its pro-Germanism as too burdensome now that it appeared the Western-dominated Entente would emerge victorious from the First World War.[24]

It was above all the leading capitalists – the Wallenbergs prominent among them – who ensured that their candidate was appointed to the central post of foreign minister. Through direct consultations between Wallenberg and representatives of the incoming government, including Branting, they agreed on the details of reforming parts of the state bureaucracy dealing with economy and trade. But it was not representatives of the labour movement that Branting wanted to place under the crystal chandeliers – it was directors and experts from the large financial empires. In the longer term, the agreement reached between Wallenberg and Branting in the autumn of 1917 was probably as important as the horse-trading of the early 1930s in developing the confidential forms of cooperation between capital and labour involved in shaping the political landscape of the twentieth century.[25]

---

23   Stråth, *Sveriges historia. 1830–1920*, pp. 203ff.
24   Sven Anders Söderpalm, *Storföretagarna och det demokratiska genombrottet: ett perspektiv på första världskrigets svenska historia* (Lund: Gleerup, 1969).
25   Ibid.

Democracy in the Glow of the Fire: 1918

In 1918, the deadlock in the fight for the right to vote was finally broken. Once again, international events drove Swedish development. On the other side of the Baltic Sea, revolutionary developments continued apace. By November 1917, the Bolsheviks had seized power in Russia, dissolved the Constituent Assembly, and proclaimed a state in which the soviets would be the platform for popular government. A month later, the Reds seized power in Finland. In the spring of 1918 the Finnish Civil War raged, before the Whites, with strong support from Germany in particular, were able to secure power.[26]

These events cut right through the Swedish labour movement. For Social Democracy, the Russian development was not a revolution but a coup d'état that had crushed a democratic development; meanwhile, the Social Democratic Left Party celebrated the new Soviet state. And they understood the Finnish development in corresponding ways: the Social Democrats saw the Finnish Social Democrats' seizure of power as 'a relapse into the methods of seeking to force a new order by revolutionary coups by organised minorities'.

The SSV, on the other hand, supported the Finnish Social Democrats, arguing that the civil war was a coup d'état by the Finnish bourgeoisie to prevent democratic development. In the spring of 1918, they initiated solidarity meetings for the Finnish workers, which were also well attended by rank-and-file Social Democrats. The meetings probably helped to make it more difficult for the government's Social Democrats to make further concessions to reactionary Finnish activism. The Swedish bourgeoisie pressed the government to intervene on the White side, or at least to provide substantial assistance in the form of arms. They financed their own Swedish brigade and sent it to Finland. The Social Democrats in the government advocated non-intervention, but at times turned a blind eye to arms smuggling to the White side from Germany.

The Finnish Civil War complicated the issue of democracy. The notion that democracy was synonymous merely with universal suffrage and parliamentarianism began to be seriously challenged. The Social

---

26   Tuomas Tepora and Aapo Roselius, eds, *The Finnish Civil War 1918: History, Memory, Legacy* (Leiden: Brill, 2014).

Democrats did not waver from their fundamental view. But the bloody revenge of the Whites against the Reds in Finland – more than 20,000 Finnish Social Democrats were executed or died in prison camps in the year after the civil war – at least gave them an idea of how reliable the bourgeois forces were if their positions were threatened by the right to vote. Slowly, the question began to surface of how democracy could be deepened after a constitutional revision.[27]

In the autumn of 1918, food supplies in Sweden deteriorated once again. As in the spring of 1917, popular protests increased. But it was another event that was to have a decisive impact on the democratic breakthrough: the German Revolution. In early November, 100,000 sailors in the German navy in the Baltic Sea rebelled. The uprising spread rapidly to soldiers all over the country, and was coordinated with hundreds of workers' councils that were formed at the same time. In Bavaria, a socialist republic was proclaimed; in the rest of Germany, power was transferred to the Council of People's Commissars. It included three representatives of the Social Democratic SPD and three of the left-wing socialist USDP. At the same time, the emperor abdicated. A conference of workers' and soldiers' councils was convened in Berlin, calling for urgent measures to socialise production.[28]

New popular mobilisations were now also emerging in Sweden. The Social Democrats called a major demonstration on 10 November demanding universal suffrage. From the left, pressure grew to go further. The SSV and what was left of the council movement of spring 1917 sent out a revolutionary manifesto entitled 'Forward to the Socialist Republic'. Its message was that it was now time for the revolutionary wave to sweep over Sweden.[29]

There was strong support also among Social Democratic workers for more vigorous measures. The Social Democratic Party leadership was flooded with hundreds of resolutions from across the country making it clear that suffrage should be seen as only one part of more far-reaching social change. A major meeting of the Social Democrats in Stockholm called for the abolition of the First Chamber and, even more controversially, the introduction of a republic. Once again, Per Albin Hansson was heard talking about a general strike. Branting refused to endorse these

---

27 Kjersti Bosdotter et al., eds, *Den röda våren 1918* (Huddinge: Arbetarnas Kulturhistoriska Sällskap, 2018).
28 Eley, *Forging Democracy*, pp. 165–9.
29 Andræ, *Revolt eller reform*, pp. 248–59.

more radical measures, however. Nothing could be allowed to jeopardise cooperation with the Liberals. Union leaders were as much against
using the threat of strike action as before.

But it is clear that the revolutionary threat was felt to be real in all
strata of society. The king feared being deposed, as his German brother-
in-law the emperor had recently been, and is said to have packed his
suitcases ready to go into exile. When the Social Democratic minister of
naval defence, Erik Palmstierna, was reached by rumours that the sailors
were threatening rebellion and asked by the commanding officer what
to do, his answer was: 'Shoot [them], half a minute before it's too late.'[30]

The capitalists calculated the costs of continued social unrest. Some of
the leaders considered the risks of violence and strikes so great that they
decided to put pressure on the parliamentary Right to accept the right to
vote. Even the king preferred this option to being forced to abdicate.

The Conservatives fell by the wayside and, during an extraordinary
session of parliament at the end of 1918, it was suddenly possible to untie
the knots it had seemed impossible to untangle for decades. But there
was no question of an unconditional surrender. The bourgeois parties
demanded guarantees that the democratic breakthrough would not be
too forceful. Most of them were accepted by the Social Democrats.[31]

The monarchy and the First Chamber would remain. The voting age
was raised sharply, from twenty-one to twenty-seven for some elections.
The young radical generation would not be allowed to vote. The decision was aimed against the 'socially alert, knowledge-seeking, vigorous
young classes who have been the driving forces of popular organisation
and education', protested one Left Party member. Even some of those
who were depending on poor relief or had tax debts could lose their
right to vote. It seemed like a punishment for illness, unemployment,
and poverty, complained Social Democrat Gustav Möller – who nevertheless chose to vote in favour of the proposal.[32]

The First Chamber would continue to act as a conservative brake.
Candidates for election to it had to be at least thirty-five, with a minimum
income of SEK 3,000 per year. This was a sum that many workers,

30   Anders Isaksson, *Per Albin*, vol. 2, *Revolutionären* (Stockholm: Wahlström &
Widstrand, 1985), pp. 254ff.
31   Annika Berg and Martin Ericsson, eds, *Allmän rösträtt? rösträttens begränsningar i Sverige efter 1921* (Gothenburg: Makadam Förlag, 2021).
32   Kjell Östberg, *Folk i rörelse: vår demokratis historia* (Stockholm: Ordfront,
2021), p. 142.

unemployed, and pensioners could not meet. In particular, the limit hit women hard. In order to ensure that the results of municipal voting were not too dramatic, some restrictions were also imposed on the scope of municipal authority. A two-thirds majority was required for decisions on major municipal investments.

It is not surprising that the SSV found it difficult to accept the Social Democrats' numerous compromises. 'Swedish democracy was born in cowardice', wrote Zeth Höglund.[33] But even many left-wing figures who still remained within the Social Democratic Party were critical. Nils Karleby – then a young editor-in-chief of a party newspaper, who ten years later formulated the party's most quoted reformist credo – spoke of 'a document of shame and pettiness'. And Ernst Wigforss, with his customary skill of verbalising radical opinions while avoiding any clear statement of his own position, wrote: 'I cannot but confess that it is extremely understandable if masses of workers perceive the tactics of the whole party leadership as a deliberate deception.'[34]

Sooner or later, universal suffrage would certainly have been implemented. But the fact that the decision was taken in the autumn of 1918 was primarily a result of the revolutionary mood that was sweeping across the continent. This is confirmed by the leading opponent of suffrage, Conservative leader Arvid Lindman. In the parliamentary debate, he stated that the real reason why the issue had come up at that particular time was the German Revolution: 'It was the spark that ignited even here at home.'[35]

The Council Movement

The revolutionary uprisings that swept across Europe in the wake of the First World War were about more than overthrowing reactionary regimes. The question was now also raised as to the forms in which the working class and its allies would exercise their power. The forms and bounds of democracy were brought into question.[36]

Strike committees and other forms of self-organisation had gradually developed in popular uprisings during the nineteenth century. The Paris

---

33 Ibid.
34 Ernst Wigforss, *Minnen*, vol. 2, *1914–1932* (Stockholm: Tiden, 1951), p. 97.
35 Östberg, *Folk i rörelse*, p. 144.
36 Eley, *Forging Democracy*, pp. 156–64.

Commune of 1871 had shown that workers could create their own organs of power. The 1905 Russian Revolution saw the coordination of local workers' councils, the Petersburg Soviet being the best known. The model was replicated on a national scale in the 1917 Revolution, to such an extent that workers', soldiers', and peasants' councils became the basis for alternative power structures. The Bolshevik slogan 'All power to the soviets' was raised as the alternative to the newly elected Constituent Assembly.

Over the next few years, workers' and soldiers' councils spread briskly across Europe. In some places, such as Hungary and parts of Germany, power was transferred to central councils. The councils arose spontaneously in the wave of strikes that swept across war-weary Europe, and among the soldiers who rebelled against their officers to end a hopeless war. In the crumbling authoritarian political structures of the Romanov, Wilhelmine, and Habsburg empires, however, the councils soon evolved into local and central organs of power.

In Germany, the Social Democrats initially participated actively in the leadership of the councils – but it was clear that they were not prepared to build the new Germany on these popular forms of organisation.[37] On the contrary, it soon became a priority for party leaders to restrain the new organs of power. Their leader, Friedrich Ebert, chose instead to forge alliances with the old imperial officer corps, gave the military a free hand to intervene against social unrest, and authorised the creation of the paramilitary detachments that were to become the main tools of the forces of reaction. When the agreements between the Social Democrats and the old ruling classes were challenged during the Spartacist uprising in January 1919, Ebert did not hesitate to unleash the forces of repression, crush the uprising, and even legitimate the murders of left-wing leaders Rosa Luxemburg and Karl Liebknecht.

But the council movement did not come to an end.[38] In Germany, social unrest in the workplace continued, and the idea of the council developed in an increasingly radical direction. Council communism – a movement often independent of the major left parties – formulated advanced demands for workers' control and social ownership. The Hungarian council republic lasted until the summer of 1919. With Turin

---

37 Heinrich August Winkler, *Arbeiter und Arbeiterbewegung in der Weimarer Republik der Schein der Normalität* (Berlin: Dietz, 1985).
38 Eley, *Forging Democracy*, pp. 162–4.

as their centre, a large number of factory committees emerged during
Italy's 'Red Years' of 1919–20. In England and Scotland, the Shop Stewards' movement swept across the nation's workplaces. These movements
were strongly supported by the Communist International, formed in
1919. The propagation of the council idea quickly became one of the
central tasks of the International.

In the new democracies of central Europe, there was also pressure to
join the council movement. In Germany and Austria, special works-
council laws were passed, giving workers the right to elect their own
representatives with the right to transparency and some influence over
their workplaces. But the legislation never fundamentally shifted the
balance of power. By the early 1920s, interest in council-inspired
experiments had waned.

This turn of events must be seen in the light of the disruption of the
council movement's triumphant procession. In Germany and Hungary,
it was crushed in bloody confrontations with more effective state
powers. In Italy it ebbed away, and was soon trumped by the mass
mobilisations of fascism. In Finland, the Red regime was defeated
without having had time to establish viable alternative forms of government, and was subjected to the bloody revenge of the Whites. In general,
authoritarian forces grew strong after 1920. In the United States, too,
the labour movement had to cower in the face of the state-sponsored
repression of workers.

This weakening of labour was also a result of the fact that the rift
within the labour movement had now become permanent. The disagreement developed to a large extent precisely around questions
relating to the forms of democracy.[39] The Social Democrats had definitively taken the side of parliamentary democracy and, as we have seen,
had not hesitated to use force as a last resort to put down popular
uprisings that challenged it. The majority of the left was united in the
communist movement, and for the Comintern (the Communist International) the council system was a natural part of the socialist strategy.
It was insufficient that the participation of citizens in the democratic
process should be limited to elections, upon which direct political
control would be relinquished to a political and bureaucratic elite.
Democracy would be extended to all parts of society, and the role of
factory committees was central in this process. Antonio Gramsci, who

39 Ibid., Chapter 11.

witnessed the rapid development of the council movement in Italy in the early 1920s, argued that the committees were the first building block of an entirely new international socialist economy.[40]

The road to council democracy was paved with difficulties, though – even where the revolution had triumphed. The civil war that followed the Russian Revolution did not provide fertile ground for the development of new democratic structures. Rosa Luxemburg – who emphatically argued that the workers' and soldiers' councils should be the lever of the state machine in all respects – was merciless against restrictions on democratic rights in the young Soviet state: 'Without general elections, without unrestricted freedom of press and assembly, without a free struggle of opinion, life dies out in every public institution, becomes a mere semblance of life, in which only the bureaucracy remains as the active element.'[41] This did not mean that there was a straight line from the dreams of the broader and more active form of democracy expressed by the council to the one-party state of Stalinism. But the period when the struggle to realise these dreams was at its height, 1917–23, ended in disappointment for revolutionaries and reformists alike.

During the growing social unrest in the autumn of 1918, the ideas of the council movement also appeared in Sweden.[42] In an appeal on 9 November, the SSV called for a socialist government 'based on workers', soldiers' and peasants' councils', and on workers' control over industry. But such councils hardly existed at this time, and hopes for the mass uprisings that had occurred elsewhere in Europe were left unanswered when the struggle for suffrage was over. Nevertheless, the question of broadening democracy had a major impact. The propaganda of the SSV, and of the syndicalists in particular, in favour of workers' control, and of some form of councils, together with the influence of the council movement around Europe, meant that the question of workers' control over

---

40   Antonio Gramsci, *Selections from Political Writings*, vol. 1, *1910–1920* (London: Lawrence & Wishart, 1977), pp. 65ff.

41   Rosa Luxemburg, *The Russian Revolution* (New York: Workers Age, 1940 [1918]), Chapter 6, available at marxists.org.

42   For the following section, see Christer Lundh, *Den svenska debatten om industriell demokrati 1919–1924*, vol. 1, *Debatten i Sverige* (Lund: Studentlitteratur, 1987); Lars Ekdahl, 'Demokratisk socialism? Svensk arbetarrörelse inför en revolutionär situation', in Kjersti Bosdotter et al., eds, *Början på en ny epok: arbetarrörelsens vägval i nordisk samhällsutveckling under 1920-talet* (Huddinge: Arbetarnas Kulturhistoriska Sällskap, 2021); Ilkka Kärrylä, 'The Contested Relationship of Democracy and the Economy: Debates on Economic and Industrial Democracy in Finland and Sweden, 1960s–1990s', PhD diss., University of Helsinki, 2019, pp. 97–101.

production was vigorously debated in the years that followed.[43] For the SSV, enthusiasm for workers' councils as the basis of a socialist Sweden was strengthened by international experience, especially after they joined the Comintern in 1919.

The Social Democratic Party was also strongly influenced by the discussion on how to deepen and broaden democracy. But the context was different. The party had been in government with the Liberals since 1917, and had accepted the terms of the electoral reform. For Branting and the trade union leaders, the question of democracy was thus settled, and the party's room for manoeuvre limited. For a younger generation of leaders – Gustav Möller, Arthur Engberg, Rickard Sandler, and Ernst Wigforss – the issue looked different. For them, it was clear that coalition with the Liberals would soon end. It was high time for the Social Democrats to formulate their own policy. The question of socialist strategy, to the extent that it had been discussed at all, had hitherto been confined to the realm of theory. It was now time to make this debate concrete.

A Social Democratic Response

For some years, especially 1919–20, there was an intense debate within the Social Democratic Party. Its outcome was to be decisive for the party for a long time to come.[44]

The discussion was strongly influenced by the international debate. A central premise was that industrial democracy – in other words, workers' power at the workplace – would play an important role in socialist development. Gustav Möller, who was secretary of the party at the time, was influenced by Otto Bauer and the Austro-Marxists. According to their ideas, workers would be able to influence production directly in the workplace, while the state would have greater influence over strategic decisions. Möller outlined a three-tier structure. Operational councils would be set up within companies. Within each sector there would be industrial councils, which would include workers along with representatives of consumers and society. These would then be united to form an economic parliament – perhaps the First Chamber could be

---

43   Ekdahl, 'Demokratisk socialism?', p. 223.
44   Ibid.

transformed into one. This tripartite division would later reappear when, after the Second World War, the LO tried to revive the discussion on industrial democracy. Inspired by Bauer, Möller argued that it should now be possible to transfer some enterprises into public ownership by legal means. Compensation, an amount determined by a court, would be paid in the form of government bonds.[45] Others, including Ernst Wigforss, expressed interest in English guild socialism. Under this model, workers in each industry would join together in self-governing local and national guilds to organise production. The means of production would only be formally owned by the state.[46]

But when it came to framing workplace power in a broader context, as a lever for broader social transformation, the debate remained vague and inconsistent. In the communist movement at this time, there was an intense discussion on how the struggle within workplaces could be developed in a socialist direction. A central concept was the transitional programme. The question was how to overcome the deep gulf that separated the struggle for the demands of the day from a dawning socialist society that remained in the far distance. 'All concrete demands arising from the economic distress of the working masses must be led into the great spear of struggle: control of production', through factory councils and trade unions, said the Comintern's 1921 *Theses on Tactics*.[47]

Such discussions were largely absent in Swedish Social Democracy – with one interesting exception. In 1919, the workers' commune in Gothenburg sent a proposal for a programme of action largely along the same lines. It was not enough simply to refer to general socialist principles, wrote the author, Ernst Wigforss. Economic restructuring was to begin immediately. The workers' commune then developed a concrete programme calling for an eight-hour working day without wage reductions, statutory paid vacation, increased wages and minimum wages, increased pensions, universal health insurance, and maternity benefits. One demand that pointed to the party's future policy was for the right to work for all, and for public jobs with decent wages for the unemployed. It also called for major state investment in high-standard housing. The economic barriers to higher education for the working class also had to be removed. A tax policy was required that not only financed social

45 Ibid.
46 Lundh, *Den svenska debatten*, pp. 149ff.
47 Communist International Congress and John Riddell, *To the Masses: Proceedings of the Third Congress of the Communist International, 1921* (Leiden: Brill, 2015).

investments, but also helped to equalise income and transfer capital into the ownership of society. For the highest incomes, the tax rate would be 95 per cent and larger inheritances would in practice be confiscated. The military system was to be essentially abolished, and all weapons training immediately suspended. The nationalisation of banks and insurance companies would begin immediately. All natural resources, as well as the transport system, were also to be nationalised.

But what made the programme especially distinctive is that it also linked the demands for reform to the ongoing experience of the council movement. The goal of a truly democratic society was to make the workers themselves responsible for managing production, through local workers' councils and corresponding national structures. And this was not a programme for some distant future, the programme concluded: 'None of the demands set out here is such that work to implement it cannot begin immediately.'[48]

However, such a radical programme found no enthusiasm in the Social Democratic Party. It did not even come up for discussion at the party executive meeting for which it had been written.

A New Party Programme

In 1920, the party adopted a new programme. The debate on it was characterised by intense discussions on industrial democracy. The violent development of the Russian Revolution and the formation of the council system and radical socialisation programme of the young Soviet state also provided an important counter-image. But, above all, for the first time, a party programme was adopted in a context in which the party in government could begin to realise some of its objectives. The question, however, was the extent to which the new programme helped to clarify the road to socialism.[49]

The general principles outlined in the programme begin in the same way as in its predecessors:

The Social Democrats differ from other political parties in that they want to completely transform the economic organization of bourgeois

---

48 Wigforss, *Minnen*, vol. 2, pp. 121–3.
49 Ekdahl, 'Demokratisk socialism?', p. 234.

society and to carry out the social emancipation of the exploited
classes for the sake of the security and development of spiritual and
material culture.

For the main cause of the ills of modern civilization is the private
capitalist mode of production.[50]

The sections dealing with the development of capitalism reflect the radical
times in which the programme was written. It contains Marxist-inflected
terms such as 'exploitation', 'impoverishment', and 'class struggle':

The class struggle between the exploited and the exploiter takes on
its modern character. The working class becomes conscious of its
historic mission to be the bearer of a new order of production, freed
from the profit motive, and emerges as the leader among the exploited
classes . . . This class struggle will not cease until society is so transformed that capitalist exploitation is completely abolished, class
society has fallen and mass poverty has been abolished. This again
can only be done by abolishing private capitalist ownership of the
means of production.[51]

This was followed by a comprehensive reform programme largely
carried over from past resolutions. It included demands for basic democratic rights, control over the state administration, popular influence
over the judiciary, democratisation of the school system, tax reforms,
the eight-hour day, protective legislation, improved working conditions,
and social security legislation.

Point XIII of the programme was an innovation, for the first time
explicitly raising the necessity of socialisation:

Into the possession of society is transferred
All natural resources necessary for the implementation of a planned
economy
Industrial companies,
Credit institutions
Transport and communication routes

---

50   Klaus Misgeld, ed., *Socialdemokratins program: 1897 till 1990* (Stockholm:
Arbetarrörelsens arkiv och bibliotek, 2001), pp. 32–8.
51   Ibid.

Expert management of social enterprises under guarantees against
bureaucratic management
   Workers and consumers participate in the governance of society
   Public control over companies that remain in private ownership

This passage represented a clear departure from the concrete reform
proposals of the other sections. The wide gap between the references to
Marxist theory, the concrete demands made, and the section on socialisation was underlined by their tenuous connection with the ongoing
debate on industrial democracy. The Social Democrats never managed
to bridge that gap.

This was also illustrated during the congress.[52] The question of
industrial democracy had its own item on the agenda, separate from
the discussion of the new party programme. And the opening speaker,
Wigforss, did not try to pick up the link between reforms and socialist
development and the role of workers' democracy from the Gothenburg
Programme. Instead, the discussion showed that the party lacked a
coherent interpretive analysis. For its more radical factions, industrial
democracy could be seen as a stage of the journey towards socialism.
For others, who saw socialist society as much more distant, it was more
a question of increasing workers' positive attitude towards making
the economy more efficient by heightening the satisfaction of work.
Industrial democracy was intended to link workers more closely to
production, and thus create an incentive to increase it, Branting argued.

When cooperation with the Liberals ended in 1920, and the Social
Democrats formed a government on their own, they set up two commissions to try to make their policy more concrete: a Socialisation
Inquiry and a Committee for Industrial Democracy.[53] But no link was
made between the two: the question of socialisation was examined
separately from the question of how to strengthen workers' power in the
workplace. The Socialisation Inquiry did not complete its work until
1935, and produced no final report. But the Committee for Industrial
Democracy submitted its report in 1923. It is difficult to describe the
result in any other way than as a sharp retreat from the hopes that had
been articulated only a few years earlier.

---

52   Sveriges socialdemokratiska arbetareparti Kongress, *Protokoll från Sverges
socialdemokratiska arbetarepartis elfte kongress i Stockholm: den 8–20 februari, 1920*
(Stockholm, 1920).
53   Ekdahl, 'Demokratisk socialism?', p. 235.

The Committee consisted of representatives from both trade unions and employers. Initially, LO chairman Herman Lindqvist led the work, but after a while he was replaced by Ernst Wigforss.[54] It proposed the establishment of company councils with a maximum of three representatives of the employers and at least three representatives of the workers, appointed by the trade unions. The councils were to be purely consultative, with the task of 'promoting good relations between the workers . . . and the management in order to ensure production'. Employers were to keep workers informed of production conditions and the financial position of the enterprises, unless this was detrimental to the enterprises, and to inform them of any cutbacks in operations.[55]

The written summary of the inquiry, by Ernst Wigforss, was clear about the limitations of the proposal's ambitions: 'It is not an attempt to legislate for workers' co-determination over industry. It is little more than a negotiating arrangement between employers and trade unions on issues of importance to both sides.'[56]

With this proposal, the party and LO leadership had put its foot down. The company councils were not part of any socialisation process; the focus was on increasing production. Wigforss, in particular, put a lot of effort into formulating the proposal so that it could also be accepted by employers. His concluding words are significant: 'The trade unions' quest for influence over industry, the working class's increasingly awakening interest in production, must be seen not as a danger but as an opportunity to rescue itself from a great danger to industry and society.'[57]

In many quarters of the LO, critical objections were made to the pale result. The president of the powerful Metalworkers' Federation objected that 'if we weigh the obligations which the workers would have to assume under this proposal against the rights which they would receive in compensation for this the obligations of the workers would be very great, while the small rights would be confined to information of perhaps often dubious value to the workers'.[58]

In the wake of the severe economic crisis of the 1920s, radicalisation was forced to retreat internationally. Gradually, Social Democracy's

---

54 Lundh, *Den svenska debatten*, Chapter 8.1.
55 State public investigation SOU 1923:29, 'Den industriella demokratins problem. I. Betänkande jämte förslag till lag om driftsnämnder'.
56 Ibid., p. 185.
57 Ibid.
58 Memorandum, Kommittén för industriell demokrati, 3–6 November 1920, vol. 1.

interest in industrial democracy – especially as a tool for a transition to socialism – diminished. Thus, Swedish Social Democracy followed the main path of Europe in general: alternative forms of popular power were rejected.

The great tragedy of 1918–19 was that Social Democrats ignored what a democratically ordered polity might be, writes the British historian Geoff Eley. They had the opportunity to expand the frontiers of democracy both by dismantling the bases of authoritarianism and by mobilising 'the new popular energies the council movement released'.[59] Alternatively, in the words of the British Marxist Perry Anderson: 'The general form of the representative state – bourgeois democracy – is itself the principal ideological linchpin of Western capitalism, whose very existence deprives the working class of the idea of socialism as a different type of state.'[60]

It would be half a century before Social Democracy again – for a brief moment – seriously raised the question of power at work.

59   Eley, *Forging Democracy*, p. 169.
60   Perry Anderson, 'The Antinomies of Antonio Gramsci', *New Left Review* I/100 (1984), p. 28.

3

Social Democracy in the Face of Reality

In the wake of the catastrophe of the First World War and the impact of the Russian Revolution, a new Europe emerged. The German and Austrian empires had been dissolved, and dozens of new states were being formed, mainly in eastern and south-eastern Europe. The vast majority of the European countries were committed to some form of parliamentary democracy with universal suffrage, although women were still waiting for the vote even in countries like France, Italy, and Belgium.[1]

There were many different views on what this new democracy should look like. In principle, the bourgeois right was still against universal suffrage. In practice they reluctantly accepted, but they tried to introduce safeguards against its having too strong an impact. Liberals often supported these restrictions. At the other end of the political scale was the radical socialist movement, which advocated ways of giving people more direct means of influencing political decisions, through council democracy or soviet rule.

The Fear of the Masses

But even for the form that triumphed in most of Europe – liberal parliamentary democracy – 'democracy' was a flexible category. Universal suffrage, and generally also parliamentarianism, was well established. Beyond that, its components could vary widely. The economic sector was left unrestricted, and workers' attempts to seize control of their working conditions were pushed back. The big question was: Could power really be handed over to the people?

Fear of the unruly masses was deeply rooted in the conservative and liberal bourgeoisie of the time.[2] The reason was not difficult to

---

1   Ian Kershaw, *To Hell and Back: Europe, 1914–1949* (London: Allen Lane, 2015).
2   Stefan Jonsson, *Crowds and Democracy: The Idea and Image of the Masses from Revolution to Fascism* (New York: Columbia University Press, 2013).

understand. The young democracies had been created in the wake of revolutionary uprisings, and many of them would indeed succumb to the lure of fascism, one of the most powerful mass movements of the time. And the Russian example attracted large parts of the working class. Sociology and mass psychology were developing as new scientific disciplines. Describing this terrifying new political phenomenon proved no easy task, but a recurring theme was its elevation of primitive impulses. When people gathered in great numbers, their moral sensibilities disappeared. They stopped thinking, acted contrary to their interests, forgot all common sense, and were guided solely by their emotions, as Sigmund Freud put it.[3]

Leading social scientists, from sociologist Max Weber to the economist Joseph Schumpeter, picked up on these concerns.[4] Weber believed that most citizens were passive and unable to understand the complexities of modern society: certainly, the people would be included by democracy, but they would not be allowed to exercise power themselves. And Schumpeter argued that democracy could only mean that the people had the power to approve or reject the individuals and parties that governed them.[5] Voters were conspicuously unintelligent, narrow-minded, and selfish. But this did not matter, as long as one did not imagine they would run the political system.

In this view, parliament's role as a leading forum for national policy had to be carefully limited. Counterweights were needed: the bureaucracy, the market, strong political leaders. It also soon became clear that the interwar period represented a democratic breakthrough with major limitations. The new democracies found it difficult to fill the new democratic structures with living content. In country after country, democratic freedoms were curtailed. In Italy, the Fascists seized power as early as 1922. Meanwhile, under the leadership of dictators and 'strongmen' such as Józef Piłsudski in Poland, Miklós Horthy in Hungary, and Engelbert Dollfuss in Austria – royal dictatorships in Albania, Yugoslavia, Bulgaria, and Romania – a number of countries developed in an authoritarian direction. When the Nazis came to power in Germany in 1933, the fascist elements in many of these regimes were strengthened. The collapse of the German Weimar Republic, in particular, has

---

3   Ibid., p. 119.
4   Jan-Werner Müller, *Contesting Democracy: Political Ideas in Twentieth-Century Europe* (New Haven, CT: Yale University Press, 2011), p. 42.
5   Ibid., pp. 149ff.

often been held up as a symbol of the shortcomings of the young democracies.[6]

Many blamed 'the masses' for this political decay. Totalitarian movements, Hannah Arendt argued, were possible wherever the masses – those without a voice and a seat in the democratic system, who felt superfluous or uninterested in the political process, who lacked shared interests or common political goals – developed an interest in politics.[7] Such a view has been rejected by the leading German historian Heinrich August Winkler, who firmly repudiates the claim that the collapse of the Weimar Republic and Hitler's rise to power had anything to do with 'the masses'. On the contrary, it was often those sections of the people who were contemptuously so called who were the ones who defended democracy when the old elites attacked it. Rather, the reason for Nazism's victory was that the German bourgeoisie traditionally lacked both democratic convictions and solid democratic parties. Nazism, as we know, came to power with the support of the bourgeois parties.[8]

Political developments were strongly influenced by the recurring economic crises of the interwar period. The depression of the early 1920s was the deepest international capitalism had so far experienced. In Sweden, industrial production fell sharply, and unemployment peaked at 25 per cent. When the economy recovered a few years later, the leading capitalists were quickly able to make large profits again. One name came to represent the winners of the roaring twenties: Ivar Kreuger. Kreuger, with his base in the match industry, had long been able to play skilfully on the growing international financial market. This in turn strengthened his position in the expansive, export-oriented industry. It was during these years that Sweden decisively entered the fold of leading modern industrial nations.[9]

For the labour movement, the 1920s were less happy. The crisis took its toll on union coffers and membership, and unemployment became entrenched.

---

6 Kershaw, *To Hell and Back*, pp. 121–48.

7 Hannah Arendt, *The Origins of Totalitarianism*, new edn with added prefaces (New York: Harcourt Brace Jovanovich, 1973), p. 311; Jonsson, *Crowds and Democracy*, pp. 23ff.

8 Heinrich August Winkler, *Arbeiter und Arbeiterbewegung in der Weimarer Republik. Von der Revolution zur Stabilisierung, 1918 bis 1924* (Berlin: Dietz, 1985), p. 15.

9 Lennart Schön, *An Economic History of Modern Sweden* (London: Routledge, 2012), pp. 180–4, 191ff.

Waiting for the Majority

The Social Democrats became the largest party in the 1921 parliamentary elections – the first with universal suffrage. But the 36 per cent share of the vote they received was far from a majority. The various parties to their left took 8 per cent between them.[10]

The left Social Democratic party, SSV, which had broken away in 1917, split repeatedly in the 1920s.[11] Underlying these schisms were relations with the Soviet Union and the world communist movement. The Swedish SSV was among the founders of the Comintern. However, it demanded firm discipline from its constituent parties, and there was dissatisfaction with this in parts of the SSV, which had been formed in protest against what it perceived as an overly authoritarian Social Democratic Party. Already in 1919, a group among them had left. In 1921, a new split occurred when a relatively large minority refused to accept the conditions set by the Comintern in its statutes, including the change in its name to the Swedish Communist Party (Sveriges Kommunistiska Parti, SKP). In 1924 there was a further split, when some of the founders of the SSV, including Zeth Höglund, broke with the Comintern altogether. After a few years, his group returned to the Social Democratic parent party, as did most of those who had previously broken with the Communist Party. In the 1924 elections, the Social Democrats increased their vote while the other left-wing parties lost ground – but together they held their position, with a total of about 46 per cent of the vote.

As in most other European democracies, it was difficult to create stable political majorities.[12] By 1920 the Liberal–Social Democratic coalition had dissolved, and a minority Social Democratic government led by Hjalmar Branting took office in that year – but resigned after less than twelve months. Over the next twelve years, changes of government were to become commonplace. The country saw eleven different governments during this period, all of them minority administrations.

For the Social Democratic Party, the question of ministerial socialism was now definitively settled. As the largest party in the Riksdag, it

---

10 Yvonne Hirdman, Jenny Björkman, and Urban Lundberg, *Sveriges historia 1920–1965* (Stockholm: Norstedt, 2012), pp. 127ff.

11 Jan Bolin, *Parti av ny typ?: Skapandet av ett svenskt kommunistiskt parti 1917–1933* (Stockholm: Almqvist & Wiksell, 2004).

12 Hirdman, Björkman, and Lundberg, *Sveriges historia*, pp. 122ff.

considered it an obligation to take on government responsibility when-
ever possible. At the same time, parliamentary conditions had changed.
The centre line in Swedish parliamentary politics, which until 1920
had run between a left wing composed of the Liberals and the Social
Democrats and a right wing, was shifting to the right. The Liberals were
henceforth to be counted among the bourgeois camp. This meant that
the Social Democrats had to form minority governments on their own.
Between 1920 and 1926, the Social Democrats led four different governments, three with Branting as prime minister and, after Branting's death
in 1925, one led by Rickard Sandler.

Shortly after Branting's death, the minister of finance, F. W. Thorsson,
also died. The deaths of these two figures signalled a generational
change in Social Democracy. The generation that had led the party
during the period of strong growth around the turn of the century, and
into parliament before the First World War, had now disappeared from
the political scene. They were replaced by the generation that would
lead it for the following decades: Per Albin Hansson, Gustav Möller,
Rickard Sandler, Ernst Wigforss, and Arthur Engberg, to name the key
characters. Most had received their initial training in the radical Youth
League, and – with the possible exception of Per Albin – had a reputation for being interested in Marxist theory. At the time of the party
split in 1917, however, they had declared their loyalty to Branting's
faction.[13] But how were the Social Democrats' long-term goals reflected
in practical policy?

Against the background of the intense discussion on council democracy and the radical tone of the new party programme, the Social
Democrats' government policies appeared remarkably pallid. And the
gap between programme and practice widened as the labour radicalisation that had sustained radical ambitions waned. Branting's second
government (1921–23) was described by the party's ideological journal
Tiden (Times) as Social Democratic in name only.[14]

On one issue, however, the Social Democrats succeeded in pushing
through a decision with a clear Social Democratic flavour: the 1925
decision on defence. Pacifist currents were strong after the slaughter of
a generation of young men in the First World War, and the Social
Democrats had actively contributed to the creation of the League of

---

13   Ibid., pp. 138ff.
14   *Tiden* 1924, p. 256.

Nations. Growing austerity made it easier for the Social Democrats to get the left wing of the Liberals on board for comprehensive cuts. The period of conscription was shortened, and many military units were disbanded.[15]

Keynes was still far ahead and no expansionary economic policy was presented to address the deep economic crisis. On the contrary, the minister of finance, Thorsson, pursued a markedly austere economic policy, including cuts in the state budget. At this time, Ernst Wigforss, in particular, supported the deflationary policy recommended by neoclassical economics. Serving foreign markets and maintaining stable prices were highly prized objectives, even if the price was higher unemployment.[16]

In the 1922 election programme, it could still be claimed that industrial democracy was an important question for the working class. But when the inquiry on industrial democracy, headed by Wigforss, presented its proposal a year later, all that remained, as we have seen, were toothless workers' councils. When the proposal was defeated in parliament, the question of industrial democracy disappeared from the party's agenda for a long time to come. Instead, imperatives such as understanding, cooperation, and harmony were to characterise relations between workers and employers.[17]

The gaps between programme and practice were widening, and increasingly resembled the unresolved prewar dilemma of the relationship between the demands of the day and a far-distant socialist future. At the same time, the party could no longer wait for the social reforms that would offer new opportunities to the working class. The right to vote had been won, and the party was in power. The need now arose to give reformism a new outfit.

---

15 Karl Molin, 'Party Dispute and Party Responsibility: A Study of the Social Democratic Defence Debate', in Klaus Misgeld, Karl Molin, and Klas Åmark, eds, *Creating Social Democracy: A Century of the Social Democratic Labor Party in Sweden* (University Park. Pennsylvania State University Press, 1992), pp. 387ff.

16 Villy Bergström, 'Party Program and Economic Policy', in Misgeld, Molin, and Åmark, *Creating Social Democracy*, pp. 136ff.

17 Anna Friberg, *Demokrati bortom politiken: En begreppshistorisk analys av demokratibegreppet inom Sveriges socialdemokratiska arbetareparti 1919–1939* (Stockholm: Atlas, 2013), p. 262.

The Karlebyan Turn

It was now, during the deradicalisation that characterised most of the 1920s, that Social Democratic reformism took a more coherent shape. How could the Social Democrats make the position of the working class as tolerable as possible? And how could the burden of unemployment be eased? Relying on some Marxist ideas, the new generation of leaders claimed that economic growth was a precondition for effective social reform.

'All men live on production', wrote Gustav Möller in his article 'The Social Revolution'. Consequently, 'achieving the highest possible level of production should be a common interest for *all* without exception'.[18] A central task for a Social Democratic government thus became that of pushing capitalism to make production more efficient and rational. It should be noted that these ideas were developed a decade before Social Democratic politics – under Wigforss's leadership – came to be governed by Keynesian ideas. Instead, they were largely influenced by the rationalisation movement that was developed at this time by American economists and business leaders.[19] In Wigforss's own words,

> Workers also had an interest in participating in the rationalisations of industry, even if in the short term they were to their own detriment. The impact of economic laws would be felt more mildly if they felt they had insight into the running of companies, and workers would show a greater understanding of the importance of wage costs for the profitability of companies.[20]

No socialist offensive was imminent. Instead, the party would have to improvise. This was the main thesis of a speech given by Ernst Wigforss in 1925 on 'Socialism as a Dogma or Working Hypothesis'. Social Democracy had to be able to feel its way between liberal economic policy and socialist demands for social intervention. A central conclusion

---

18   Gustav Möller, 'Socialiseringsproblemen', *Tiden* 12 (1920).
19   Hans de Geer, *Rationaliseringsrörelsen i Sverige: effektivitetsidéer och socialt ansvar under mellankrigstiden* (Stockholm: SNS, 1978), Chapter 4.
20   State public investigation SOU 1923:29, 'Den industriella demokratins problem. I. Betänkande jämte förslag till lag om driftsnämnder'.

was that in the economic field, cooperation produced better results than combat.[21]

From now on, this became the credo of reformism. Socialism could again be postponed. In practice, the result was a reformism that confined itself to ameliorating capitalism.

The person credited with giving the new course its theoretical makeover was Nils Karleby. Shortly before his death from tuberculosis at the age of only thirty-four, in 1926, he published his classic book *Socialismen inför verkligheten* (Socialism in the face of reality). Karleby was originally a typographer, and later a newspaper editor. In 1920 he became secretary of the Socialisation Inquiry, which investigated the possibility of socialising private companies.[22] He belonged to the pioneering generation of the Swedish Social Democratic Youth League (Sveriges socialdemokratiska ungdomsförbund, SSU) – the new youth union that the party had had to establish because the old one had left the Social Democrats for the new SSV. Much of Karleby's agitational activity, not least as a journalist, was dedicated to criticising radical demands for profound systemic change.

Karleby belonged to the limited circle of Social Democrats who had devoted themselves to a more detailed study of Marx, and his book contains extensive references to the Marxist heritage. At the same time, much of the text is impenetrable and incoherent. It should be noted that the book was written in just a few weeks in a sanatorium. In some key respects, Karleby broke clearly with Marx. These included his rejection of the law of value and the concept of exploitation. Karleby had studied economics under the leading liberal economist Eli Heckscher, and was sympathetic to the neoclassical school, which held decisive influence over the economic policy of the Social Democrats in government at that time.

But what has given Karleby an almost iconic status in the history of Swedish Social Democratic ideas are a few passages in the middle of his book. For Karleby, paraphrasing Eduard Bernstein, the reforms were everything, the goal nothing. All the reforms brought about by pressure from the working class, on the one hand, and by the problems arising

---

21 Ernst Wigforss, 'Socialismen – dogm eller arbeshypotes?', in *Från klasskamp till samverkan* (Stockholm: Tiden, 1941).

22 Örjan Nyström, 'Vem var Nils Karleby', in Nils Karleby, *Socialismen inför verkligheten: studier över socialdemokratisk åskådning och nutidspolitik* (Gothenburg: Tjänstemännens socialdemokratiska förening, 2018).

from the development of modern production, on the other – which had together resulted in an increase in the social compared to private control of property – implied a socialist transformation of society of the same nature as that which could be imagined in the future, Karleby argued.[23]

The reforms were thus not a preparation for social transformation; they were themselves the transformation of society. And these reforms could take a variety of forms, from legislation on shortening working hours and worker protections to strengthening the purchasing power of the working class through tax reform, cooperative activity, or direct state intervention. On this view, socialisation, in the sense of the working class taking control over of the means of production, became a secondary question. The ownership of enterprises had to be determined by what was most expedient. Above all, socialisation should not be pursued at the expense of production. Karleby's conclusion was thus the same as that of Wigforss and Möller: 'Improvements in the efficiency of economic activity have always been, and will always be, the only way to increase the overall prosperity of society.'[24] The primary task of Social Democracy, at least for the time being, was to make capitalism as efficient as possible.

That the measures favouring growth and rationalisation were often at odds with the interests of the working class – at least in the short term – was, as we have seen, well known to the men behind these ideas. Similarly, the ambition of intervening actively to influence the efficiency of industry was difficult to combine with the empowerment of the workers.

In retrospect, Karleby has often been singled out as the figure who first succeeded in formulating the basic features of the Social Democratic ideology of the welfare state.[25] It has been associated with what has come to be known as 'functional socialism': ownership is of secondary importance; the 'mixed economy' – a market economy where capitalism operates in a society in which the workers' movement has an increasingly strong influence – is the most appropriate objective. It is through social reform and legislation that the working class can best advance its position.

---

23 Nils Karleby, *Socialismen inför verkligheten: studier över socialdemokratisk åskådning och nutidspolitik* (Stockholm: Tiden, 1926), pp. 84–6.
24 Ibid., pp. 143ff.
25 Nyström, 'Vem var Nils Karleby?', pp. 17ff.

The party leadership gratefully accepted Karleby's ideas. The question of how to implement socialism could be taken off the agenda, as the process was already under way. But neither Karleby's ideas nor Wigforss's underlining of the importance of cooperation with capital in order not to endanger production offered any solution to the question of what policy the party should pursue in the here and now.

Communal Socialism as an Alternative?

The Social Democrats' political footprint in the 1920s was thus limited, and the party clearly lacked a more aggressive political agenda. Could the conditions for a rapid breakthrough of a new policy come about at the municipal level? In many of the big cities with large working-class populations, and in a large number of mill towns around the country, the labour parties were able to win a majority quickly. Would municipal autonomy create opportunities for radical labour politics at the local level?

The demand for communal socialism had long been enshrined in the programme of the Social Democratic Party.[26] In some areas, it advocated socialisation at the local level: 'Business enterprises of a local nature, which are of general importance for the living conditions of the population and show a monopolistic tendency, should be transferred to municipal ownership and operation.' In addition to electricity, water, and gas – which had usually already been municipalised by bourgeois parties – this applied, for example, to slaughterhouses, market halls, and dairies. The programme also called for municipal housing construction.

But, to prevent municipal experiments with socialism, the bourgeois parties made the acceptance of the electoral reforms in 1919–21 conditional on the restriction of municipal decision-making. They pushed through the requirement of a two-thirds majority for major new investments. The rule was widely applied, and proved an important barrier when left-wing majorities wanted to set up wood yards or communalise bus services. 'In a municipality like Spånga, it is difficult to pursue a

---

26 For this section, see Kjell Östberg, *Kommunerna och den svenska modellen: socialdemokratin och kommunalpolitiken fram till andra världskriget* (Eslöv: Symposion, 1996).

revolutionary social-democratic policy', sighed the Spånga Social Democratic council group, after having a municipal-owned local bakery
overturned on such grounds.[27]

Two areas of policy were at the forefront of Social Democratic municipal activities: unemployment and housing. Both were complicated by
the enforced restrictions. The housing question had occupied a prominent place in the Social Democrats' municipal policy from the very
first programme, in 1901. But the Social Democratic majority won in a
number of municipalities after 1919 left virtually no impression on
the construction of municipal-owned housing. At the beginning of the
1920s, it came to a complete halt. The bourgeois minorities were able to
stop most proposals by requiring a two-thirds majority.

Proposals to make support for the unemployed more humane than
the abhorrent labour market policy were blocked by the same means.

Unemployment

The issue that undoubtedly represented the greatest challenge to the
labour movement, and to the Social Democratic governments of the
1920s, was unemployment.[28] At most, a quarter of LO members were
out of work; but even after the crisis turned into a boom in the middle
of the decade, unemployment remained significantly higher than before
the First World War. Since the war, state unemployment policy had
been organised through the Unemployment Commission (Statens
Arbetslöshetskommission – AK). It was a part-based commission, in
which the LO and the SAF had equal representation. The directives were
laid down by the Riksdag.

The task of the AK was not only to provide financial help to the
unemployed. It was also to support the government's economic policy,
which, in the early 1920s, was decidedly depressive, and thus to help
bring down wages. As a consequence, payments to the unemployed had
to be well below the minimum wage usually paid. There were a number
of other conditions that made the so-called AK jobs deeply unpopular:
the unemployed could be directed to work far from home, and workers

27   Ibid., p. 112.
28   For this section, see Nils Unga, *Socialdemokratin och arbetslöshetsfrågan 1912–
34: framväxten av den 'nya' arbetslöshetspolitiken* (Lund: Arkiv, 1976).

who refused AK jobs would be cut off from all forms of public assistance, including poverty relief. The trade unions, and especially the
municipal workers, argued that many of the AK jobs were jobs that
would otherwise have been done by regular workers at market wages –
the result being wage-dumping. Particularly controversial was the
AK's decision to assign the unemployed to workplaces where there was
trade union conflict, thereby forcing the AK workers to become
strike-breakers.[29]

The AK was a state agency, but a large part of its activities were
organised by municipalities through state subsidies. Local AK committees were obliged to implement AK directives. For example, a
municipality was not allowed to pay higher benefits to the unemployed
from its own budget. Any attempt to override these requirements for the
sake of a more humane unemployment policy was contrary to state
regulations, and municipalities that did not follow the directives would
lose their state funding.

Not surprisingly, the AK policy quickly came to be thoroughly
despised by the unemployed. At the same time, it created severe tensions
within Social Democracy. At the local level, it was often a Social Democrat official who set the low level of payment, sent the unemployed off
to work far from home, or was forced to administer jobs that would
otherwise have been worked for regular wages.[30] At the central level,
leading Social Democrats were thus co-responsible for the directives
issued by the AK. As we have seen, the party leadership, including
Wigforss, fully accepted deflationary economic policy – and, by extension, the very low remuneration of AK workers. It never advanced the
idea that higher wages for the unemployed would be a way to stimulate
the economy. That policy was still a decade away.

On some points, the Social Democrats took issue with the AK. The
most important was the possibility of forcing the unemployed to take
jobs where there was trade union conflict. When parliament refused to
overturn a decision to refer the unemployed to the Stripa mine in
Guldsmedshyttan, where there was a strike, the Sandler government
chose to resign.[31]

29   Ibid., pp. 89–97.
30   Östberg, *Kommunerna och den svenska modellen*, pp. 181ff.
31   Hirdman, Björkman, and Lundberg, *Sveriges historia*, pp. 142ff.

The State of the Labour Movement

Towards the end of the 1920s, political and social tensions increased in Sweden. The economic boom was coming to an end, and internationally there was evidence of increasing political polarisation in the wake of the growing influence of fascism.[32] The political contradictions culminated in the autumn of 1928, during the so-called Cossack elections.[33] The Conservative Party used the election campaign to launch a virulent attack on the Social Democrats. They pursued two lines of attack.

One was anti-communism. The Russian threat had constantly been used to mobilise nationalist sentiment in Sweden, and it reached a new peak with the rise of the Soviet state across the Baltic Sea. Many strikes were claimed to be directed from Moscow. In addition, the Soviet Union was said to be preparing a military attack on Sweden. The Social Democrats were accused of complicity because, for technical reasons, they used the same party name in the elections as the Communists – the Workers' Party – even though they used different ballot papers.[34] 'Anyone who votes for the Workers' Party is voting for the disintegration of the family, the degeneration of children and the decline of morality', read large election posters, illustrated with women who had been sold into slavery.

The second line of attack related to a motion on inheritance tax written by Ernst Wigforss. The aim of the motion was modest: merely to set up an inquiry to examine the possibilities of a higher inheritance tax. Wigforss began the motion by pointing out, as he often did, the importance of increasing production: 'Increased production is the basis for increased prosperity, is a truth that everyone recognises. But that must not blind us to another truth', he continued: 'increased production means greater prosperity for all people only if the returns to common labour are fairly distributed.' What followed shortly afterwards would be the sentence that the Right deployed as its main trump card in the debate: 'Poverty is borne with equanimity when it is shared by all.' It was quickly, and with great impact, reinterpreted in bourgeois newspapers as the desire of the envious Social Democrats to drive everyone into

---

32   Ibid., p. 147.
33   Bengt Schüllerqvist, *Från kosackval till kohandel: SAP:s väg till makten (1928–33)* (Stockholm: Tiden, 1992), Chapter 5.
34   Ibid., pp. 80f.

poverty. They carefully avoided Wigforss's continuation: '[Poverty] becomes unbearable when it can be compared daily with the abundance of others, and if it appears unnecessary, as a temporary result of such arrangements in society as can be changed.'[35]

At the same time, the Social Democrats came under unexpectedly heavy attack from the left, the Comintern recently having taken an ultra-left line. The Social Democratic 'social fascists' were portrayed as the main enemy of the working class, and the party was now labelled 'an agent of capitalism' and 'auxiliary of imperialism.'[36]

The ensuing elections were a major defeat for the Social Democrats, whose share of the vote fell from 41 per cent to 37 per cent. The winners were the fringe parties. The Communists almost doubled their vote, although 6.4 per cent fell far short of the vote the Social Democrats had secured.

At the same time, there were rising attacks on trade unions' right to strike. Bourgeois governments had come under substantial pressure from employers to implement legislation restricting trade unions' room for manoeuvre. Such a law was implemented in 1928, criminalising strikes that took place where there were binding collective agreements. Unions that supported or did not sufficiently oppose an illegal strike could be ordered to compensate employers for their losses, which could amount to very large sums. Individual workers could be fined the equivalent of a month's wages. A special labour court was set up to monitor labour disputes, consisting of two members each from the unions and employers, as well as three senior lawyers.[37] Not surprisingly, the court usually ruled in favour of the employer.

The reaction against the law was strong among LO members, and several thousand protest statements were adopted. The LO leadership also objected to the bill, and called a short political general strike that produced a large turnout. The Social Democrats voted against the law, as did the other left-wing parties.

However, both the LO and the party leadership were in fact sympathetic to the thinking behind the new law. 'It means more peace and job

---

35   Ernst Wigforss, 'Egendomsutjämning och arvsskatt', in *Från klasskamp till samverkan*, pp. 196–216.

36   Schüllerqvist, *Från kosackval*, p. 80; Geoff Eley, *Forging Democracy: The History of the Left in Europe, 1850–2000* (Oxford: Oxford University Press, 2002), pp. 254ff.

37   Klas Åmark, 'Social Democracy and the Trade Union Movement: Solidarity and the Politics of Self-Interest', in Misgeld, Molin, and Åmark, *Creating Social Democracy*, pp. 74ff.

satisfaction for both sides if agreement on working conditions can be reached amicably without conflicts and litigation, which often arouse resentment and discontent', the LO's consultation response stated. Once the law was in place, both the LO's and the party leadership's objections also disappeared, and any proposal to abolish the law was rejected. It later became a central part of the famous 'spirit of Saltsjöbaden'.

In fact, the LO leadership endorsed further initiatives to improve relations with employers. At the same time as the new law was being implemented, the new right-wing government invited the LO and the employers to a 'Labour Peace Conference'. The inspiration for it came from the British industrialist Alfred Mond, who had tried two years earlier to heal the wounds of the 1926 General Strike. A joint resolution from the conference stressed the importance of trustful cooperation between the social forces, and of course of increasing economic growth. In particular, it emphasised the need for the export industry to preserve markets already won and to conquer new ones. This required serene and undisturbed production 'for the investing capital to be remunerated and for the workers for whom the enterprise is to provide a livelihood'.[38]

The LO's leadership fully accepted the party's main line that the labour movement should approve and support industry's potential to increase production. This is how LO chairman Edvard Johansson chose to respond to the trade union opposition's demands for a tougher fight for higher wages: 'Wages – I'm speaking of real wages – can be raised only insofar as improvements in production methods and economic organisation create conditions therefore . . . For us to believe that unions' influence alone is decisive for wage increases is as much folly as it would be for the rooster to believe the sun rises because he crows.'[39]

Important steps towards an institutionalised, corporate labour market were taken – built on a shared desire for economic and industrial growth.[40] But the backing within the LO was far from unanimous. The parties to the left of the Social Democrats had much stronger influence in the trade union movement than was reflected in electoral contests. When parts of the left returned to the Social Democrats, many union

---

38 Schüllerqvist, 'Från kosackval', pp. 104ff.
39 Quoted in Jonas Pontusson, *The Limits of Social Democracy: Investment Politics in Sweden* (Ithaca, NY: Cornell University Press, 1992), pp. 41–2.
40 Anders L. Johansson and Lars Magnusson, *LO: 1900-talet och ett nytt millennium* (Stockholm: Atlas, 2019).

leaders joined them – brought back with them much of the class struggle-inspired rhetoric.[41]

The Communist Party took advantage of dissatisfaction with the pro-business attitude of the LO leadership. It initiated an opposition movement, the Unity Committees, with the aim of 'instilling a new spirit of class struggle' in the trade union movement. In response to the LO's participation in the Mond Conference, an 'anti-Mond Conference' was organised to which unions representing one-fifth of the LO's membership sent representatives. Communist influence grew particularly strong in several of the industrial workers' unions.

The LO leadership quickly went on the counter-offensive. Membership of the Unity Committees was declared incompatible with membership of the LO, and expulsions were initiated in some unions. But the Communist Party was divided over which tactic to choose. The background was the ultra-left line taken by the world communist movement after the Sixth Congress of the Comintern. A minority within the Swedish party wanted to challenge the LO's exclusion directive – but the majority wanted to take a step back, and accept that local unions could no longer actively support the Unity Committees. The result was that by 1929, Sweden had two communist parties. A minority of affiliates – about one-third – were still affiliated to the Comintern. However, Sweden was one of the few countries where the majority of communists broke with Moscow and formed an independent party, which a few years later was renamed the Socialist Party.[42]

But the LO was not alone in attacking the Communists. In fact, the pressure was on from the Social Democratic leadership to attack communist influence. Just as the communists had already begun to build cells in workplaces, the Social Democrats would form their own clubs within the local unions. One aim was to mobilise their own members to attend meetings, in order to ensure that communists were not elected to union posts. But its aims were more ambitious than that. With the help of the trade union clubs, the party set up its own intelligence forces to keep track of communists and other radicals. At the same time, the LO employed a special functionary to organise the fight against the communists. Anti-communism has since been a prominent feature of the Social Democratic–dominated labour

---

41   Schüllerqvist, *Från kosackval*, pp. 108ff.
42   Ibid., pp. 113–18.

movement – and a prerequisite for the further development of pro-business policies.

The first success of this hard line was precisely the split in the Communist Party, which occurred as a direct consequence of the LO's ultimatum.[43]

A People's Party?

The 1928 election loss was the party's first serious setback, and led to extensive internal discussions. One question was the extent to which the party should more actively seek to reach voters outside the traditional working class, to develop in the direction of a broader People's Party, or whether its primary focus should be as a party for the working class. It was a debate that would influence the political orientation of the Social Democrats for years to come.[44]

But this was far from a new debate. In fact, Social Democracy had from the outset directed its activities towards much broader groups. Many intermediate groups, such as teachers and small businessmen, were early recruited to Social Democracy. When male suffrage was extended in 1911, the new electorate consisted mainly of the rural poor, and the party made great efforts to win them over.[45] Indeed, the new party programme adopted in 1920 clearly emphasised the alliance between workers and other oppressed groups.

Per Albin Hansson – the person most closely associated with the 'People's Party' line – wavered for a long time. Sometimes he argued vigorously for deals with the bourgeois left, celebrated consensus, and criticised trade union strikes. At other times, he spoke of class struggle and the need for a more direct socialist policy, and hailed the Wigforss inheritance tax motion as an essential attack on the existing capitalist order.[46] His most celebrated speech, the 'People's Home Address' of 1928, was a clever amalgam of both positions:

---

43   Ibid., p. 118.

44   Francis Sejersted, *The Age of Social Democracy: Norway and Sweden in the Twentieth Century* (Princeton, NJ: Princeton University Press, 2011), pp. 161ff.

45   Clas-Erik Odhner, 'Workers and Farmers Shape the Swedish Model: Social Democracy and Agricultural Policy', in Misgeld, Molin, and Åmark, *Creating Social Democracy*, p. 185.

46   Schüllerqvist, *Från kosackval*, pp. 119ff.

At ceremonial and sometimes also at everyday occasions we like to speak of society – the state, the municipality – as the home, the people's home, the citizen's home, common to us all.

The foundation of the home is community and togetherness. The good home knows no privileged or backward people, no pets and no stepchildren. There is no looking down on one another. No one tries to gain an advantage at the expense of others; the strong do not oppress and plunder the weak. In the good home there is equality, caring, cooperation, helpfulness. Applied to the great home of the people and the citizen, this would mean the breaking down of all the social and economic barriers which now divide citizens into the privileged and the backward, the ruling and the dependent, the plunderer and the plundered.

Swedish society is not yet the good home of the citizen. Although there is formal equality, equality in political rights, the class society still exists socially and the dictatorship of the few prevails economically. The inequalities are sometimes glaring; while some live in palaces, many consider it fortunate if they can remain in their colonial cottages even during the cold winter; while some live in plenty, many go from door to door to get a loaf of bread, and the poor anxious for tomorrow, where sickness, unemployment and other misfortunes lurk. If Swedish society is to become the good home of the citizen, class distinctions must be eliminated, social welfare must be developed, economic equalization must take place, the working people must be given a share in economic management, and democracy must be implemented and applied socially and economically as well.[47]

Hansson gave many concrete examples of the depredations of the prevailing class society, and sharply attacked the recently enforced labour legislation. At the same time, he severely criticised the current bourgeois government for rejecting any attempt at consensus.

This speech was delivered before the 1928 election. After the election, we can see how Hansson increasingly took a 'People's Party' line. In several articles in the autumn of 1929, he argued that 'class' should be replaced by 'people' in the party's rhetoric. The working class was too

---

47   Per Albin Hansson, speech, Swedish parliament, Second Chamber, 18 January 1928, available as '19280118 – Per Albin Hansson: Folkhemstalet', Svenska tal, 15 June 2012, svenskatal.se.

small to form a majority in parliament; the electorate had not been ready to embrace the party's policies. He now viewed Wigforss's inheritance tax motion as a mistake, and likewise the criticism of the labour peace legislation. He openly pleaded for cooperation with bourgeois parties when possible. An agreement in which workers were given some code-termination by agreeing to limits on strike activity was one example he offered.

At the same time, Hansson advocated tougher action against the Communists. For him, the decline of the Communists would smooth the pathway for the Social Democrats' evolution into a broader, less radical 'People's Party'.[48] As his phrasing makes clear, Hansson's 'People's Party line' was not just an effort to win over non-working-class voters to Social Democracy. The party had had this ambition from the start. It was also about toning down the party's class rhetoric to facilitate political alliances with parties on the right.

Hansson's line did not stand unchallenged. By the time of Branting's death in 1925, the party had undergone its first major generational transition. Initially it proved impossible to agree on a replacement for Branting. Rickard Sandler took over as prime minister, while Hansson was elected temporary party chairman. Others in top leadership positions included Ernst Wigforss, Arthur Engberg, and, after a while, the former editor of *Stormklockan* and founder of the SSV Zeth Höglund, who returned to the party in 1925. A number of looser factions gradually emerged, based on a mixture of personal and political disagreements, and sometimes perhaps on a lack of policy. Hansson was appointed as the party's regular chairman in 1928, but his position was not uncontroversial. Arthur Engberg was editor of the party's main organ, *Social-Demokraten*, and soon allied himself with Höglund. Based in the Stockholm workers' commune, they formed a kind of left-wing faction within the party, and also became the main representatives of the class party line. Disagreements with Hansson became so extensive that the party chairman was not allowed to write in the main party organ, but was instead forced to publish his articles in the Gothenburg-based *Ny Tid*.[49]

---

48 Schüllerqvist, *Från kosackval*, pp. 119–26.
49 Ibid., pp. 75ff.

4

The Crisis of the 1930s and the Social Democratic Breakthrough

The 1930s were a time of deep polarisation and widespread radicalisation on both right and left. The economic crisis that would be symbolised by the Wall Street Crash in 1929 was a decisive factor. The consequences were global: world trade more than halved in a few years, companies went bankrupt on a regular basis, and many millions of workers were thrown into unemployment. Farmers all over the world were forced off their farms. At the same time, basic social safety nets were absent. Hunger lines and soup kitchens became commonplace.[1] In Sweden, the spectacular Kreuger Crash of 1932 became emblematic of the crisis of capitalism.[2]

Needless to say, those affected were deprived of their human dignity. In the phrase of the unemployed Tåbb in Lars Ahlin's classic novel *Tåbb med manifestet* (Tåbb with the manifesto): 'You only live as long as you have a job.'

The political consequences were far-reaching. The disintegration of liberal democracies, which had already begun in the 1920s, accelerated sharply. Hitler's rise to power in 1933 pointed to a political solution attractive to some: the totalitarian fascist state.[3] For others, the Soviet Union, which did not seem to have suffered from the capitalist crisis, provided an alternative model. Some branches of the labour movement, especially the Social Democrats and Communists, initially stood idly by – or, as in Germany, fought one another.[4] By the middle of the decade, various attempts at a counter-offensive could be discerned. In

---

1 E. J. Hobsbawm, *The Age of Extremes: The Short Twentieth Century, 1914–1991* (London: Joseph, 1994), Chapter 5.

2 Lennart Schön, *An Economic History of Modern Sweden* (London: Routledge, 2012), pp. 216ff.

3 Enzo Traverso, *Fire and Blood: The European Civil War 1914–1945* (New York: Verso, 2016).

4 Leon Trotsky, *The Struggle against Fascism in Germany* (New York: Pathfinder, 1987).

countries like France and Spain, popular fronts were built to defend democracy and seek social reforms. At the same time, Spain soon became the scene of the most symbolic – and bloody – struggle between democracy and fascism. General Franco's rebellion against the legitimate government in Madrid was strongly supported by Nazi Germany and Fascist Italy. An exemplar of democracy was bombed to pieces.[5]

Sweden in no way escaped the depression of the 1930s. The most severely affected industries were those that were all-important for exports: the ironworks, sawmills, and pulp mills.

For Swedish capital, the crisis of the 1930s was turbulent. The financier Ivar Kreuger had invested in international financial markets, using the profits from the match industry as a base – partly by brokering capital flows from the United States to Europe. In the 1920s, he challenged the Wallenberg family's position as the leading Swedish financial dynasty. Kreuger was also an important lender to indebted countries. During the deep economic crisis many struggled to pay their debts, and Kreuger's financial empire began to crumble. The liberal Swedish government intervened for a period, and large loans were granted by the Riksbank – Sweden's central bank – and the major commercial banks. Soon, however, it was discovered that Kreuger had engaged extensively in dubious financial dealings. In 1932, Kreuger took his own life.

The Kreuger Crash had far-reaching consequences for the financial markets. Several financial companies collapsed, and many individuals lost their assets. Kreuger's own bank, one of the largest in the country, was threatened with bankruptcy.[6] A significant part of Kreuger's industrial empire – including LM Ericsson, AB SKF, the Swedish forestry company SCA (Svenska Cellulosaaktiebolaget), and the iron and mining company Gränges – was taken over on favourable terms by other Swedish financial families. The Wallenberg family played a key role in the buyouts.

The economic crises also had significant political consequences. It turned out that the Liberal prime minister Carl Gustaf Ekman, who had arranged the substantial loans to Kreuger, had at the same time received substantial financial support for his party, which he initially denied.

---

5 Traverso, *Fire and Blood*, pp. 54ff.

6 Stig Hadenius, *Swedish Politics during the 20th Century: Conflict and Consensus* (Stockholm: Svenska Institutet, 1997), pp. 43ff; Yvonne Hirdman, Jenny Björkman, and Urban Lundberg, *Sveriges historia. 1920–1965* (Stockholm: Norstedt, 2012), pp. 180–3.

Distrust of the bourgeoisie, both economic and political, grew during the 1930s crisis.[7]

The working class was hit hard. Unemployment rose to 25 per cent – in the forestry industry, to more than 50 per cent – and the insufficient policy of the Unemployment Commission was unable to keep up. Meanwhile, wages were squeezed.[8] Workers responded with strikes, and Sweden once again rose to the top of the international strike statistics. Parts of the trade union movement were radicalised; communist influence increased despite the constant party splits. Employers responded, as usual, by deploying strike-breakers.

Conflicts escalated, reaching a tragic climax in Ådalen, not far from Sundsvall, in the spring of 1931.[9] Further south, workers at a paper mill had been on strike for a long time, and sympathy strikes spread along the coast. When strike-breakers, with the approval of the Liberal government, were deployed in Ådalen, a large trade union demonstration was organised against their barracks. The authorities recruited the military to protect the scabs. As the demonstrators approached the camp, the order to fire was given. Four workers and a young girl, who was among the bystanders, were shot and killed. These events exacerbated social and political tensions – especially after the worker identified as the leader of the demonstration was sentenced to two and a half years in prison, while the officer in charge was given eight days in unguarded detention.

Outraged reaction was widespread. In Stockholm, hundreds of thousands of workers demonstrated, declaring 'a flaming protest against the employers, the authorities, the brutal servants, who jointly bear responsibility for the crimes committed'.[10] Arthur Engberg, editor-in-chief of the *Social-Demokraten*, was among those who condemned the murders in the strongest terms. In a trial that tested the state's commitment to press freedom, he was convicted for having defamed the officer in charge. When the victims were buried, the LO proclaimed a general work stoppage.

Not surprisingly, the political right defended the military's actions. The bourgeois newspapers baselessly claimed that it was the workers who had started the shooting.

---

7   Hirdman, Björkman, and Lundberg, *Sveriges historia*, pp. 180–3.
8   Schön, *Economic History*, pp. 216ff.
9   Roger Johansson, *Ådalen 1931: kampen om historien: sociala konflikter, historie-medvetande och historiebruk 1931–2000* (Stockholm: Hjalmarson & Högberg, 2021).
10   Ibid., p. 93.

Victory for the People's Party

But these two perspectives were not the only ones. The Ådalen Commission, appointed by the Liberal government, attempted to share the blame equally between workers and employers. Blame was also placed upon the workers who had managed to stop the work of the strike-breakers: it was the workers' fault that the conflict had intensified and that the military had to be called in. Behind the Commission's conclusions, unimaginably, were also two prominent Social Democrats, Östen Undén and Fritjof Ekman from the LO leadership. The Commission's conclusions also became those of Per Albin Hansson, and gradually of the Social Democratic Party itself.[11]

That Hansson gave his support to an interpretation so sharply at odds with the reactions that had immediately come from the entire labour movement, trying to divide responsibility between the military and the striking workers, can only be understood as a function of his 'People's Party' line, which underlay attempts to build political alliances with parts of the bourgeoisie: in order to achieve such broad political cooperation, the class perspective had to be avoided. For a long time, this interpretation became the official interpretation of Social Democracy. The events in Ådalen thus morphed into a 'tragedy' created by 'political extremes' – in other words, by communists. This reading had a decisive impact on the political options in Swedish domestic politics for long into the future.

Today, however, the memory of Ådalen is an indisputable example of the heroic past of the labour movement, even for the Social Democrats. In the wave of research into radical labour history that emerged in the wake of the radicalisation of 1968, the Ådalen shootings again came to be understood in terms of attacks by bourgeois forces on struggling workers – a view that also influenced the broader labour movement. This reinterpretation was marked on the fiftieth anniversary of the killings, in 1981. When Olof Palme inaugurated a well-known memorial, he unequivocally placed blame for the events on a 'hard, unforgiving and obdurate bourgeoisie'. The alleged responsibility of the communists was now completely erased.[12]

---

11   Ibid., pp. 75–7.
12   Ibid., pp. 430ff.

In the 1930s, however, the various interpretations of the tragedy in Ådalen were used as ammunition in the struggle between supporters of the 'People's Party' and the 'Class Party'.[13] These contradictions escalated in the run-up to the 1932 Party Congress. Two themes dominated the many motions submitted by members: the questions of socialisation and disarmament. Several motions demanded development in a socialist direction to be reflected in daily politics as well. Meanwhile, the strong pacifist current within the party demanded that the disarmament carried out in 1925 be continued in the direction of full disarmament. Both views challenged Hansson's 'People's Party' line. But these motions of the radical opposition enjoyed strong support among party members, and it was not impossible that the congress would support them.

Before the congress, however, the supporters of the People's Party and Class Party lines joined forces.[14] Hansson had shortly beforehand demanded that the party leadership take over control of *Social-Demokraten*, which had undermined the position of the Class Party supporters. It was now agreed that a power-sharing arrangement would be implemented, based on both factions submitting to stricter party discipline. The two faction leaders, Per Albin Hansson and Arthur Engberg, jointly outlined the party board's response to the motions. On the disarmament motions, the proposal was to reject them. As for the socialisation motions, it was proposed that the party wait for the results of the Socialisation Commission, which had been set up as early as 1920 but had not yet completed its work – and a final report never appeared.

By and large, it was Hansson's more cautious line that prevailed. At the same time, the leading class politicians retained their positions in the party leadership; when Hansson formed his government a few months later, Engberg became one of his ministers.

Party discipline worked. The party leadership acted in unison, regardless of the views previously expressed. The disarmament motion was rejected by a relatively large majority. The demand for socialisation to be given a clear place in the party's day-to-day policy was rejected by a narrow margin of 157 votes to 149, despite the fact that the entire party leadership, led by Wigforss, had argued against it.[15] These decisions

---

13   Bengt Schüllerqvist, *Från kosackval till kohandel: SAP:s väg till makten (1928–33)* (Stockholm: Tiden, 1992), pp. 135ff.

14   Ibid., Chapter 5.

15   Ibid., pp. 161ff.

definitively transformed the party programme's treatment of socialism into a text in the history of ideas, as one Social Democrat put it. It survived on paper, but had no role in practical politics.[16]

Demands for party discipline also led to a centralisation of the party's decision-making structures. Particular emphasis was placed on unified behaviour on the part of the party press. The Social Democratic newspapers were to show 'considerable caution in their statements' on controversial issues. Hansson set up a special information department, which provided ready-made articles on how the press should 'view the government's positions'. The decision reflected concerns that too much criticism of the bourgeois parties would hamper attempts to reach agreements with the right.

For Hansson, it was also important to get the LO to keep pace with the party's political initiatives. Attempts to isolate the communists had been an important part of his political programme for several years, and now he was pressing the LO leadership to drive them out of the trade union movement. The issue became particularly topical as several strikes in the construction sector complicated the implementation of the new unemployment policy. Hansson's work was ultimately successful.

In a special 'Circular 807' from the LO leadership, the trade unions were called upon to expel 'trade union trouble-makers' – in practice, communists and syndicalists. Trade union members were to 'profess the democratic principles which the Swedish labour movement has made its own' and 'pursue the struggle for the transformation of society by peaceful means'. The LO also employed several functionaries to monitor and register communists.

In short, as historian Bengt Schüllerqvist notes, the Social Democrats underwent a fundamental organisational change in 1928–33 from a loose to a tightly managed organisation.[17] This change would prove crucial when the party regained power in 1932.

---

16   Villy Bergström, 'Party Program and Economic Policy', in Klaus Misgeld, Karl Molin, and Klas Åmark, eds, *Creating Social Democracy: A Century of the Social Democratic Labor Party in Sweden* (University Park: Pennsylvania State University Press, 1992), p. 144.

17   Schüllerqvist, *Från kosackval*, p. 204.

Election Victory and Horse-Trading

The 1932 elections were a great success for the Social Democrats. The party received 42 per cent of the vote, an increase of almost 5 percentage points. At the centre of the election campaign was the issue of unemployment, and here the Social Democrats were on the offensive. It was Ernst Wigforss, in particular, who formulated and agitated for the party's programme.[18]

For Wigforss, the issue of unemployment had been prominent throughout the 1920s. As minister of finance he had pursued a Liberal-influenced deflationary policy that helped to keep unemployment relatively high even during boom years. As we have seen, the Social Democrats also accepted the tight wage policy of the Unemployment Commission.

Gradually, however, Wigforss began to question the dominant economic doctrine that unemployment could be fought only by lowering wages.[19] He was inspired early on by Marxist theories of underconsumption as a cause of economic crises. Towards the end of the 1920s, he also came into contact with the new currents developing in English economics, under the guidance of J. M. Keynes. Wigforss found himself in sympathy with their suggestion that money spent by the state to combat unemployment stimulated the economy, providing work for far more people than just the unemployed themselves. He first made use of these ideas in a motion to parliament in 1930.

Unemployment was due to excessive saving, low consumption, and low investment, Wigforss argued. By under-balancing the budget to create public jobs with market wages, the supply of money would increase, demand would rise, and unemployment would fall. At the same time, the much-criticised system of jobs overseen by the Unemployment Commission would be abolished, and unemployment insurance introduced.

In the run-up to the 1932 elections, the Social Democrats made the fight against unemployment their main issue. A hundred-page motion was presented to the spring session of the parliament, in which

---

18   Hirdman, Björkman, and Lundberg, *Sveriges historia*, pp. 193ff.
19   Leif Lewin, *Planhushållningsdebatten* (Stockholm: Almqvist & Wiksell, 1967), pp. 60–9.

Wigforss's new perspective was developed further. Wigforss also popularised his ideas in the high-profile pamphlet 'Can we afford to work?'[20] When he was appointed finance minister, he immediately set about trying to turn them into policy.

The origins of Wigforss's ideas have been intensely debated ever since among political scientists, economists, and historians. Some have argued that Wigforss was a predecessor of Keynes, whose *General Theory of Employment, Interest and Money* was first published in 1936.[21] But Wigforss had followed the debate among British economists from an early date.[22]

Another milieu that increasingly drew inspiration from Keynes's ideas was the group of economists that came to be known as the Stockholm School. Wigforss was in close contact with several of them, not least Gunnar Myrdal. Wigforss himself liked to refer to the fact that the Social Democrats, before the First World War, had already actively promoted the idea of publicly financed jobs with market wages to combat unemployment. He may have been inspired by Beatrice Webb's *The Minority Report of the Poor Law Commission*; but her ideas were intended to mitigate the effects of cyclical unemployment, and lacked expansionary ambitions characteristic of Keynesianism. They appeared in various forms during the 1920s, notably in motions from parties to the left of the Social Democrats. In 1928, before Wigforss had formulated his new ideas on unemployment policy, the LO called for the abolition of the Unemployment Commission system, and for the unemployed to be paid labour market wages. In general, the trade unions' growing criticism of the Unemployment Commission system played an important role in their Social Democratic reorientation.[23]

Wigforss was perhaps the first politician to attempt to pursue a policy inspired by theories of expansionary government policy enabled by an under-balanced budget as a means of combating unemployment. But the ideas sometimes subsequently attributed to Wigforss were by no means unknown among contemporary economists and other social

---

20 Ernst Wigforss, 'Ha vi råd att arbeta?', in *Från klasskamp till samverkan* (Stockholm: Tiden, 1941).

21 Otto Steiger, 'Bakgrunden till 30-talets socialdemokratiska krispolitik', *Arkiv* 1 (1971).

22 Karl-Gustav Landgren, 'Socialdemokratisk krispolitik och engelsk liberalism', *Arkiv* 3 (1972); Lewin, *Planhushållningsdebatten*, p. 61.

23 Lewin, *Planhushållningsdebatten*, pp. 61–3.

scientists. The promise to tackle unemployment was a key reason for the Social Democrats' election victory in 1932. But the aftermath of the shootings in Ådalen and the diminished credibility of the bourgeoisie symbolised by the Kreuger Crash also contributed. The Social Democratic share of the vote thus rose to 42 per cent. The divided Communists together received just over 8 per cent. The Farmers' Union also made headway, gaining just over 14 per cent. The Right lost out by a large margin, losing over 5 percentage points, and the combined vote of the two liberal parties fell by over 4 points.[24]

Per Albin Hansson was given the task of forming a government. No one could have imagined at the time that this moment inaugurated a period of forty-four consecutive years of Social Democratic prime ministers (with a short 'summer vacation' in 1936). The government was filled by the new generation of Social Democrats. Ernst Wigforss became minister of finance, Gustav Möller minister of social affairs, Rickard Sandler minister of foreign affairs, and Arthur Engberg minister of education. But the balance of seats in the Second Chamber was still 118:112 in favour of the bourgeoisie, and the prospects of implementing any of the Social Democratic unemployment policies were uncertain.

The impasse was resolved by one of the most spectacular political compromises of the twentieth century: the 1933 agreement with the Farmers' Union, or so-called 'cow-trade'.[25] In the spring of 1933, the government presented the new policy in the draft budget, as well as several other bills. SEK 200 million was requested for the implementation of the unemployment programme: SEK 160 million was to be spent on productive emergency work, with wages in line with those for regular jobs. In addition, the Unemployment Commission was to be abolished and unemployment insurance introduced. The budget was underbalanced, and provided for some borrowing to finance aid to the unemployed, but otherwise it was by no means expansionary. Most ministers had to resign themselves to cuts. It was 'a show of austerity', wrote the minister of finance, Wigforss.[26]

All the bourgeois parties – the Conservatives, the Liberals, and the Farmers' Union – were opposed to this programme. Opposition was focused on the increase in benefits for the unemployed, of which the

24   Hirdman, Björkman, and Lundberg, *Sveriges historia*, pp. 193–6.
25   Ibid., p. 196.
26   Ernst Wigforss, *Minnen*, vol. 3, *1932–1949* (Stockholm: Tiden, 1954), p. 17.

farmers were the most critical of all. Intense negotiations throughout the spring did not seem to produce any result, and the fall of the government looked increasingly likely. At the same time, the political situation was complicated by the fact that the bourgeois parties were divided among themselves, and bruised by their election losses. Although the Farmers' Union was obviously included among the bourgeois parties, it had little sympathy for the liberal economic doctrines of the other bourgeois parties.[27]

Against all odds, the Social Democrats managed to persuade the Farmers' Union to agree to a deal that was to their mutual advantage. The government pushed most of its unemployment programme through. In addition, the odious directive that could force the unemployed into workplaces where strikes were taking place was abolished. But it was not a complete victory. The Unemployment Commission was to be retained, and no unemployment insurance was included in the agreement. In addition, the most symbolic decision – that the unemployed would be paid market wages – was watered down: their maximum full-time working hours were reduced from forty-eight to forty hours. As it was difficult to find enough 'productive' jobs, more and more people resorted to unproductive emergency-relief work.

At the same time, the Social Democrats abandoned their traditional line on free trade. The slogan 'Away with hunger tariffs!' had been raised in the party's first programmes. Food tariffs were hitting workers particularly hard. In the 1932 election campaign, the party had been clear that it wanted to support only the poorer part of the farming population. This view was now completely revised. The Farmers' Union was supported by a comprehensive protectionist agricultural subsidy.[28] The agreement meant that cereals continued to be regulated, while aid was given to beet farming as well as animal production. In 1934, price supports were introduced for meat, pork, and eggs. Even some tariff increases and import regulations were introduced. Most controversially, the Social Democrats accepted a margarine tax. The party had long argued in its propaganda that the tax enriched the already-rich by exploiting the poor.

In retrospect, many have argued that it was natural that the workers' and peasants' political parties should ally with each other. The two parties have

---

27   Lewin, *Planhushållningsdebatten*, pp. 89–96.
28   Odhner, 'Workers and Farmers Shape the Swedish Model', pp. 191ff.

been described as having been built on the popular movements of the cities and the countryside, respectively. But this is a gross oversimplification. The self-employed farmers who formed the basis of the Farmers' Union were traditionally a strong conservative force in Swedish politics. They had long opposed democratic reforms that threatened their strong position in the Riksdag; the members of the Farmers' Union were the most vocal in their opposition to the 1918–21 voting reforms. It was also among farmers that hostility towards trade unions was at its strongest. There was no obvious ideological affinity between the two parties.

The bargain did not change the conservative values of the political peasant movement.[29] At the same time as the Farmers' Union was forming its alliance with the Social Democrats, the pro-Nazi currents within it remained prominent. In radical Ådalen, the Farmers' Union mobilised against the workers, influenced by the fascist Lappo movement in Finland. Openly racist thinking was not uncommon. The party programme stated that it was a national task to preserve the Swedish people 'against the interference of inferior foreign racial elements', and to prevent the 'degenerating influence' of undesirable foreigners – in other words, Jews. A leading party representative could declare without objection from his party colleagues in the Riksdag: 'I readily admit, Mr Speaker, without shame that I am today an anti-Semite.'[30]

The Social Democrats made no concessions to these ideas, although the inclusion of a party with such values in the government may of course have helped to normalise that way of thinking. It also made it more difficult for the government to articulate robust criticism of Nazi Germany; the Farmers' Union advocated a more restrictive policy on accepting Jewish refugees.

The deal was primarily a pragmatic agreement with farmers' interest organisations. Alongside their political party, the farmers had built up an economic movement, the Riksförbundet landsbygdens folk (RLF) – a kind of farmers' equivalent of the labour movement's LO – and it was the men behind the RLF that were the driving force behind the agreement with the Social Democrats.[31] The farmers were a social force with

---

29   Anders Björnsson, *Skuggor av ett förflutet: Bondeförbundet och trettiotalet: en idéhistorisk essä* (Lund: Sekel, 2009).

30   Hirdman, Björkman, and Lundberg, *Sveriges historia*, pp. 242–53, quote p. 253.

31   Bo Rothstein, 'Managing the Welfare State', *Scandinavian Political Studies* 3 (1985); Per Thullberg, *Bönder går samman: en studie i Riksförbundet Landsbygdens folk under världskrisen 1929–1933* (Stockholm: LT, 1977).

their own class organisation. The programmatic support of the other bourgeois parties for free trade, and their scepticism about state support for the agricultural industry, made closer cooperation with the Right difficult.

It was not only in Sweden that the independent organisation of the peasantry facilitated alliances across the political divide.[32] Shortly before the Swedish bargain, the Danish Social Democrats reached an agreement with the farmers' party, Venstre. It guaranteed calm in the labour market and extensive state support for both agriculture and construction. In Norway a few years later, a crisis agreement was reached between the Social Democrats and the Farmers' Party. And the 1937 Red Soil government in Finland – an alliance between farmers and Social Democrats – was not only a political agreement between the two groups that had suffered most during the deep crisis of the 1930s, but also the first political alliance between two parties that had been on opposite sides in the civil war that had divided the Finnish nation for twenty years.

In Sweden, the political agreement between the Social Democrats and the Farmers' Union lasted a few years, but in the summer of 1936 there was a crisis around the question of rearmament.[33] The disarmament of the Swedish armed forces, pushed through by the Social Democratic government in 1925, was reconsidered in the mid 1930s in light of growing international unrest and, in particular, Germany's increasing militarism. The Social Democrats also supported increased funding, but did not want to go as far as the bourgeois parties. When, in the spring of 1936, the opposition pushed through an increase in defence spending, while at the same time voting down a proposal for an increase in pensions, the Hansson government resigned. It was replaced by a government based on the Farmers' Union, and had a very weak parliamentary base.

But the Social Democrats, it turned out, were only taking a short break from government. The parliamentary elections in September were a great success for the party, which won 112 seats in the Second Chamber against 107 for the bourgeois parties. With 11 seats for the communists and socialists, the left now commanded a majority there.

---

32 Francis Sejersted, *The Age of Social Democracy: Norway and Sweden in the Twentieth Century* (Princeton, NJ: Princeton University Press, 2011), pp. 84ff.
33 Hirdman, Björkman, and Lundberg, *Sveriges historia*, p. 269.

In the First Chamber there was still a bourgeois majority; on important budget votes, where the chambers voted together, the score was 190:190. To the surprise of many, the Social Democrats chose to invite the Farmers' Union to cooperate once again, and this time also to join the new government. Promises were made to the farmers that their economic position would continue to be improved.[34] Most importantly, the party promised not to pursue any radical policies of a socialist character. 'I preferred a coalition government', Wigforss wrote in his memoirs. 'We wanted to secure a parliamentary majority sufficient to implement social reforms and hoped that the Farmers' Union would see the reasonableness of such a policy . . . Neither the party nor the government was prepared to pursue a policy which in earlier party-political language would have been called socialist.'[35]

An important reason for the Social Democratic victory of 1936 was that the economic crisis was quickly overcome. Already in 1934, growth was higher than before the crisis. Despite the sharp downturn at the beginning of the decade, the 1930s were one of the most successful decades ever for the Swedish economy. But the reason was not Wigforss's policies. Researchers today agree that he did not have time to put his economic policies into effect before the upturn. The much-discussed under-balancing was too small to have played a major role; and for the rest of the decade, economic policy was instead restrictive, with surpluses in government finances.[36]

More important was that Sweden followed Britain's example by abolishing the gold standard. The result was a fall in the value of the Swedish krona, which in turn created major expansion opportunities for export-oriented Swedish industry. Exports to Germany grew particularly rapidly. In fact, a major reason for the rapid recovery of Swedish industry was that Swedish companies were able to supply the German armaments industry with iron ore and ball-bearings. In 1940, half of Sweden's exports went to Nazi Germany.

Real wage increases remained low, partly because of a labour surplus. Despite the much-vaunted expansionary unemployment policy, unemployment remained high, at over 10 per cent, and the agricultural crisis freed up labour in rural areas. But the crisis was also lifted by strong

34   Ibid.
35   Wigforss, *Minnen*, vol. 3, p. 93.
36   Schön, *Economic History*, pp. 218–27.

growth in the domestic market, which was not the product of expansionary economic policies either, but was largely demographic in origin. The proportion of the population aged between twenty and thirty was higher than ever. Family formation stimulated housing construction and demand for capital goods.[37]

Social Movements and Democracy in Danger

Sweden has often been singled out as one of the few exceptions to the general trend in Europe during the 1930s. There has been talk of a Swedish *Sonderweg*. The economic crisis did not, as in many other countries, lead to increased polarisation or a stronger position for fascist and anti-democratic currents. Instead, a party with deep popular roots was able to develop strong social support for a future welfare state. As early as 1936, the American journalist Marquis Childs's book *Sweden: The Middle Way* attracted international attention. Sweden was presented as pursuing a successful middle path between planned and market economies, and Child particularly highlighted the importance of social reforms as an explanation for the rejection of totalitarian ideologies.[38]

Two conditions have usually been highlighted as explanations for the country's success in developing a stable democracy: first, the ability of the Social Democrats to pursue Keynesian policies early on that were able to counteract the economic and social consequences of the crisis; second, their successful attempts to build class alliances – in Sweden's case the parliamentary cooperation between workers and farmers.[39] These explanations are not uncontroversial. As we have seen, the impact of Keynesian-influenced policies was limited; other circumstances lifted Sweden out of the economic crisis. And the deal with the Farmers' Union was hardly a class alliance. It was, rather, a pragmatic agreement with the farmers' economic interest groups.

Instead, I will highlight another factor that played a decisive role in the relative survival of Swedish democracy in the dark 1930s: the increased social radicalisation and broad mobilisation of popular movements that characterised this period. The decade was marked by the

37 Ibid.
38 Marquis William Childs, *Sweden: The Middle Way* (New Haven, CT: Yale University Press, 1936).
39 Several articles in Misgeld, Molin, and Åmark, *Creating Social Democracy*.

rapid growth of traditional social movements and the emergence of new ones – and their influence on social development was significant. In fact, this revitalisation of social movements played a decisive role in the success of the Social Democratic project.[40]

The radicalisation that characterised the 1930s can be seen in the sharp increase in the number of strikes – an area in which Sweden once again took top billing internationally. Although successes alternated with defeats – the Ådalen being a tragic climax – it was clear that the trade union movement was not prepared to accept employers' wage pressures or to be thrown into unemployment on benefits that were impossible to live on. It may be worth noting that the Social Democratic political breakthrough did not reduce strike activity: it was as high at the end of the 1930s as at the beginning.[41]

But radicalisation can also be seen in efforts to strengthen collective organisation. This trend was most evident in the trade union movement. After the crisis of the 1920s, the LO's membership was down to just under 350,000. By 1930 it had risen to over 600,000, and by 1939 it had reached almost a million. The rate of organisation of the Swedish working class rose from 45 per cent in 1930 to 66 per cent in 1940 – one of the highest in the world. A contributing factor to the increase in unionisation at the end of the 1930s was that the unemployment insurance scheme introduced in 1935 was based on the Ghent model: unemployment funds were administered by the trade unions, but with state support. This provided a powerful additional argument for joining the unions.[42]

Since the LO mainly organised blue-collar workers, the strong growth in the unionisation of white-collar workers was also an important factor. In thoroughly organised Sweden, white-collar workers in different sectors had also joined together in their own organisations at an early date. Often, these were interest groups in which more traditional trade union issues such as wage negotiations played a secondary role; relations with employers were often much less confrontational. But

---

40   For this section, see Kjell Östberg, *Folk i rörelse: vår demokratis historia* (Stockholm: Ordfront, 2021), pp 173–83.

41   Klas Åmark, *Hundra år av välfärdspolitik: välfärdsstatens framväxt i Norge och Sverige* (Umeå: Boréa, 2005), p. 227.

42   Anders Kjellberg, *The Membership Development of Swedish Trade Unions and Union Confederations since the End of the Nineteenth Century* (Lund: Lund University, Department of Sociology, 2017).

the interwar crises hit white-collar workers hard. Unemployment was high even for them, and many struggled to maintain their incomes.

A major problem for white-collar workers was that their right of association was not recognised. The LO had already won the battle for the right to belong to a trade union in the December Compromise of 1906, but it was not yet regulated by law. By studying the LO, middle-class employees could see the benefits that more widespread unionisation could bring. Interestingly, they also drew support from Sigfrid Hansson, editor of the LO's magazine *Fackföreningsrörelsen* and brother of Per Albin Hansson. In 1936, the white-collar workers recorded their first major success, when the Riksdag passed a law on the right to organise and, for those employed in the private sector, to negotiate. Unlike the LO, the white-collar unions retained their party-political neutrality, and within some unions the bourgeois influence was significant. However, most of the central leaders of the Confederation of Professional Employees (Tjänstemännens Centralorganisation, TCO), the white-collar equivalent of the LO, had been active Social Democrats; among public-sector employees in particular, Social Democratic influence has been dominant.[43]

Disaffected and economically stricken middle-class groups across Europe were under significant pressure from the emerging fascist movement. The significance for democratic development of the fact that Swedish officials chose the popular-movement route can hardly be overestimated.

As we have seen, it was important for the political development of the 1930s that the farmers had created their own trade union, the RLF, which was aimed at strengthening the economic organisation of the peasants, and much less tied to the conservative ideological heritage of the political farmers' movement.[44] Several new branches of the tree of popular movements emerged during the interwar period. They were usually closely linked to the labour movement. Among their founders were not only Social Democrats, but usually also communists and left-wing socialists of various kinds.

Rent disputes had been ongoing since the end of the nineteenth century. They increased during the turbulent year of 1917, and in the following decade widespread conflicts broke out, particularly in

---

43   Tommy Nilsson, *Från kamratföreningar till facklig rörelse: de svenska tjänstemännens organisationsutveckling 1900–1980* (Lund: Arkiv, 1985).
44   See above.

Stockholm and Gothenburg. But it was during the 1930s crisis that the real surge occurred. Strikes and blockades were widely used; landlords who raised their rents too rapidly were declared blockaded and boycotted. The membership of the National Union of Tenants doubled during the 1930s and by the middle of the decade it approached 50,000. At the same time, a housing cooperative developed – the Savings and Construction Association of Tenants (Hyresgästernas sparkasse- och byggnadsförening).[45] As the tenants' movement grew, it also widened its focus to housing policy in general. It made extensive demands on the Social Democratic government to produce more and better-quality housing. Many of these demands were incorporated by the major Social Housing Commission that was working at the time.[46]

The impressive breadth of the radical movement's ambitions is perhaps best illustrated by the fact that even sexual politics became the basis of a popular movement in the 1930s through the Swedish Association for Sexuality Education (Riksförbundet för sexuell upplysning – RFSU). The struggle for the right to contraception, abortion, and sexual education had been driven by the radical movement for fifty years, both within the labour movement and by radical doctors and social reformers.[47] But it says something about the spirit of the 1930s that they chose to organise their activities through a popular movement. A range of trade union, political, and women's organisations were actively involved. By 1940, organisations representing 65,000 members were affiliated to the RFSU – and their support was not merely passive. Local chapters were formed all over the country, including in smaller mill towns. The RFSU set up advice bureaus, cooperated with doctors, published information brochures, and sold carefully tested contraceptives. Its clearly stated aim was to try to reach out to working women.[48]

---

45   Hannes Rolf, 'A Union for Tenants', *Radical Housing Journal* 3, no. 1 (May 2021); Hannes Rolf, *En fackförening för hemmen: kollektiv mobilisering, hyresgästorganisering och maktkamp på hyresmarknaden i Stockholm och Göteborg 1875–1942* (Stockholm: Ersta Sköndal Bräcke högskola, 2020).

46   State public investigation SOU 1945:63, *Bostadssociala utredningens slutbetänkande*, part 1.

47   Gunnela Björk, *Lust och nöd: Karin & Nils Adamsson – sexualupplysningens pionjärer* (Lund: Historiska Media, 2021).

48   Lena Lennerhed, 'Sex Reform in the Welfare State: RFSU, the Swedish Association for Sex Education, in the 1930s and 1940s', in Paul Pasteur, Sonia Niederacher, and Maria Mesner, eds, *Sexualität, Unterschichtenmilieus und Arbeiterinnenbewegung* (Leipzig: Akademische Verlagsanstalt, 2003), pp. 157–65.

During the 1930s, a whole generation of writers with roots in the working class came to occupy a leading position in the Swedish literary world. These 'proletarian writers' were usually autodidacts, and have described their own upbringing in several autobiographical accounts. At the same time, they were strongly influenced by contemporary European literature, and their literary themes were gradually broadened. A couple of them – Pär Lagerkvist, Eyvind Johnson, and Harry Martinsson – became Nobel laureates. They also participated actively in the political debates of the time. Their texts were spread through the newspapers of the labour movement, where the trade union press – not least economically – played an important role. Through publishers owned by the labour movement, their books were distributed in hundreds of thousands of copies.[49]

The Popular Movement's Party at Work

I have already stressed the importance of the fact that several political parties in Sweden can be described as popular-movement parties. They were built up by members who were also active in the major popular movements of the time. With the widening of democracy, these parties soon became the basis of local politics. This was particularly true of Social Democracy. After some initial uncertainty about how the party would use its new influence, confidence soon grew. By the end of the 1930s, the Social Democrats alone, or with the support of parties on the left, held a majority in most major cities, as well as in many hundreds of mill towns and industrial communities. In ever more places, Social Democratic politicians were running local government. They represented a movement that was active in many different parts of society. Those who participated were also often active in their trade unions, women's clubs, educational organisations, or temperance societies, and were thus deeply rooted in their communities.[50]

The hubs of the Social Democratic people's movement were the workers' communes, of which there were several thousand around the

49   Lars Furuland and Johan Svedjedal, *Svensk arbetarlitteratur* (Stockholm: Atlas, 2006).

50   Kjell Östberg, *Kommunerna och den svenska modellen: socialdemokratin och kommunalpolitiken fram till andra världskriget* (Eslöv: Symposion, 1996); and Östberg, *Folk i rörelse*.

country. In the workers' communes, politics was discussed in all its aspects, from the road to socialism to municipal budgets, and many proposals and ideas were hatched there that were later translated into political action. All important issues of local politics were initially debated in detail before they came up in local councils and assemblies, and party representatives were given clear instructions on how to vote. At the same time, a significant proportion of active Social Democrats were elected as local politicians. The workers' communes and their leaderships were dominated by male representatives – usually workers active in various LO unions. This does not mean that women were not politically active; women drove many of the issues that became the backbone of the Swedish welfare model through their organisations.

All parts of the Social Democratic movement grew strongly during the 1930s.[51] Between 1929 and 1939 the party's membership almost doubled, from 235,000 to 460,000, and the number of workers' communes grew from 1,480 to 2,522, which meant that there were now local branches in virtually every municipality. The membership of the Women's Federation quadrupled in the 1930s. The Swedish Social Democratic Youth League (Sveriges Socialdemokratiska Ungdomsförbund – SSU) had to start from scratch when the old youth union had exited Social Democracy along with the SSV in 1917. During the 1930s, its membership grew from 42,000 to almost 100,000. Soon, there were SSU clubs in every major industrial town. In the late 1920s, Per Albin Hansson highlighted the presence of the organisation in the mill town of Surahammar, where the local SSU club had 250 members. 'This means that the club has mastered the youth of the place. And that's how it is in many other places. The Social Democratic youth movement controls a youth that numbers in the tens of thousands.'[52]

The People's Houses, of which there were well over a thousand around the country during the 1930s, were obvious meeting places. In many localities, they were supplemented by People's Parks, which were used for outdoor meetings and summer parties – not least for dancing. Cultural activities were important. In 1933, the Social Democratic minister of education and culture, Arthur Engberg, had founded the National Touring Theatre (Riksteatern): 'It is not only the population of the capital that has a legitimate claim to enjoy first-class theatrical art. The

51   Östberg, Folk i rörelse, pp. 190–5.
52   Schüllerqvist, Från kosackval, p. 101.

rest of the nation can justifiably make a similar claim.' For a long time, the People's Houses and Parks provided the most important stages for the National Touring Theatre's performances. There were several other important meeting places, including consumers' cooperatives for material needs. In the Workers' Educational Association, workers continued their education uninterrupted.

In the 1930s, the pioneer generation of the labour movement reached retirement age. Naturally, they then formed the first pensioners' organisations. The Swedish National Pensioners' Organisation (Pensionärernas riksorganisation) soon became an important advocate for a better pension system. And for those at the other end of the age-scale, the children's organisation Young Eagles (Unga Örnars Riksförbund) was formed at the same time. In the broad world of labour movement organisations, one could exist from cradle to grave.[53] And, for those beyond that span, the labour movement also established Fonus – a chain of undertakers.

Women Organising

In the 1921 parliamentary elections, women were able to vote and be elected on the same terms as men for the first time. Hopes of a significant political breakthrough were high, and not unfounded. Through the women's suffrage movement, as well as in a number of women's political, trade union, and other organisations, women had trained themselves in political discussion and parliamentary work. In the leadership of this broad women's movement there was an expansive layer of highly competent, experienced, and well-educated women who could easily compete with the male candidates.

The women of the labour movement could also claim to have lit the spark and led the hunger revolt of spring 1917 – the greatest social uprising the country had ever seen. But the women's experience was forgotten. In 1921, just five women were elected out of 380 members in parliament, and only two were Social Democrats.[54] The situation was little better in the municipal assemblies, where fewer than 5 per cent of

---

53 Östberg, *Folk i rörelse*, p. 194.

54 For this section, see Kjell Östberg, *Efter rösträtten: kvinnors utrymme efter det demokratiska genombrottet* (Eslöv: Symposion, 1997), including quotes in the following pages.

those elected were women. And it was not just an unfortunate start. After ten years, the Social Democrats still had only two women in parliament, out of a total of four.

Within the women's movement, a sense of backlash spread. They could expect harsh attacks, from the right as well as from the left: 'Feminism is a phenomenon of degeneration. Its politics have triumphed in the face of a tired and resigned zeitgeist and under the leadership of manly women', wrote the leading Social Democratic student politician Arnold Sölvén, who after a few years would become the LO's chief lawyer. Sölvén continued, 'Feminism seeks to sharpen and extend the competition for work between the sexes in areas where women lack the opportunity for self-assertion and self-development, and where their activities lead only to the degeneration of work and their own withering away.'

Next came attacks on women's right to work. Proposals for legislation targeting working married women appeared in parliament, initially from Social Democrats. This, in turn, can be seen as part of a concerted offensive by men from different political camps to drive women back from public life into the home.

But why were women not elected? For the men who tried to explain it at the time, the answer was, in most cases, obvious. From right to left on the political spectrum, the same answer was given: it was the woman's own fault. A number of character traits were attributed to women that, taken together, would explain their lack of success. The women were *immature and uninterested* in politics. 'The working woman, who lives the same life as her male comrade, has not the same degree of political enlightenment as he. She lacks the social and political overview of a situation which for thinking people is the reason for joining organisations for a united struggle towards a certain goal', wrote a leading Social Democratic couple. Women were *unqualified and ignorant*. The editor of the *Social-Demokraten* argued: 'women have the most brilliant chances of acquiring influence, but they cannot fill all the posts for which they should be qualified, because the experienced and competent women are so few.' There was another important characteristic attributed to women by all sides: their propensity for *gossip, division, and jealousy*. In a communist newspaper one could read: 'Woman herself has often been women's worst enemy, their greatest obstacle, in that the female sex has never been able to free itself from intrigue and gossip, from petty envy and conventional prejudices.'

It would not be surprising if representatives of the right held such views, as they had consistently opposed women's suffrage. But even members of the labour movement endorsed the view that women had no place in the political arena. This was also reflected at the top of the Social Democratic Party. Throughout the interwar period, there was only one woman in the party leadership – and in the government they were completely absent. Only in 1921 did the Social Democratic Party allow women to form their own national union – now that women's votes were needed.

From the very beginning, the activities of the Women's League were questioned. Male Social Democrats felt that 'women are not yet mature enough to manage themselves in organisational terms'. They should be involved in workers' communes, not isolating themselves in women's clubs'. The Women's League, on the other hand, argued forcefully for the right of women to organise themselves in their own organisations: 'If the party is to be merely an electoral apparatus, we can do away with the women's organisations, but if women are to be trained as citizens, they must have some means of fulfilling that role.'[55]

Women's powerful response to this position was Joe Hill's *Don't Mourn – Organize!* They created their own organisations, networks, and meeting places. In the 1930s, women's organising exploded. This was the great period of women's separate organisation in Sweden – not least Social Democratic women.

As we have seen, there was a general opinion among men that women were far too immature and ignorant for politics, as well as uninterested in it. But a study of Social Democratic women's activities at the local level gives a different picture. Women bore a heavy responsibility for the material structure of the movement. They collected money for sick members, for striking workers all over the country, for the youth club, for the election fund, and for monuments to the movement's male leaders. Bazaars and festive events were common sources of income, in addition to what was handed over from the household budget. All of this activity went so far that the Women's Federation had to try to limit the clubs' generosity.

Above all, however, the minutes of the women's clubs were filled to the brim with municipal politics. But they dealt with different issues than men, often adopting broader perspectives. The recurring issues discussed were children, schools, health, maternity, nursing, hygiene, and sobriety.

---

55   Ibid., pp. 60ff.

Already at its first meeting, in 1908, the Karlskoga Women's Club had demanded free dental care for schoolchildren. The following year, they persuaded the workers' commune to push the issue at the school assembly – which, after initial resistance, appointed a committee to investigate the proposal. After three years, the Social Democratic member of the committee was able to inform the women that the committee had not yet held its first meeting. In 1919, the Social Democrats gained a majority in Karlskoga's municipal council, and several times during the 1920s the issue was raised again by the women's club. In 1934, a positive decision was finally taken on the matter.

What happened in the school was discussed extensively and from many directions. The clubs were often critical of the excessive teaching of religion and the influence of priests. But they were not content only to discuss this issue – they also took action. During the economic crisis of the 1930s, women demanded that school exams be cancelled because many parents could not afford to buy graduation clothes. In addition, teachers were to be banned from accepting gifts from children. They also demanded better school meals and free textbooks.

Municipal decisions on childcare centres or nurses to care for the sick at home often originated in discussions in women's clubs. Hygiene issues played a prominent role in work for a more tolerable everyday environment. Women's clubs often called for bathhouses or communal laundries, which were crucial when most homes lacked bathrooms and hot water. They made their demands to a variety of bodies: the workers' communes, municipal and ecclesiastical councils, county councils, state authorities, trade unions, and employers.

Contrary to male prejudices about women's lack of political consciousness, it is obvious that women developed an extensive practice of municipal politics. The most prominent issues were those linked to the reproductive sphere, raising children, and care – issues that have now largely moved beyond the exclusive realm of the family, and have been broadly politicised.

That women accepted socially defined 'women's issues' as their special domain can be understood in several ways. It may be an expression of a distortion of women's political activity caused by men's refusal to let women into their domains. It may also be a deliberate strategic choice by women to advance their position. In any case, the result was that, although women were excluded from the formal municipal political arena, they still managed to pursue and develop the issues that would later become central to the construction of welfare: schools, health care, and social services. In fact, it was to a decisive extent women's local political action that laid the foundations for the Swedish welfare state during this period.

Women's Networks

An alternative female public sphere existed during the interwar period – a myriad of women's organisations. Alongside the political women's associations and the traditional women's associations, there were house-wives' associations, women's temperance associations, charity associations, church societies, sports associations, peace societies, and pro-defence organisations.[56]

There were many reasons why women chose to organise separately. Anti-feminism and the marginalisation of women in public life have already been mentioned. Working life was more divided into male and female arenas than it is today. Higher education, in particular, was seg-regated. All this had consequences for the most important women's associations of the 1930s: the women's trade unions.

The LO never accepted women's separate organisation. Women's unions were forced into unions dominated by men at the beginning of the century.[57] But most working women were in areas not organised by the LO at the time – office workers, teachers, shop workers, medical staff, telegraph and postal workers, and so on – where separate organi-sation was the rule. The women's unions largely served the social interests of their members, with canteens, lounges, holiday homes, and housing for women. But, in the 1930s many of the women's unions became radicalised. Their precarious position in the labour market and their role as a reserve army meant that they were hit harder by the 1930s crisis. They came under severe pressure to relinquish their jobs to unemployed men. The situation became truly threatening when an unholy alliance between right-wing MPs from the Farmers' Union and conservative Social Democratic trade unionists demanded legislation to ban married women from public employment. One of the first actions

---

56   Ibid., pp. 175–98.
57   Eva Schmitz, *Arbetarkvinnors mobiliseringar i arbetarrörelsens barndom: en studie av arbetarkvinnors strejkaktiviteter och dess inflytande på den svenska arbetar-rörelsen* (Lund: Lund University, Department of Sociology, 1999), pp. 53ff.

of the Social Democratic government when it took office in 1932 was to set up an inquiry into the matter.[58]

It is striking how this women's community was able to mobilise women from different social backgrounds. The fight against the ban on married women's right to work involved not only professional associations, from brewery workers to clerks, lawyers, and doctors. Political women's associations from all camps, socialists and right-wing women, and even housewives' associations, took part in the struggle. Women's organisations mobilised all the power their hundreds of thousands of members could muster. They held mass meetings, wrote petitions and newspaper articles, conducted their own investigations, and influenced all the men they could. Although women's sympathies extended across the political field, Social Democratic women took a leading position, making skilful use of their contacts with their party colleagues in the corridors of government.[59]

The result was a tremendous success. Instead of a ban on married women's right to work, the result was a law banning the dismissal of pregnant women. The decision was also in line with the social policy offensive that the Social Democratic government had just launched in the wake of the debate on the 'population crisis'. Several of the leading women also came to be associated with these projects.

The struggle for married women's right to work reflected a recurring feature in the history of the Swedish women's movement: a remarkable ability to unite, even across class boundaries, on issues concerning women's fundamental rights, and above all women's right to work. This applies to the women's suffrage movement as well as to the broad women's movement of the 1970s.

With their own organisations, women were able to lead and educate themselves, and largely to formulate their own agenda. The aim was to be equal to men and to enter politics and the labour market without being discriminated against. Separate organisation became one of the main tools of the struggle for equality.

---

58 Renée Frangeur, *Yrkeskvinna eller makens tjänarinna? Striden om yrkesrätten för gifta kvinnor i mellankrigstidens Sverige* (Lund: Arkiv, 1998).
59 Östberg, *Efter rösträtten*, pp. 172–5.

The Welfare Bureaucracy

The Social Democratic movement was effectively organised from the outset, and produced strong leadership on all levels. In Gramscian terms, the movement's leaders, who were primarily of proletarian origin, were organic or movement intellectuals. They were products of social movements, rather than of traditional educational institutions and elite power groups.[60]

The initial task of these intellectuals had been to establish and organise the Social Democratic movement. As the party established decisive political influence, the role of its intellectuals changed to that of developing the welfare state. At the same time, the party experienced a growing need to recruit a more specialised type of intellectual: those traditionally belonging to the educated elite.[61]

The construction of the Swedish welfare state was largely a local-government affair. Traditionally, towns and municipalities had been responsible for poverty relief, elementary education, and care for the elderly. The rapid development of the postwar years entrenched this arrangement. The vast expansion of the education system, a considerable housing programme, the explosion in public childcare – all were assigned to the local administration.[62]

The Social Democrats won a majority in local-government assemblies at an early point. By the end of the 1930s, three-quarters of Sweden's towns were run by a left-wing majority. The issue of how the party was to create a competent and powerful leadership at the local administrative level was thus a political question of the first rank. This problem was aggravated by the fact that a significant portion of local-government administrative functions were assigned to volunteers serving on elected but unpaid commissions. This applied, for instance, to most of the poor

---

60   Antonio Gramsci, *Selections from the Prison Notebooks of Antonio Gramsci* (London: Lawrence & Wishart, 1971), pp. 12, 16; Ron Eyerman and Andrew Jamison, *Social Movements: A Cognitive Approach* (Cambridge: Polity/Basil Blackwell, 1991), pp. 97ff.

61   Kjell Östberg, 'The Swedish Social Democracy: Civil Servants, Social Engineers and Welfare Bureaucrats', in Mathieu Fulla and Marc Lazar, eds, *European Socialists and the State in the Twentieth and Twenty-First Centuries* (Cham: Palgrave Macmillan, 2020).

62   Bo Gustafsson, *Den tysta revolutionen: det lokala välfärdssamhällets framväxt: exemplet Örebro 1945–1982* (Hedemora: Gidlund, 1988).

relief, including its coercive measures. Outside big cities, local officials were rare before the Second World War, and most local governments lacked a modern administrative structure.[63] Up until the 1950s, there were 2,500 separate cities and municipalities.

The vast majority of the Social Democrats elected were industrial workers. As the scope of local political assignments grew, it became obvious that social divisions between manual and intellectual labour would make it impossible to combine this work with the municipalities' governing functions. It was necessary to create a material basis for local political work. This, in turn, would lead to the creation of a local labour elite.

It soon became common to elect leading Social Democrats to the administrative posts of municipal manager or clerk. There were also other jobs, lacking formal political connections but appointed by municipal bodies, to which Social Democrats sought to get their candidates elected – posts such as teachers, social administrators, local policemen, and even clergymen. There could, of course, have been many reasons why Social Democrats wanted to politicise these appointments. It may have been in the interest of the labour movement to secure the appointment of teachers or policemen who were sympathetic to the workers' cause. The politicisation of these posts could also be seen as an expression of clientelism. In the interpretation offered here, however, the process constituted the means of creating a material basis for wider influence over local politics.

A second source from which it was possible to recruit Social Democrats for top municipal positions consisted of those who already worked full-time within the labour movement as journalists, managers of the cooperative stores, janitors of the People's Houses, and so on.[64]

Finally, as a result of Gustav Möller's project, described below, thousands of state-employed 'street bureaucrats' were recruited to local labour exchanges and social insurance bureaus. A vast majority of them were also Social Democrats.[65] The result was a large number of full-time functionaries who constituted a thickly woven and cohesive social group that could be defined as a local Social Democratic welfare-state

---

63   Östberg, 'Swedish Social Democracy', pp. 210ff.
64   Ibid., p. 211.
65   Bo Rothstein, *The Social Democratic State: The Swedish Model and the Bureaucratic Problem of Social Reforms* (Pittsburgh, PA: University of Pittsburgh Press, 1996).

bureaucracy, which played a central role in building the welfare state on the local level.[66]

Gradually, local parliamentary political work occupied an increasing share of the attention of local party leaders. Municipal issues took up gradually more space on the agendas of the workers' communes, at the expense of ideological and general political discussions. In addition, a new centre of local power emerged: the Social Democratic City Council group. Soon the question arose: Who should decide on the party's local policy – members of workers' communes, or elected representatives in council groups?

Conflicts between local politicians and party members became so widespread in some places that the central party leadership was forced to intervene. In a special pamphlet from 1940, it sided with the municipal politicians. It was undemocratic that the decisions of members should bind municipal politicians. If such a system were accepted, the deliberations of municipal bodies would be 'nothing but a spectacle and a fundamental attack on democracy as such'.[67]

This was, of course, an uncontroversial exposition of the consequences of representative democracy. But it also illustrates how party democracy had to be subordinated to parliamentary rules. By extension, this meant a necessary centralisation and hierarchisation of the party's decision-making structures, which was simultaneously taking place at the central level. The scope for workers' communes to take their own initiatives was reduced, while central control was increased.

At the same time, both the LO and the party's central organisation also implemented organisational changes that would shift power away from members and towards the central leadership.

The Social Engineers

Whether or not they had formal secondary schooling, the political education and skills of the Social Democratic leaders entering the government in 1932 were equal to those of any other politician. But it was necessary to recruit new supporters to fulfil other essential functions

---

66   Ernest Mandel, *Power and Money: A Marxist Theory of Bureaucracy* (London: Verso, 1992).

67   Östberg, *Kommunerna och den svenska modellen*, p. 208.

in government departments and the administration. If the party had left the execution of the reforms it sought to implement to the bourgeois-minded civil servants already in place, there was a risk that they would be delayed or sabotaged.[68]

The traditional Swedish state bureaucracy could generally be characterised as a Weberian, relatively well-paid, and non-corrupt stratum. Long after the end of the Second World War, all levels of the Swedish state bureaucracy remained dominated by civil servants with conservative values. In some government offices – not without reason – the joke went that the only Social Democrats were the minister and the janitor. Most senior civil servants had a law degree, and recruitment to law school was very much socially biased. Until the 1960s, few posts inside the ministries – aside from those of the ministers themselves – were assigned on political grounds.[69]

Swedish public administration differed in some respects from that of many other countries. The ministries were rather small. Responsibility for the implementation of public policy belonged, as it still belongs, to semi-autonomous national boards. The ministries were not supposed to intervene in the work of these boards. These factors, of course, made it even more complicated for the Social Democratic government to implement its policy.

In order to solve this problem, the Social Democratic government started by forging links with those young academics who had become radicalised during the 1930s. This attempt was fruitful: the first generation of social engineers was formed at this time. This cohort developed and implemented reform projects on behalf of the new government.

A circle formed in Stockholm around Alva and Gunnar Myrdal. Its members managed effectively to combine the roles of scientists, agitators, political actors, expert investigators, and state bureaucrats. They included economists, architects, physicians, sociologists, and psychologists, as well as writers, artists, and other creative intellectuals. The circle's members took part in some of the central social and political discussions of the time: the housing question, new economic policies, unemployment, population issues, education, childcare, health care. They composed governmental reports, academic papers,

---

68   Rothstein, *Social Democratic State*.
69   Thomas J. Anton, *Administered Politics: Elite Political Culture in Sweden* (Boston: Martinus Nijhoff, 1980).

and pamphlets, and published cultural magazines. Some also entered
the administration and became practical reformers. Alf Johansson,
perhaps the most talented economist of the Stockholm School, left
academia and became head of the Housing Board. It is striking that
several of those partaking in this circle were women, some of whom
later became members of government: Alva Myrdal, Karin Kock, and
Ulla Alm-Lindström, for example.[70]

The Social Democratic Party was, for the same reasons, also interested in maintaining good contacts with the interwar, radical, sometimes
Marxist-influenced student movements. The party recruited a number
of young radical academics from this background who were to play
prominent roles in the party and in the Swedish state. Tage Erlander,
later party leader and long-time prime minister, was for some time
linked to this milieu.[71] As a result, in the late 1930s a number of central
national boards of particular interest for the government were directed
by Social Democrats: the Boards of Health and Welfare, the Board of
Housing, the National School Board, and what was to become the
National Labour Market Board.

Another innovative solution to the problem of changing the bureaucracy was advocated by the minister of social affairs, Gustav Möller:
that of consciously establishing a new type of administration in certain
key areas. In these areas, bureaucrats were largely recruited from the
labour movement or from other popular organisations. This was true
in particular of the National Labour Market Board, which played a key
role in implementing the government's extremely important labour
market policy. In contrast to the Weberian model of bureaucracy, no
specific consideration was to be given to formal merit, though 'the
existence of theoretical education should, of course, not be looked
upon as a disqualification', Möller told his critics.[72] However, this
unconventional way of running government activities by recruiting
'street-level bureaucrats' was limited to spheres where activities were
decentralised to a significant degree.[73]

70   Eyerman and Jamison, *Social Movements*, pp. 150–61; Yvonne Hirdman, *Alva Myrdal: The Passionate Mind* (Bloomington, IN: Indiana University Press, 2008).
71   Crister Skoglund, *Vita mössor under röda fanor: vänsterstudenter, kulturra-dikalism och bildningsideal i Sverige 1880–1940* (Stockholm: Almqvist & Wiksell, 1991).
72   Gustav Möller, minutes 1943:35, Swedish Parliament, Second Chamber, no. 35, 13 December 1943, p. 31.
73   Rothstein, *Social Democratic State*.

These Swedish social engineers developed a unique form of welfare bureaucracy with close ties to the state-run Social Democratic Party. It came to play a central role in the development of the Social Democratic welfare society. For the social engineers, it was natural to put their knowledge at the disposal of politics – or, in the words of Alva Myrdal: 'They must now move from the mere recording of facts and the analysis of causal relationships to the formulation of rational plans for appropriate change.'[74] The echo of Marx's words that philosophers should not only explain the world but also change it is clear enough.

The economists of the Stockholm School provided an important source of inspiration and a sounding-board for Ernst Wigforss as he tried to make policy out of the Keynesian ideas that were in vogue during the 1920s and 1930s. The Myrdals' 1934 book, *Crisis in the Population Question*, was a central initial source of inspiration for the social policy reform agenda formulated after the Social Democratic government came to power.[75] The background to this agenda was one of the key social issues of the interwar period: too few children were being born. The solution in most European countries was to reward women who stayed at home and gave birth to many children.[76] The labour market was to be reserved for men. The Myrdals turned the issue around. To encourage young families to have children, it was necessary to introduce social reforms that would make it easier for them financially: housing allowances; free schooling, including free school lunches, educational materials, and health care; and subsidies on healthy basic foods. Instead of making it more difficult for women to work, it was essential to make it easier for those who wanted to combine work with raising a family.[77]

Crisis in the Population Question had an immediate impact. It was discussed in all parts of society and became an obvious point of focus for the many study circles organised by the labour movement around the country. 'The left had stolen the population issue from the right', as leading historian Yvonne Hirdman notes.[78] In 1935, the social affairs minister, Gustav Möller, set up a major government inquiry, the

74   Hirdman, Björkman, and Lundberg, *Sveriges historia*, p. 210.
75   Alva Myrdal and Gunnar Myrdal, *Kris i befolkningsfrågan* (Stockholm: Bonnier, 1934).
76   Hirdman, Björkman, and Lundberg, *Sveriges historia*, p. 215.
77   Ibid., pp. 212–15.
78   Ibid., p. 219.

Population Commission, to turn its ideas into policy. Three years later, it had presented seventeen volumes. The proposals spanned a wide range of areas: day care centres, tax issues, maternity allowances, child support, and sexual policy. The proposal to legislate to prohibit married women from public employment was buried once and for all. Instead, the dismissal of women on grounds related to marriage and child-bearing was prohibited. And state-employed women were allowed to stay at home with pay when they gave birth.[79] Only a small proportion of the proposals were implemented immediately. The minister of finance, Wigforss, commanded a reform freeze in the last years of the 1930s, and during the Second World War there was no room for costly social policies. But most of the proposals were to reappear and form the backbone of postwar radical family policy.

The image of the welfare society as a dwelling – the people's home – was firmly established by Per Albin Hansson's classic speech from 1928. But housing in a more material sense was a recurring theme during the 1930s, not least among social engineers. The 1930 Stockholm exhibition is also regarded internationally as an important milestone in the break-through of functionalism in architecture. Like so many other ideas harboured by social engineers, housing was intended both to help modern people live rationally and to make the most of technological advances to build as efficiently and economically as possible.[80]

Social housing policy soon became a hallmark of the construction of the people's home – and here the need was great. For a long time, Sweden was among the countries in Europe with the worst housing standards, the highest levels of overcrowding, and the highest rents. In the wake of the housing crisis, a militant renters' movement emerged. Housing construction figured prominently in the 1933 crisis programme. It was relatively easy to engage the unemployed in construction jobs. But it had no real effect on the housing crisis, as crisis aid was not allowed to affect market-economic conditions. In addition, the efforts that were nevertheless made were hampered by widespread conflict in the construction industry.

More important was another decision taken by the government in the same year: the establishment of the Social Housing Commission, headed by leading economist Alf Johansson. The inquiry worked for fourteen

---

79 Frangeur, *Yrkeskvinna eller makens tjänarinna?*
80 Hirdman, Björkman, and Lundberg, *Sveriges historia*, p. 210.

years, and its main findings, presented only after the Second World War, were to influence state housing policy for generations to come.[81] Housing policy now became an integral aspect of the construction of Social Democratic 'Folkhem' ('the people's home' – the symbol of the Swedish welfare state), indeed sometimes leading it. Alf Johansson brought with him the Keynesian-influenced thinking of the Stockholm School, and housing policy became an important part of the government's economic policy. But Johansson also belonged to the Myrdal network, and was thus in close contact with the reform-oriented architects and social politicians of the time.

Some of the proposals of the Social Housing Commission were implemented before the Second World War. Most notable were state subsidies for housing for families with many children. They were often built in a functionalist architectural style, and were popularly known as 'Myrdal houses'. Families with many children were also eligible for grants to build their own homes in rural areas. Both of these initiatives were in line with the Population Commission's ambition to facilitate childbearing through social policy measures.

But the home also became central to the more radical utopia of the Folkhem developed by the social engineers.[82] Alva Myrdal sketched the collective house where cooking, cleaning, laundry, and childcare were lifted from families – that is, women – and socialising took place in common spaces. She wanted to create the 'comrade family' (kamratfamiljen), but above all to provide 'walls for a new social life, a new human being who better corresponded to the demands made on her by technological and social development', writes historian Yvonne Hirdman.[83]

This creation of the new man (and woman) was to begin at an early age. Alva Myrdal was an early proponent of preschool education – a high-quality physical and intellectual upbringing that allowed for children's individuality and initiative, as well as for interaction with other children. The entire new social policy outlined by the social engineers was aimed at 'producing a better human material'. It was about control and surveillance in the service of democracy and freedom, in Hirdman's summary.[84] A good illustration of this view is the fact that Alva Myrdal

---

81   SOU 1945:63.
82   Yvonne Hirdman, *Utopia in the Home: An Essay* (Armonk, NY: Sharpe, 1992).
83   Yvonne Hirdman, *Att lägga livet tillrätta: studier i svensk folkhemspolitik* (Stockholm: Carlsson, 1989), p. 109.
84   Hirdman, Björkman, and Lundberg, *Sveriges historia*, pp. 217–19.

advocated 'supervision of consumption'. Support for families with children should primarily take the form of contributions in kind: parents might not have been knowledgeable enough to buy what was best for their children.

In recent decades, social engineers and their projects have come under severe criticism. Their ambition 'to put life right' has been interpreted as an affront to individual freedoms and an attempt to abuse omnipotence. This criticism has been linked to a broader questioning of the politics of the Folkhem – a criticism especially intense when the neoliberal project was launched in the 1990s.

There have also been extensive attempts to associate the rise of the welfare society with racial biology and forced sterilisations. A leading critic argued that one motive for the introduction of sterilisation laws had been to fund increases in child benefits and other social reforms planned by the Social Democrats at the time. For some, the links to the racial laws of the Third Reich were also obvious. The Swedish sterilisation policy was simply a kind of reverse Nazism; the difference was that in Sweden, it was social maladjustment, not the concept of race, that was its governing concept. Racial biology was presented for some years as a kind of supremacist ideology of Folkhem.[85]

However, neither racial biology nor sterilisation policy was a Social Democratic invention.[86] They had already had a major impact before the First World War, particularly in the United States. During the interwar period, they constituted a mainstream trend in international politics and science. At the heart of biological racism was an eminently traditional fear of the 'masses' – the new citizens who claimed influence and challenged the previous ruling elites. Not only were they to be restrained by political bureaucracies – it was also necessary to reduce the physical proliferation of the masses themselves. Eugenic thinking was elaborated through overtly class-based arguments.

In 1922, a racial biology institute was established in Sweden, at the suggestion of members of parliament from the Social Democrats and the Farmers' Union. Inspired by neo-Darwinian thinking and the research

85   Maciej Zaremba, *De rena och de andra: om tvångssteriliseringar, rashygien och arvsynd* (Stockholm: Bokförlaget Forum, 1999).

86   Gunnar Broberg and Mattias Tydén, 'Eugenics in Sweden: Efficient Care', in Gunnar Broberg and Nils Roll-Hansen, eds, *Eugenics and the Welfare State: Sterilization Policy in Denmark, Sweden, Norway, and Finland* (Lansing, MI: Michigan State University Press, 2005), pp. 77–149.

of the time on heredity, its aim was to investigate how to improve the human material. Avoiding miscegenation was an obvious starting point. In Sweden, the mapping of the Sami was an important component of this endeavour.[87]

In the 1930s, the emphasis was on how to prevent 'inferior elements' from reproducing. This included those who were considered to have a poor genetic make-up, hereditary diseases, or intellectual disabilities. In 1934, the first sterilisation law was passed unanimously, allowing those suffering from 'disturbed mental activity' to be sterilised against their will.

Support for this measure was strong in many parts of society. The year before, over 1,000 women had petitioned the government, representing the entire women's political elite, from right to left. A key demand was for sterilisation legislation, while others concerned the right to abortion and sexual education. No arguments were advanced based on racial biology – the demand was that women should be given the opportunity to create a decent life. In 1941, the law was extended to include people with 'asocial lifestyles'. This time there was greater opposition, several Social Democrats and Liberals voting against the proposal.

The application of the sterilisation laws is a dark part of Sweden's modern history. Approximately 63,000 people, mostly women, were sterilised before the law was abolished in the late 1970s. Nearly 6,000 are estimated to have been sterilised under coercion. A further 15,000 accepted sterilisation as a condition for release from institutions. For several others, pressure from the authorities was intense. A significant group of those who voluntarily applied for sterilisation were emaciated pregnant women who, as a result, were also able to obtain an abortion.[88]

According to leading researchers, sterilisation was driven by two main actors: doctors and local poor-relief bureaucrats. Responsibility falls heavily both on them and on politicians. On the other hand, claims that the sterilisations were driven mainly by the Social Democrats, that they were part of a social policy project or were a prerequisite for social reforms, have little empirical support. Certainly, eugenics and sterilisation policies were not peculiar to Social Democratic Sweden.[89]

---

87   Hirdman, Björkman, and Lundberg, *Sveriges historia*, p. 224.
88   Ibid., p. 229.
89   Broberg and Tydén, 'Eugenics in Sweden'.

The Fight against Fascism

Explicitly fascist and Nazi movements never succeeded in recruiting large numbers of followers in Sweden.[90] Taken together, the various parties received a maximum total of 25,000 votes – well under 1 per cent of the electorate. More problematic was the fact that Nazism had the support of a relatively large number of police officers and military officials. This is not to say that fascist ideas did not attract groups within the Swedish bourgeoisie, some of whom also sympathised with Mussolini's programme for addressing the shortcomings of Italian society. Indeed, many in the bourgeoisie showed their appreciation for the new order Hitler was implementing. The Conservative Party Youth League went so far in supporting Nazism that the party had to break off contact. Parts of the business community had their traditional pro-Germanism strengthened by their interests in good business relations with Hitler's Germany.

The pro-Nazi opinion that rejected Nazism as a solution for Sweden but accepted it for Germany was in some parts more dangerous than the openly Nazi parties, argues historian Klas Åmark in his seminal study of Sweden's relationship with Nazism, *Att bo granne med ondskan* (Living next door to evil). That opinion was anchored in the social strata in a way that open Nazism was not.[91]

At the local level, there were frequent confrontations between Nazi groups and an alliance of Social Democrats and Communists. The SSU sent its members to Nazi meetings, where – especially in southern Sweden – they interrupted and heckled the speakers, and sometimes sang the Internationale. 'We implemented a reporting system, which kept us informed of every Nazi meeting that was organised', writes Torsten Nilsson, later Social Democratic minister of social affairs and foreign affairs, in his memoirs. 'We trained emergency squads that went around demanding debate.'[92]

The biggest anti-fascist mobilisations took place during the Spanish Civil War. The various sections of the labour movement formed a joint

90   For the following pages, see Klas Åmark, *Att bo granne med ondskan: Sveriges förhållande till nazismen, Nazityskland och förintelsen* (Stockholm: Bonnier, 2011); Stig Ekman, Klas Åmark, and John Toler, eds, *Sweden's Relations with Nazism, Nazi Germany and the Holocaust: A Survey of Research* (Stockholm: Vetenskapsrådet, 2003).

91   Åmark, *Att bo granne med ondskan*, p. 459.

92   Torsten Nilsson, *Människor och händelser i Norden* (Stockholm: Tiden, 1977).

solidarity committee with more than 400 local aid committees that held 3,000 meetings and demonstrations. Money was collected equivalent to half a million daily wages. Communists and socialists were most active locally, while the LO and the trade unions provided financial support centrally. Some 500 Swedes, most of them communists, volunteered in the war. A third of them were killed.

There is no doubt that the labour movement was the main force in the fight against Nazism and fascism in Sweden during the interwar period. At the same time, it is clear that the Social Democratic government increasingly pressed for controversial concessions to its powerful neighbour to the south. When Hitler came to power, the LO supported an international boycott of German goods, but not without reservations – the boycott would not put Swedish companies in immediate difficulties. And the foreign minister, Rickard Sandler, strongly discouraged any action.

At the same time as many in the labour movement took the side of the Spanish people, the Social Democratic government adhered to the British-initiated non-intervention pact. Laws were passed in Sweden criminalising the provision of arms and volunteers to fight on the side of the Republic. A request from the last ambassador of the Spanish Republic to buy Bofors anti-aircraft artillery was refused by the Social Democratic government, while the Basque town of Guernica was bombed to pieces.[93]

One area where the Social Democratic government has been heavily criticised in retrospect is its very restrictive policy on accepting refugees from Nazi Germany.[94] During the 1930s, hundreds of thousands of Jews and a large number of political opponents left Germany to escape persecution. Only a few thousand came to Sweden, and the reason was the government's reluctance to grant residency permits. Initially, the motives were mainly economic. In general, Sweden required refugees to show that they could support themselves. In order to process Jewish refugees more easily, Sweden joined an agreement between Germany and Switzerland that Jewish passports would be stamped with a capital 'J' – a de facto acceptance of the German Nuremberg Laws.[95]

93   Åmark, *Att bo granne med ondskan*, p. 77.
94   Klas Åmark, 'Sweden and the Refugees, 1933–1945', in Mikael Bystrom and Pär Frohnert, eds, *Reaching a State of Hope: Refugees, Immigrants and the Swedish Welfare State, 1930–2000* (Lund: Nordic Academic Press, 2013).
95   Steven Koblik, *The Stones Cry Out: Sweden's Response to the Persecution of the Jews 1933–1945* (New York: Holocaust Library, 1988).

But the major adjustment in relation to the south was trade policy: exports to Germany increased sharply towards the end of the decade, and in 1940, half of Swedish exports went to Nazi Germany.[96] The main reason for this was that Germany's rearmament created an ever-increasing demand for Swedish iron ore and ball-bearings. The country became increasingly dependent on Swedish ore, and was keen to ensure that supplies could be made without risk of disruption – even during a war. In a special agreement in the autumn of 1939, the two states regulated their trade policy. Sweden increased its exports of ore and ball-bearings in exchange for large imports of coal and coke. These mutually beneficial contacts with Nazi Germany were underpinned by strong pro-German currents in the diplomatic corps and the military – two spheres entirely without Social Democratic representation and sympathies.

The End of a Decade: A First Balance Sheet

At the end of the decade, the Social Democratic Party could look back on the 1930s with satisfaction. The mere fact that it had managed to retain government power for seven years – longer than any other twentieth-century Swedish government before then – was itself an achievement. No one could question its ability to run the country, although many questioned its policies.[97]

The movement was bigger, broader, and better organised than ever. A young generation of intellectuals had joined, and were making their contributions to radical politics – and the voters approved.

The government had shown its willingness to reform: unemployment policy had changed direction, unemployment insurance had been implemented, and the position of women in the labour market had been strengthened. Parliament had decided on a statutory two-week paid holiday, and pensioners had received some additional benefits. The Population Commission had proposed a series of family policy reforms, some of which had already been implemented. Journalists from other

96   Åmark, *Att bo granne med ondskan*, Chapter 5; Marin Fritz and Birgit Karlsson, 'Dependence and National Supply: Sweden's Economic Relations to Nazi Germany', in Ekman, Åmark, and Toler, *Sweden's Relations with Nazism*.
97   Hirdman, Björkman, and Lundberg, *Sveriges historia*, esp. pp. 200–30.

countries were already materialising to study the extent of the ambitions for social transformation in Sweden.[98]

Socialist aspirations had been postponed. But reforms could not wait – and the party's firm belief was that this now required growth and a well-managed economy; and here the government was going to help. But how much would it be able to intervene? How much would business accept interference from a Social Democratic government?

It is clear that the government was not content simply to stimulate the economy during recessions. The depression seemed to have faded, but the forces of recovery remained weak, Ernst Wigforss argued in 1934. Even now, a public investment programme was needed. The forces of the free market were insufficient to deliver the required stimulus to the economy – and the Social Democrats could not be satisfied with a business sector operating below its potential. They demanded 'a business community running at full speed'.[99]

The Social Democrats, wrote the ideological journal *Tiden*, would inject new vitality into the capitalist system through their expansionist policies. Efforts were needed at both the micro and macro levels.[100] The LO and the party were also inspired by Austro-Marxist Otto Bauer, who warned of 'misrationalisation' if responsibility for the economy was left to the market alone.

The government set up a series of sectoral inquiries to facilitate the 'planned expansion' of the economy, targeting large and small enterprises including the export industry, the timber industry, housing construction, and agriculture. A state credit institute was set up, and the oil and coffee monopolies were examined.[101]

Capitalists were initially sceptical, as it was still a strange idea that the state would so actively interfere in free enterprise; they therefore sensed socialist ambitions behind these initiatives. As it turned out, the results of the inquiries were not very impressive, and few led to concrete results.

---

98   Childs, *Sweden: The Middle Way*.
99   Lewin, *Planhushållningsdebatten*, p. 99.
100   Ibid., pp. 105ff.
101   Jonas Pontusson, *The Limits of Social Democracy: Investment Politics in Sweden* (Ithaca, NY: Cornell University Press, 1992), pp. 43–7; J. Magnus Ryner, *Capitalist Restructuring, Globalisation and the Third Way: Lessons from the Swedish Model* (London: Routledge, 2002), pp. 72–8; Hans de Geer, *Rationaliseringsrörelsen i Sverige: effektivitetsidéer och socialt ansvar under mellankrigstiden* (Stockholm: SNS, 1978), pp. 345–9.

To reassure the reluctant capital, both Ernst Wigforss and Per Albin Hansson repeatedly stressed their desire to find forms of cooperation and consensus. There would be no adventurous experiments, from which, Hansson declared, it would be the workers who suffered most.[102]

A concrete expression of these efforts to foster consensus was the commission with the inviting name of 'National Supply and Labour Peace'. It was set up to examine the possibilities of 'intervention by society in certain areas of economic life'. One impetus behind this move was the business community's demand for action against strike movements that did not seem to give in. The Social Democrats now hinted that they might consider legislating against 'socially dangerous strikes'. In exchange, they wanted to raise questions of industrial democracy, more secure employment conditions, and social control over banks, and to discuss with the business community how production could be made more efficient. A series of new sub-inquiries was also initiated. The broad scope of this initiative has caused it to be remembered by historians as the 'Mammoth Inquiry'.[103] Although its concrete results were again limited, it nevertheless came to symbolise a step towards greater understanding between the parties.

The growing consensus was also helped by the government's deceleration of reforms in 1938, which reduced the need for tax increases. At the same time, it cut taxes for the most prosperous companies, and introduced business-friendly investment funds.[104]

A symbolic culmination of the government's efforts towards collaboration was a speech by Ernst Wigforss - ten years earlier the main enemy of the bourgeoisie - to business leaders in Gothenburg on the issue of cooperation between the state and the business community.[105] His main theme, once again, was the importance of collaboration to increase production, including through improved use of new technologies and more rational scientific research. Wigforss strongly emphasised the importance of promoting the export industry, and also called for formal consultations between government and industry. The speech was

---

102   Lewin, *Planhushållningsdebatten*, p. 113.
103   Ibid., p. 155.
104   Ibid., p. 169.
105   Ernst Wigforss, 'Om samarbete mellan staten och det enskilda näringslivet', 1938, in *Från klasskamp till samverkan*.

well received. Cooperation soon began, and a joint working group even managed to agree on various export-promotion measures before the outbreak of the Second World War.[106]

At the same time, there was a spectacular rapprochement between the LO and employers, against a backdrop of demands for further legislation to deal with workers' strikes.[107] The Social Democrats' reluctance to introduce such legislation changed when the party came into government, and was given direct responsibility for industrial peace. On several occasions, the Social Democratic government intervened with mediation proposals that were unfavourable to the workers; in 1934, only the threat of coercive laws persuaded the unions to accept the contract they were being offered.

But with little sign of such conflicts abating during the 1930s, demands from employers and the political right for further legislation only increased. They focused in particular on laws to protect 'third parties' not directly involved in the conflict – among whom they included strike-breakers!

The government took several initiatives to meet the demands of employers. As we have seen, one of the aims of the Mammoth Inquiry was to make proposals in precisely this direction.

The Saltsjöbaden Agreement

Before any concrete proposal was presented, however, the LO and the Swedish Employers' Association (SAF) had taken matters into their own hands.[108] On the initiative of the SAF, five people from each organisation met in secrecy to discuss possible ways of solving the problems through agreements between the actors in the labour market instead of by legislation. To the surprise of many, the two organisations were able to reach a main agreement at the end of 1938, the legendary Saltsjöbaden Agreement (Saltsjöbadsavtalet), which would regulate labour relations for a long time to come.

---

106 Lewin, *Planhushållningsdebatten*, p. 173.
107 Klas Åmark, 'Social Democracy and the Trade Union Movement: Solidarity and the Politics of Self-Interest', in Misgeld, Molin, and Åmark, *Creating Social Democracy*, pp. 74ff; Anders L. Johansson and Lars Magnusson, *LO: 1900-talet och ett nytt millennium* (Stockholm: Atlas, 2019).
108 Ibid.

The contents of the agreement that was signed were not very extensive. A negotiating mechanism was agreed that was designed to facilitate
solutions to disputes before conflict broke out. A special joint labour
board was set up to assess, among other things, whether conflicts were
socially dangerous. But the great significance of the Saltsjöbaden
Agreement lay in its subtext.[109] The LO and the SAF committed themselves to avoiding open conflict as far as possible – an object that would
be facilitated by a centralised bargaining system. Furthermore, the
government was to be kept out of the negotiations.

Leading scholars have also pointed to some other effects of the agreement. In wage negotiations, the export industry would set the tone. The
SAF promised to refrain from using strike-breakers, while the LO
pledged to go after communists and syndicalists. The industrial peace
necessary to maintain production would be the guiding priority for both
employers and unions.

For the LO, the Saltsjöbaden Agreement also had far-reaching organisational consequences.[110] It had never been a monolithic organisation.[111]
The various unions had different interests, sometimes opposed to each
other, and to the LO's leadership. Although no one questioned the close
relations with the Social Democratic Party, there was always a desire to
mark the unions' organisational autonomy. This was true both for the
moderate union leaderships, who were reluctant to jeopardise the
unions' resources in political action, and for the sometimes strong left-
wing currents, among whom there was no desire to act as support
troops for Social Democratic governments. The LO's ability to influence
the activities of individual unions was limited, the unions themselves
deciding how wage campaigns should be conducted, when conflicts
should be called, and so on. A recurring demand of the left opposition
was that the LO should be transformed into an 'attack organisation' that
would more actively initiate and support trade union struggles.

But the Saltsjöbaden Agreement put all of that on hold. The new statutes adopted in 1941 mandated a major centralisation. The federations

---

109   Christer Lundh, ed., *Nya perspektiv på Saltsjöbadsavtalet*, (Stockholm: SNS
förlag, 2009).
110   Sune Sunesson, *Politik och organisation: staten och arbetarklassens organisationer* (Lund: Arkiv, 1974).
111   Lars Ekdahl, 'Fackföreningen – en socialistisk resurs. Makten över arbetarrörelsen och samhällsutvecklingen', in Håkan Blomqvist, ed., *Arbetarrörelsen inför
socialismen* (Stockholm: Carlsson – forthcoming, 2024).

inside the LO were obliged to seek the views of the LO leadership on all significant matters of principle. The LO was given the right to participate in the unions' contract negotiations, and to put forward proposals – which the union leaders had to accept if they wanted financial support. All strikes involving more than 3 per cent of a union's members were to be approved by the LO leadership. The same applied if a conflict risked leading to lockouts by employers. At the same time, the right to a decisive membership vote was abolished.[112]

Sweden gained one of the world's strongest, and at the same time most centralised, trade union confederations. But it was not used for radical trade union struggles. Its aim was different: to achieve the most efficient economic development possible through cooperation with the business community in order to create the conditions for the future welfare of the working class. To quote the English historian Donald Sassoon, the Saltsjöbaden Agreement was 'a class compromise in which the organisations of the working class agreed to accept the capitalist definition of growth and productivity'.[113] This description could also apply to the Social Democratic government's ambitions to stimulate Swedish industry. The government took a number of initiatives and set up several inquiries to this end, without much success. And the Social Democrats showed their willingness to cooperate by considering further measures to curb strike activity.

The Second World War

The Swedish policy of neutrality and Sweden's relationship with Nazi Germany during the Second World War are among the most hotly contested questions in twentieth-century Swedish history. A few issues in particular have taken centre stage.[114]

One of them is the extensive German troop and material transports that took place across Swedish territory. Swedish trade policy, in which extensive iron ore exports were central to Germany's armaments, is another. In 1940, iron ore from Sweden accounted for about half of that

---

112   Sunesson, *Politik och organisation*, Chapter 5.
113   Donald Sassoon, *One Hundred Years of Socialism: The West European Left in the Twentieth Century* (London: I.B. Tauris, 1996), p. 61.
114   Ekman, Åmark, and Toler, *Sweden's Relations with Nazism*; Åmark, *Att bo granne med onskan*.

consumed by Germany. A third topic concerns Sweden's initial reluctance to accept Jewish refugees. The final issue is that of restrictions on democratic rights – perhaps above all freedom of the press – that were imposed in order not to displease Germany, and which were also sometimes justified in domestic political terms.

At the outbreak of war in September 1939, the Swedish line was to avoid doing anything that might draw Sweden in. Above all, it was important not to provoke Germany's indignation. Although Sweden had begun to re-arm in 1936, it was clear that it would have little chance of resisting a German attack.

The Russian war on Finland at the end of November of the same year did not pose an immediate threat to Sweden, but it had a major impact on the domestic political situation. Firstly, Per Albin Hansson took the initiative of forming a national coalition government with the three bourgeois parties – the Conservatives, the Liberals, and the Farmers' Union. The communists were, of course, left out.[115] Social Democracy dominated the government. Hansson was still prime minister, Wigforss minister of finance, Möller minister of social affairs, and Per Edvin Sköld minister of defence. But the post of foreign minister was given to a conservative diplomat, and the post of minister of justice to Karl Gustaf Westman of the Farmers' Union – who quickly showed an interest in curtailing important democratic rights.

Sympathy for Finland was very strong in Sweden. Large parts of the military and the political right believed that Sweden should support Finland actively. The government declared Sweden a 'non-combatant', which allowed for the sending of munitions and for Swedish officers and volunteers to participate in the war. Extensive humanitarian aid was also provided, including joint fundraising by the LO and the SAF.[116]

In the spring of 1940, the threat of war suddenly became acute. In April, Denmark was occupied, and, after a few months of fighting, Norway too. Many feared that Sweden was next in line. But Hitler did not want to risk jeopardising the vital transport of ore through an extensive war. Germany skilfully exploited the Swedish unrest to push through extensive concessions from Sweden that seriously damaged the policy of neutrality. Germany demanded to be allowed to send troop

---

115   Åmark, *Att bo granne med onskan*, pp. 82–6.
116   Alf W. Johansson and Torbjörn Norman, 'Sweden's Security and World Peace', in Misgeld, Molin, and Åmark, *Creating Social Democracy*, p. 353.

transports to Norway on Swedish railways. Formally, the transport was called 'Permittenttrafik', meaning that it would involve German soldiers going home on leave. In reality, it also involved combat soldiers and extensive transport of war materials. Growing German pressure caused the traffic to swell rapidly. By November 1941, 680,000 German soldiers had travelled – more than 1,000 a day – on Swedish railways, as well as between 1,000 and 1,500 freight wagons, half of them carrying war materials.[117]

The most controversial concession was made in the context of the German attack on the Soviet Union in 1941. Germany insisted on the transport of an entire division of 18,000 combat-ready soldiers from Norway to Finland, which had joined Germany, and on to the Russian front. This time, there was more resistance in the Social Democratic parliamentary group, but Per Albin Hansson managed to get the demand accepted.[118]

More important than troop transport for Germany's success in the war was the possibility of continued supplies of iron ore and ball-bearings from Sweden.[119] A first trade agreement, in the autumn of 1939, set the course. Sweden was to continue exports at the same level as before, while at the same time being guaranteed imports of coal and coke at comparatively low prices. A year later, Germany tightened its stance: ore imports would be allowed to increase while Sweden would have to pay more for the coal. As the fortunes of the war turned, the Western powers increased their demands on Sweden to reduce exports. But it was not until the end of 1944 that a more significant cut was made.

The Swedish policy of adaptation also targeted anti-Nazi groups and currents. The Swedish government devoted considerable effort to monitoring and intervening against a critical press.[120] The government also actively tried to influence what the press wrote, and newspapers were asked not to publish negative information about the warring states, primarily Germany.

The most drastic intervention against free speech was the government's transport ban, under which disreputable newspapers could not

117   Åmark, *Att bo granne med onskan*, pp. 103–8.
118   Ibid., pp. 122–43.
119   Klaus Wittmann, *Schwedens Wirtschaftsbeziehungen zum Dritten Reich 1933–1945* (Munich: Oldenbourg, 1978).
120   Åmark, *Att bo granne med onskan*, Chapter 5.

be sent by public transport such as mail, rail, and buses. Communist newspapers in particular were affected. Attacks increased sharply during the Finnish Winter War, in which the Communist Party supported the Soviet Union. Party members were purged from positions of trust in unions within the LO.

The scope for more active popular mobilisations sharply diminished, and pressure to endorse the Swedish policy of neutrality increased. The strikes came to an end, and the 1 May marches were transformed into unity demonstrations in which Swedish flags now shared space with the Reds.

The newly established State Information Board brought together social movements and political parties in campaigns to 'maintain a good social spirit and counter un-Swedish propaganda'. One element of this project was a study circle titled 'The Swedish Way of Life', which aimed to strengthen the sense of Swedishness and democratic traditions. Unsurprisingly, these traditions were presented as free of conflict. In describing the general strike of 1909, this initiative heaped praised on both the self-discipline of the workers and the 'firmness and wisdom' of the right-wing government. The Second World War served to strengthen nationalist currents within Social Democracy.[121]

---

121 Samuel Edquist, *En folklig historia: historieskrivningen i studieförbund och hembygdsrörelse* (Umeå: Boréa, 2009), pp. 113ff.

5

Harvest Time?

A new world emerged from the ruins of the Second World War. Authoritarian and fascist ideals were discredited, while communism received a temporary boost. The Soviet Union had borne the brunt of the war against Hitler's Germany, and communists had played a prominent role in partisan movements across Europe. Widespread social unrest also erupted in many places, triggering civil wars in countries such as Italy and Greece. At Yalta, the victorious powers divided Europe into spheres of interest. The countries liberated from Nazism by the Soviet army were incorporated into a Soviet-dominated Eastern Bloc.

Demands for social reform grew strongly after the hardships endured during the Second World War. As a result, the Left, Communists, and Social Democrats won major victories in many elections. The Beveridge Plan and the 'Spirit of '45' raised hopes for welfare for all.[1] In Sweden, the national consensus of the years during the war was broken by the great metalworkers' strike of 1945. Living standards had been depressed during the war, partly by the government's wage freeze, and now demands were being made for proper wage increases. The ban on Communists holding positions of trust in the LO, introduced after 1939, was lifted, and the Communists' influence greatly increased – especially in the Metalworkers' Union, which was the largest and most influential union in the LO. A strike broke out in the spring of 1945 and lasted for five months. In four membership referenda, wage proposals were rejected, and the executive board had to adopt a proposal against the will of the membership in order to end the strike. The Communists also made strong electoral wins, more than doubling their vote to over 10 per cent in 1944. These gains were at the expense of the Social Democrats, who lost the Second Chamber majority they had enjoyed since 1940.[2]

---

1 Tony Judt, *Postwar: A History of Europe since 1945* (New York: Penguin, 2005), Chapter 3.

2 Yvonne Hirdman, Jenny Björkman, and Urban Lundberg, *Sveriges historia. 1920–1965* (Stockholm: Norstedt, 2012), pp. 413ff.

This did not mean the Social Democrats were a broken party. On the contrary, they began planning for peace with great confidence as soon as the end of the war was in sight. It was harvest time.

The Postwar Programme

In the summer of 1943, a Postwar Council of the Labour Movement was formed, which included representatives of the Social Democratic Party, the LO, and the various branches of the movement. In light of the experience of the 1930s, the fundamental question was how to achieve full employment. It was considered out of the question that business could eliminate unemployment without government intervention. The result of work done by the Council was presented in the proposal for the labour movement's 'Postwar Programme', one of the most celebrated works of Social Democracy. The 200-page document sold 130,000 copies, and was widely read in study circles throughout the movement.[3]

'The world in which our people will live after peace is restored must be very much a new world', the programme began. 'The economic system of the past will not be able to solve the problems of the future. It gave rise to recurring crises of unemployment and reduced production.' The experience of the war showed the potential of production placed under the direction of society: 'We need not resign ourselves to unemployment and we can do away with want if the productive power that the war shows we possess is used equally fully for peace.'[4] One of the main tasks would therefore be to coordinate economic activity within a planned economy, so that labour and material resources were used for efficient production under the direction of society.

The concrete programme of the Social Democrats for the postwar period was thus elaborated in the twenty-seven paragraphs included in this document. They were grouped under three main headings: full

---

3   Villy Bergström, 'Party Program and Economic Policy', in Klaus Misgeld, Karl Molin, and Klas Åmark, eds, *Creating Social Democracy: A Century of the Social Democratic Labor Party in Sweden* (University Park: Pennsylvania State University Press, 1992), pp. 144–56; Jonas Pontusson, *The Limits of Social Democracy: Investment Politics in Sweden* (Ithaca, NY: Cornell University Press, 1992), pp. 47–56; Leif Lewin, *Planhushållningsdebatten* (Stockholm: Almqvist & Wiksell, 1967), pp. 213ff.

4   Ernst Wigforss, ed., *Arbetarrörelsens efterkrigsprogram: de 27 punkterna med motivering* (Stockholm: Victor Pettersons bokindustriaktiebolag, 1944), pp. 3ff.

employment, fair distribution and higher living standards, and greater efficiency and democracy in industry. The programme was written in a context of fear that the war, like the First World War, would be followed by a postwar depression. Its central idea was a Keynesian-influenced policy and an effective labour market policy to maintain the strength of purchasing power. But the state would also support the export industry and pursue low interest rates.

The second section outlined the main features of the welfare policies that were largely implemented over the coming decades: unemployment and health insurance, increased pensions, shorter working hours, support for families with children, democratisation of education, and the levelling out of economic differences between the classes, with a central role for a 'solidarity-based wage policy'.

But it was the third part of the programme that attracted the most attention. This section further developed the Social Democrats' basic commitment to the necessity of increasing industrial production, and their ambition to contribute actively to such a development. Full employment and fair distribution were not enough: those parts of the economy that increased society's productive assets were to be strengthened. At the same time, citizens were increasingly demanding a greater say in the activities in the workplaces on which they depended. These objectives were not incompatible. Empowering workers would help make production more efficient – but within the framework of capitalism: 'Citizens' collective control over economic production should not be a constraint on private enterprise.'[5]

At the same time, the state was to take greater responsibility for business investment, stimulate exports, and support technological and economic research. The planned economy was the organising idea to which Social Democratic aspirations were henceforth subordinated. These were no longer socialist aspirations in the classical sense; instead, they gave full expression to Nils Karleby's principle that the most efficient forms of production in each context should be actively supported. The very idea of the planned economy already entailed the assumption that it should be tested under the changing economic conditions; thus, 'any schematic demand for a certain division of individual and common ownership . . . is excluded from the beginning'.[6] It was essentially only

---

5   Ibid., p. 21.
6   Ibid., p. 197.

in industries where companies were clearly failing that a transfer to state ownership would be considered at all.

Efforts to stimulate business efficiency were thus combined with demands for greater worker influence over production. But these demands were narrowly instrumental: workers would be given the opportunity to influence the technical and economic conditions in the workplace so as to increase their well-being and security, and so that companies were better able to pay higher wages. The debate on broader forms of industrial democracy, including workers' councils, had receded into the mist.

As the end of the war approached, the coalition government faced dissolution. The Social Democratic Party's losses in the 1944 parliamentary elections strengthened the Social Democrats' resolve to govern on their own. Collaboration made it more difficult to pursue a more offensive reform policy. To the surprise of many, Per Albin Hansson hesitated. He had long sought to transform the Social Democrats into a People's Party, and perhaps the ideas of the Folkhem could have been more easily realised in a coalition government. It is well known that Hansson thrived in the role he had been given during the war as father of the country. He may also have been concerned that the increasing radicalisation of the working class would lead to demands for over-reaching reforms, and a coalition government might act as an effective brake on this.[7]

In this he had little support, however. In the summer of 1945, the government was transformed into a Social Democratic one, still with Hansson as prime minister, Wigforss as minister of finance, and Gustav Möller as minister of social affairs. A dynamic addition to the government was Gunnar Myrdal, as minister of trade – and it was Myrdal who was given direct responsibility for putting the Postwar Programme into action.

The government set up the Commission for Postwar Economic Planning, which soon came to be known as the Myrdal Commission, after its chairman. Its task was to collect the ideas already expressed in various parliamentary initiatives, based on which it would draw up concrete action plans.[8] With such a vague mandate, the Commission could choose which issues it would address.

---

7   Alf W. Johansson, *Per Albin och kriget: samlingsregeringen och utrikespolitiken under andra världskriget* (Stockholm: Tiden, 1985), pp. 379–81.

8   Stig Hadenius, *Swedish Politics during the 20th Century: Conflict and Consensus* (Stockholm: Svenska Institutet, 1997), pp. 72ff; Hirdman, Björkman, and Lundberg, *Sveriges historia*, pp. 410ff.

Myrdal was among those most convinced that a postwar depression was inevitable and – not surprisingly, given his background as a leading member of the Stockholm School – he was a keen advocate of expansionary economic policies to counter the potential crisis. But it was now not just a matter of keeping consumption up through unemployment policy, as Myrdal placed greater emphasis on stimulating business investment. A couple of new priorities that pointed forward to the economic policies of the 1950s were also given greater prominence: a flexible labour market, and limiting wage rises so as not to drive up inflation.[9]

The effort to improve the efficiency of business soon became Myrdal's main interest. His ambition was to take a broad approach. As in the 1930s, the Social Democrats' favoured response was always to set up a commission. In all, some forty sectoral commissions were set up after the war, investigating everything from the shoe industry to insurance companies. But their results were generally modest, and their proposals were mainly of a generic or technical nature – increased specialisation, better staff training, changes in customs duties or quality declarations for goods – and far from all of them were implemented. Industrial rationalisation was a failure, writes political scientist Leif Lewin, the scholar who has most thoroughly and enthusiastically examined the Social Democrats' ambitions for a planned economy.[10]

Two reasons have been proposed for the lack of results delivered by the Postwar Programme, or by the Myrdal Commission's attempts to implement a more coherent and state-led planned economy. The first is the inaccuracy of economic forecasts. A postwar depression never materialised. Instead, the capitalist economy entered its longest sustained period of expansion, for thirty golden years. This strong growth required fundamentally different interventions than the crisis policies of the 1930s, and the programme for this had yet to be developed. The second reason was the strong opposition that even the rather modest proposals advanced by the Social Democrats aroused within the bourgeoisie.[11]

An active economic policy to counteract the consequences of a recession was something that the bourgeoisie could gradually come to

9 Örjan Appelqvist, *Bruten brygga: Gunnar Myrdal och Sveriges ekonomiska efterkrigspolitik 1943–1947* (Stockholm: Santérus, 2000).
10 Lewin, *Planhushållningsdebatten*, p. 326.
11 Ibid.

accept – especially after Bertil Olin, one of the driving forces of the Stockholm School, was elected chairperson of the leading bourgeois party, the Liberals. But the prospect that a Social Democratic–led government would interfere in the operations of private enterprise was unthinkable – even if the basic aim was said to be to support business efficiency.

Resistance increased as the upsurge of radicalism at the end of the war was transformed into Cold War, demobilisation, and anti-communist reaction. Industry was able to meet its own needs and had no use for outside advice, it was said. There was a stiff refusal of any involvement of workers' representatives. They could not 'be presumed to possess sufficient qualifications for the task'.[12] Implementation of the postwar planned economic programme would instead lead to 'the strangulation of individuality under centralist domination'. The influence here of Friedrich Hayek's *The Road to Serfdom*, published in Swedish in 1944, was clear.

The mobilisation of the business community against the intended move towards a planned economy is among the classic political struggles in contemporary Swedish history. A large battle fund was built up, which was invested in bourgeois newspapers and propaganda activities. Conflict on this question came to a head in the 1948 elections. With the support of the Communists, the Social Democrats managed to retain their Second Chamber majority by a single seat. But there was no longer any scope for enacting more extensive state influence over business. Gradually, such ambitions disappeared from the Social Democratic agenda.[13]

A New Party Programme

In 1944 the Social Democrats also adopted a new party programme.[14] It was a final confirmation of the profound changes the party had undergone over the previous twenty years.[15] In the 1920 programme, there

12   Lars Ekdahl, *Mot en tredje väg: en biografi över Rudolf Meidner*, vol. 1, *Tysk flykting och svensk modell* (Lund: Arkiv, 2001), p. 212.

13   Pontusson, *Limits of Social Democracy*, pp. 50–3.

14   Klaus Misgeld, ed., *Socialdemokratins program: 1897 till 1990* (Stockholm: Arbetarrörelsens, 2001).

15   Villy Bergström, 'Party Program and Economic Policy', pp. 144–9.

had still been clear echoes of the party's Marxist roots – there was talk of class struggle and exploitation. And among all the demands of the day there were paragraphs about extensive socialisation and social control over the economy. In the new programme, essentially written by Wigforss, all such wording was gone. The opening paragraph stated: 'The aim of the Social Democrats is to transform the economic organisation of bourgeois society in such a way as to place the right to control production in the hands of the whole people.'[16]

The means of achieving this power was no longer socialisation, but the planned economy: a planned economy of the people 'which makes it possible to make full and efficient use of the productive resources of society', and at the same time to provide the whole population with secure employment and a standard of living corresponding to 'the returns of common labour'.[17] The forms of ownership were, in accordance with the ideas of Karleby and Wigforss from the interwar period, of secondary importance: 'Whether economic activity is based on individual property rights or on various forms of collective property rights, it must be coordinated into a planned economy if labour and material resources are not to be wasted through unemployment or inefficient production. Such coordination can only be achieved under the direction of society.'[18] Socialisation was only relevant to the extent that 'it is necessary for the implementation of such a planned economy'. But socialisations had, in reality, long since been removed from the party's programme and practice.

And soon the demands for a planned economy, in the sense of the Postwar Programme, also subsided. After the 1948 elections, the government instead sought new forms of closer cooperation with the business community, which would soon lay the foundations for the corporate Swedish model. But it was not only the state's ambition to take the lead in making business more efficient that was abandoned. Employers defended their monopoly of power in the workplace. The agreement to set up 'joint work councils' (*företagsnämnder*) reached between the LO and the SAF in 1946 gave no real influence to employees.[19]

---

16 Misgeld, *Socialdemokratins program*, p. 40.
17 Ibid., p. 44.
18 Ibid.
19 Pontusson, *Limits of Social Democracy*, pp. 52ff; J. Magnus Ryner, *Capitalist Restructuring, Globalisation and the Third Way: Lessons from the Swedish Model* (London: Routledge, 2002), pp. 80f.

The wave of radicalisation that swept the world at the end of the war – and which was a key reason for the Social Democrats' raised voices in the Postwar Programme – had in most places ebbed away by the turn of the decade, to be replaced by the rise of the Cold War. This further reduced the pressure on the Social Democrats to realise the more far-reaching ambitions of the Postwar Programme.

The 1950s

From the ruins after the Second World War emerged a whole new society. The decades following the end of the Second World War were a period of unprecedented economic growth. Terms such as 'the Golden Years' or *les trente glorieuses* show that this was an international phenomenon. Economic historians have given the prevailing economic ideology of this period a name: Fordism. They point to the fundamental change in working and production conditions: assembly lines and standardised products, a hierarchical organisation of work. In the postwar period, the term took on a broader meaning. A prerequisite for Fordist mass production was that it could find its outlet – mass consumption. But Fordism also stands for a form of society built around a historical compromise between workers and capital, trade unions and employers, and the expansion of state institutions to guarantee people's welfare.[20]

Fordism presupposed a new type of economic policy – and, even within the economy, values changed after the war. The dominant doctrine of the interwar period had been a pronounced market liberalism. It had resulted in economic crises and mass unemployment, and created a political climate conducive to the emergence of political extremes. In planning for peace, Western economic and political leaders had learned from their mistakes. A much more structured and organised capitalism was needed, and Bretton Woods formulated the economic rules of the game for the coming decades. The dollar became the hard currency of the international economy.[21]

---

20 Lennart Schön, *An Economic History of Modern Sweden* (London: Routledge, 2012), pp. 231ff.

21 Ibid., pp. 200, 366ff. On Fordism, see also Werner Schmidt, *Antikommunism och kommunism under det korta 1900-talet* (Lund: Nordic Academic Press, 2007), pp. 219–21.

With increased support from the United States, the capitalist econo
mies were reconstructed. The Marshall Plan, introduced in 1947, played
an important role. Seventeen European countries, including Sweden,
received $12 billion, mainly in the form of grants, to stimulate economic
growth. The motives were hardly altruistic. A strong European market
was of great importance to the US economy, and Europe used a significant proportion of the grants to buy American goods.[22]

But the purpose of the Marshall Plan was also overtly political. Aid
was originally part of the Cold War that was developing at the time.
Making Europe economically strong would tie the western part of the
continent to American interests and create a strong barrier against
the Soviet Union. From now on, European development would take
place in the shadow of the Cold War. This would also have major repercussions for the Swedish labour movement.

The view of the state changed. Keynes's previously controversial theories
that the state should actively step in to stimulate the economy during
recessions became commonplace, even though it was the problem of
economic overheating rather than recessions that preoccupied economists and politicians in the postwar period. It came to be widely accepted
that the state should take on an increased role in creating the infrastructure required by the modern industrial and welfare society: roads
for transport and private motoring, housing for the workers needed by
industry, health and social care – and, not least, schools and higher
education to meet the need for an increasingly skilled workforce.

All this required a rapidly expanding public sector, financed by
increased taxes. This was very much an international trend. Certainly,
the size, focus, organisation, and ambition of the public sector differed
from country to country. But the emergence of the well-organised welfare
state of the postwar era is not something that can be associated exclusively with Swedish Social Democracy; German Christian Democrats,
British Conservatives, Japanese Liberal Democrats – and sometimes
even American Democrats, too – accepted increased government intervention in economic policy.

It can also be argued that Fordism contributed to the relative political
and ideological consensus that characterised postwar welfare states. The
Cold War worldview, which dominated the scene from the late 1940s
onwards, implied in public discourse a strong endorsement of Western

22 Judt, *Postwar*, pp. 90–9.

democracy and the market economy, and a corresponding rejection of communism and other forms of strong radicalism. Liberal *Dagens Nyheter*'s leading editor, Herbert Tingsten, argued that words like conservatism, liberalism, and socialism 'as systems of ideas about what will happen and what should be done' were no longer valid. Instead, there was far-reaching agreement on fundamental political issues across party lines.[23]

The death of ideologies was a phenomenon proclaimed not only in Sweden, but by leading social scientists and intellectuals throughout the Western world. Daniel Bell's *The End of Ideology* and Raymond Aron's *The Opium of the Intellectuals* expressed the same ideas. At the same time, for those who refused to take a stand in the conflict between East and West, excommunication from public discourse awaited. The group of writers in Sweden who advocated a third position came under fierce attack, including from leading Social Democrats.[24]

The Social Democrats thus managed to retain government power by a hair's breadth in the 1948 elections. But the bourgeois mobilisation against planned economy had not passed the party by unnoticed. The proud plans of 1944 were gone. Under the leadership of the new minister of finance, Per Edvin Sköld, the government took a series of measures to restore confidence in the business community. Of great symbolic importance was the so-called Thursday Club, where representatives of government and business met regularly to discuss economic issues.[25]

At this time, there was a change of attitude within the bourgeoisie. With a generational shift, many of those raised under the harsh market liberalism of the interwar period disappeared. A new generation had a much more pragmatic attitude towards state intervention and cooperation with the state. Inspiration for this approach often came from American management and social science.[26] This generational shift was also taking place within Social Democracy itself. Per Albin Hansson died in the autumn of 1946, and Ernst Wigforss and Gustav Möller left the government a few years later. Thus disappeared the last representatives of the generation that had received its basic ideological, Marxist-influenced schooling during the party's most radical period,

23   Alf W. Johansson, *Herbert Tingsten och det kalla kriget: antikommunism och liberalism i Dagens Nyheter 1946–1952* (Stockholm: Tiden, 1995), p. 14.

24   Ibid., pp. 277–86.

25   Pontusson, *Limits of Social Democracy*, p. 52.

26   For this development, see Lewin, *Planhushållningsdebatten*, Chapter 4.

the years around 1910. Per Albin's unexpected successor, Tage Erlander, had received his early political apprenticeship in politically radical Lund, but spent the last decade on social and education policy in the chancellery in Stockholm. And Wigforss's successor, Sköld, was among the party's most pro-business representatives.[27]

On one level, the Social Democratic government fared well as the 1950s began. Swedish industry emerged unscathed from the war, and got off to a flying start. Economic growth reached 5–6 per cent, and unemployment dropped like a stone. The problems were the opposite of what had been expected: economic overheating, inflation, excessive profits, wage increases, and labour shortages in the fast-growing parts of industry. But what did a Social Democratic strategy that might solve these problems look like? There was no ready-made programme.

In the early 1950s, instead of the socialist harvest promised by the Postwar Programme, the Social Democrats found themselves deeply involved in the day-to-day work of making the capitalist economy function as smoothly as possible. Or, in the words of Eric Hobsbawm: 'As for the socialist parties and workers' movements which had been so prominent in Europe, they adapted easily to the new, reformed capitalism, for in practice they had no economic policy of their own.'[28] This was certainly true of Swedish Social Democracy.

The 1952 elections were an unexpectedly big setback for the Social Democrats. In his diary, Tage Erlander describes the period with great gloom. Erlander's diaries have attracted attention not least for the unexpected streak of misanthropy that runs through them. To some extent, this is probably because Erlander used the diary as a safety valve, where he could give vent to feelings that a prime minister found difficult to express to his colleagues. The election campaign was boring. The party's programme was weak; there was no ideological discussion within Social Democracy. 'And, of course, people ask whether we have become too old in power, so that we no longer have anything to give.'[29]

---

27 Hirdman, Björkman, and Lundberg, *Sveriges historia*, pp. 442ff.
28 E. J. Hobsbawm, *The Age of Extremes: The Short Twentieth Century, 1914–1991* (London: Joseph, 1994), pp. 310–11.
29 Tage Erlander, *Dagböcker 1952* (Hedemora: Gidlund, 2002), pp. 150, 181.

The Rehn–Meidner Model

It was not, then, within the Social Democratic Party that new thinking was to be found. Instead, it was within the LO. The great innovation came with new theories for dealing with economies undergoing strong growth and maintaining high employment, with the associated risk of over-heating, developed by LO economists Gösta Rehn and Rudolf Meidner. Unemployment was no longer a major issue, but inflation was.[30]

Their starting point was clearly business-friendly: a well-functioning business sector was a prerequisite for full employment and equality. The main problem was how to persuade wage-earners to hold back on wage demands. It was, of course, a sensitive matter for LO economists to argue that wage rises should be kept under tight control, especially when exports were making huge profits while at the same time crying out for labour. The solution was the so-called 'solidaristic wage policy'. The scope for wage increases would not be based on what each sector could offer its employees. Instead, it was to be determined on the basis of developments in the profitable and more productive export industry, and then distributed in solidarity across the entire labour market.[31]

In practice, this meant that the LO refrained from demanding maximum wage increases from the profitable export industry. At the same time, wages in low-paying industries rose more than many compa-nies could bear. As well as aiming to keep inflation down and reduce wage differentials among workers, this policy therefore had major con-sequences for the reconstruction of industry. By providing the most expansive and export-dependent industries with more favourable wage agreements than would otherwise have been possible, the 'solidaristic wage policy' made it easier for these companies to assert their position on the world market.

At the same time, companies with lower profitability were eliminated. It might seem an undesirable effect of a union-originated wage policy that workers lost their jobs in this way. However, in a labour market with significant growth, it was possible to offer them new jobs if they

---

30   For the following pages, see Ekdahl, *Mot en tredje väg*; Åmark, 'Social Democ-racy and the Trade Union Movement: Solidarity and the Politics of Self-Interest', in Misgeld, Molin, and Åmark, *Creating Social Democracy*; Pontusson, *Limits of Social Democracy*, pp. 60–4; Ryner, *Capitalist Restructuring*, pp. 82–6.

31   Pontusson, *Limits of Social Democracy*, pp. 62ff.

were prepared to move to the expanding industrial towns in southern
Sweden. A tangible effect of this wage policy was thus significant relocation of the population. The redundant workforce was to be induced,
with the help of a greatly strengthened labour market policy, to seek
out the industries and places where jobs were available. Both the stick
and the carrot were used to this end. The Labour Market Board became
the engine of this project, and thus the most important of all government agencies. It had a broad repertoire of measures at its disposal. It
developed a comprehensive retraining programme under which the
unemployed were trained as welders or lathe operators, or whatever
the modern engineering industry needed. Those who moved to other
cities received generous relocation allowances. Large areas of modern
housing sprang up around the expanding industrial towns. But none
of this prevented the relocation policy from being widely opposed.[32]
Folk humour in Norrland, the part of Sweden hardest hit by mass
migration, jokingly changed the abbreviation of Board in Swedish –
AMS – to *Alla Måste Söderut* (All must go southwards!). Labour market
policy had thus come a long way since the concerns of the 1930s to
alleviate the social consequences of acute unemployment. Instead, it
became an active component of the rationalisation of Swedish
industry.

Another part of the model concerned tax policy. The trade union
movement accepted a relatively high tax burden as a way of fighting
inflation – particularly, of course, the taxation of growing corporate
profits. At the same time, high tax revenues provided opportunities for
the state to enact social reform of various kinds. But the Rehn–Meidner
model was mainly about wage and labour market policy, and did not
include other measures that intruded into the economic system or
demanded industrial control. There were no demands for workers'
influence over their working conditions, either from the LO or from the
Social Democratic Party.

---

32 Lewin, *Planhushållningsdebatten*, pp. 412–15; Pontusson, *Limits of Social
Democracy*, pp. 64–8.

The Swedish Model

The Rehn–Meidner model became an important part of the corporate system that is a cornerstone of what has come to be known as 'the Swedish model'. It is often summed up in three concepts: first, institutionalised cooperation between labour market partners – 'the spirit of Saltsjöbaden'; second, a corporate political system, often referred to as a 'Harpsund democracy', in which formal and informal cooperation between the state and other interested organisations plays an important role; and third, a relatively large and tax-financed welfare state, often referred to as 'Folkhemmet'.[33]

The labour market conditions drew the most attention. What came, from the 1930s onwards, to be known as 'the spirit of Saltsjöbaden' enjoyed international triumph in the 1950s. A key priority of the 1938 agreement between the LO and the employers' organisation SAF was to avoid strikes at all costs; to that end, the LO's new statutes had made it more difficult for affiliated unions and local branches to enter into conflict on their own. For the LO leadership, the 1945 metalworkers' strike was an unfortunate exception, provoked by the communists. Great efforts were made to reduce the communist influence in the unions, which was facilitated by the heightened tensions of the Cold War.

Social scientists and politicians from all over the world came to study the country from which strikes were said to have disappeared. LO and SAF leaders went arm in arm on celebrated tours of the United States to teach the Swedish experience and emphasise the country's climate of cooperation between labour and capital. In 1967, Sweden had 0.2 strikes per 100,000 workers, compared with 6.2 in the United States and 14 in Italy.[34]

This policy would hardly have been possible without the extraordinarily centralised contractual system that characterised the Swedish labour market at that time. In practice, wage agreements that became binding on the majority of Swedish wage-earners were concluded by a small group of gentlemen from the LO and the SAF, who met for a few

---

33   Kjell Östberg and Jenny Andersson, *Sveriges historia. 1965–2012* (Stockholm: Norstedt, 2013), pp. 29–31.

34   Christer Thörnqvist, *Arbetarna lämnar fabriken: strejkrörelser i Sverige under efterkrigstiden, deras bakgrund, förlopp och följder* (Gothenburg: HIstoriska Institutionen, 1994), p. 49.

nights in the smoke-filled premises of the Employers' Association. It is hardly surprising that the employers, represented mainly by delegates from the large Swedish companies, also favoured a wage policy that so greatly benefited the Swedish export industry.

The LO now became a key social player beyond the trade union field.[35] As early as 1941, in its report 'The Trade Union Movement and Business', the LO had signalled its ambitions to influence government policy, noting: 'it cannot be said of the Swedish state that it is an instrument of capitalist oppression. Nor can it be claimed that it is a tool in the hands of a few.'[36] This gave the LO an opportunity to gain influence over the development of society of a kind that it had not enjoyed before.

This corporatist approach is also prominent in another expression of the Swedish model, the 'Harpsund democracy'. The phenomenon takes its name from a series of conferences initiated by Tage Erlander in the mid 1950s. The prime minister regularly invited representatives of big business, the trade union movement, the cooperative sector, and other important interest groups to his summer residence, Harpsund, to deliberate and exchange information on key social issues. The meetings were much appreciated by all parties, and symbolised the close cooperation between government, business, and other parties that was also evident elsewhere.[37]

One example of this is that major interest groups were often represented on the boards of government agencies. In this way, they also had an influence on the formulation of government policy – and even more on how it was implemented in practice. Naturally, both the LO and the employers in the SAF were represented on the Labour Market Board. They could thus directly influence the formulation of policy in this area.[38] Another route to political influence was participation in government inquiries. These inquiries played an extraordinarily important role in shaping the policy reforms of the twentieth century. The fact that, for example, farmers' representatives were included in all the important agricultural inquiries naturally gave these organisations great

35 Lars Ekdahl, 'Fackföreningen – en socialistisk resurs. Makten över arbetarrörelsen och samhällsutvecklingen', in Håkan Blomqvist, ed., *Arbetarrörelsen inför socialismen: Socialdemokratin inför verkligheten* (Stockholm: Carlsson – forthcoming, 2024).

36 *Fackföreningsrörelsen och näringslivet* (Stockholm: LO, 1941), p. 147.

37 Hirdman, Björkman, and Lundberg, *Sveriges historia*, p. 465.

38 Ryner, *Capitalist Restructuring*, p. 94; Bo Rothstein, *The Social Democratic State: The Swedish Model and the Bureaucratic Problem of Social Reforms* (Pittsburgh, PA: University of Pittsburgh Press, 1996).

opportunities to influence the shaping of policy and legislation on the issues that were close to their hearts.

Corporate representation was extensive. Political scientist Bo Rothstein estimates that the LO had at its peak more than 1,100 representatives in 663 government agencies, investigations, delegations, and committees. If the local and regional levels are added, this number rises to around 4,000.[39]

Welfare – but How?

The Rehn–Meidner model, while boosting economic growth and strengthening public finances, also provided the conditions for the third leg of the Swedish model: the strong welfare state.[40]

The promises of social reform made by the Social Democratic government in the 1930s, not least those formulated by the Population Commission, could only be implemented in a limited way before the Second World War put all reform plans on hold. In 1946, the minister of social affairs, Gustav Möller, outlined the four reforms he wanted to prioritise: pensions, health insurance, housing policy, and child allowances. The following year, a decision was taken to introduce universal child allowances for all children. Other reforms had to wait until the following decade.[41]

Until now, Sweden had not been a pioneer in the area of social security. Health insurance was administered by voluntary insurance funds with state subsidies, and did not cover all citizens. The universal pension was a patchwork of reform implemented in 1913, albeit supplemented by a low extra allowance in 1946, so that many elderly people would not have to ask for poor relief to meet their living expenses. Housing standards, especially in the big cities, were among the lowest in northern Europe. And the unemployment insurance scheme implemented in the 1930s was linked to trade union membership, and initially provided low benefits. It was only in the 1950s that the Swedish welfare system, through universal health insurance and the new supplementary pension system (*allmän tilläggspension* – ATP), began to take on the contours of

---

39   Rothstein, *Social Democratic State*.
40   Ryner, *Capitalist Restructuring*, pp. 85ff.
41   Gøsta Esping-Andersen, 'The Making of a Social Democratic Welfare State', in Misgeld, Molin, and Åmark, *Creating Social Democracy*, pp. 45ff.

the solidarity-based welfare state that later became the distinctive hall mark of Swedish Social Democracy.[42]

But the road was not smooth – and, above all, was not determined by a Social Democratic master plan. When Möller presented his proposal for universal state health insurance, it was inspired by Beveridge's ideas for the UK. Möller proposed a relatively low general level that would provide basic security for all, which could then be augmented through voluntary supplementary insurance. The state would guarantee every-one a certain minimum standard in case of illness 'but leave it to the individuals themselves to arrange for what is required in addition', Möller wrote.[43] He also wanted universal unemployment insurance, also at a low basic level.[44] In one respect, however, Möller's model differed from Beveridge's: the state was to take sole financial responsibility for basic security.

But Möller's proposal was never implemented. His successor as minister of social affairs, Gunnar Sträng, came from the trade union movement, which instead advocated income security in the event of illness and unemployment. In practice, this meant differentiated benefits based on income. In 1953, a state health insurance fund was also introduced along these lines.[45]

Unemployment insurance benefits were also reformed on the same basis. The maximum levels were raised to make it attractive also for white-collar workers to join an unemployment fund, and thus to join a trade union. As far as unemployment insurance was concerned, the LO made sure that it would not be state-run, but would continue to be administered by the trade unions, albeit with generous state subsidies. The link between trade union membership and membership of the unemployment fund has been an important reason for the high

---

42   Sven E. O. Hort, *Social Policy, Welfare State, and Civil Society in Sweden*, vol. 1, *History, Policies, and Institutions 1884–1988* (Lund: Arkiv, 2014); Klas Åmark, *Hundra år av välfärdspolitik: välfärdsstatens framväxt i Norge och Sverige* (Umeå: Boréa, 2005).

43   Göran Therborn, 'Arbetarrörelsen i välfärdsstaten', in *Klass, allianser och välfärdsstat: analys och teori i arbete 1967–2021* (Lund: Arkiv, 2021), p. 236; Göran Ther-born, 'Nordiska konferensen för forskning i arbetarrörelsens historia', in *Det nordiska i den nordiska arbetarrörelsen: femte nordiska konferensen för forskning i arbetarrörelsens historia Tammerfors, den 23–27 augusti 1983: Papers Presented at the Fifth Nordic Confer-ence for Labour History* (Helsingfors: Finnish Society for Labour History and Cultural Traditions, 1986).

44   Åmark, *Hundra år av välfärdspolitik*, Chapter 4.

45   Ibid.

membership rate of the Swedish trade union movement. To this day, Sweden lacks universal state unemployment insurance – an anomaly in an otherwise uniform and universal welfare system.

The next task was to resolve the pension issue. The low level of the general national pension meant a sharp drop in the standard of living for most people, especially the working class. White-collar workers often had pension benefits in their wage contracts and greater opportunities to save for their own retirement. The demand for a state-guaranteed supplementary pension, income-based and linked to employment, was increasingly driven by the LO from the late 1940s. An important priority, apart from financial security, was fairness between blue-collar and white-collar workers.[46]

The Social Democratic government was under severe pressure, but hesitated about which path to take, not least because reform would be very costly. Should it build on national pensions, and increase them? Would it introduce a system of state-subsidised supplementary pensions? Would they be compulsory or voluntary? And would the level be income-related? Several studies were commissioned and in 1955 the party decided to go for a compulsory supplementary pension. The decision was strongly criticised by the bourgeois parties, which saw the proposal as part of an increased state influence over people's finances. The issue became central to the 1956 election campaign, which led to another Social Democratic setback.[47]

The pension question had now become the dominant issue in Swedish domestic politics. After a further investigation, three proposals emerged. The Social Democrats maintained their allegiance to a compulsory, income-based supplementary pension for all wage-earners. One innovation was that pension payments would be pooled in state-controlled funds. The Conservatives and Liberals, together with the employers in the SAF, advocated a system of increased national pensions and voluntary pension agreements between unions and employers. The Farmers' Union, which broke off cooperation with the Social Democratic government because of the disagreements over pensions, went all in on increasing basic pensions.

---

46   On this, see Bo Stråth, *Mellan två fonder: LO och den svenska modellen* (Stockholm: Atlas, 1998), Chapter 2; Francis Sejersted, *The Age of Social Democracy: Norway and Sweden in the Twentieth Century* (Princeton, NJ: Princeton University Press, 2011), pp. 249–57.

47   Lewin, *Planhushållningsdebatten*, pp. 409–16.

The bourgeois parties, strengthened by their success in the parliamentary elections, demanded an advisory referendum on the pension issue. The Social Democrats hesitated. In principle, the party was against the use of referenda, which in Sweden are usually consultative. They risked weakening the strong governments that had been the Social Democrats' ideal. The party was also demoralised by the defeats in the last elections, and pursued possibilities for compromise with the bourgeois parties to the last. The LO did not want a referendum either. But in the end the party gave in, and in 1958 an advisory referendum was held offering a choice between the three platforms presented above.

The ATP election is one of the classic political mobilisations in modern Swedish history. Despite the initial pessimism of the Social Democratic leadership, it marked the beginning of a new turning point for Social Democracy. It was transformed into a class election, above all through the strong involvement of the LO in the referendum campaign. The simultaneous involvement of several white-collar unions and leading figures from the TCO was also crucial. Many of their members also lacked more comprehensive pension agreements, and the ATP proposal would also guarantee most of them a better pension.

The result was that the Social Democratic line received 45 per cent of the vote, the Liberals and the Right 35 per cent, and the Farmers' Union (now renamed the Centre Party) 15 per cent. The Social Democrats felt they had a mandate to go enact their proposal, but they lacked a majority in the Riksdag. The government therefore decided to call new elections. The 1958 off-year election was a success – but not by a large enough margin. The vote in the Second Chamber was 115:115, and the outcome risked being decided by lot. The dramatic denouement, however, was that one of the few workers in the Liberal Party parliamentary group declared that he could not vote against a reform that would mean so much to his fellow workers at the Gothenburg shipyards. This may seem a fortuitous end to one of the most high-profile political battles of the twentieth century, but at the same time it reflects the impact of the class mobilisation for the ATP reform. Once the reform was passed, it quickly gained broad popular support. In retrospect, the ATP came to be seen as the 'jewel in the crown' of Social Democratic welfare reforms.

The ATP, like the health insurance and unemployment reforms implemented a few years earlier, was based on the principle of income security. Thus it can be argued, as Gøsta-Esping Andersen does, that the foundations were laid for a Social Democratic 'welfare state regime' that came to grow stronger in the 1960s, and stronger still in the 1970s.[48]

But it is difficult to argue that this was the result of a programmatic policy on the part of the Social Democrats. The universalist dimension of the reform, for example, was not the result of any conscious Social Democratic ambition, but the overall outcome of a complicated process in which the party repeatedly prioritised other sub-goals, writes historian Klas Åmark: 'The essence of Social Democracy, the hard core, is not given from the start or determined by purely internal factors such as class interest or ideology. Social Democratic politics – and thus Social Democratic society – becomes what the environment allows and what the context makes possible.'[49]

The concrete design of the ATP reform was not the result of any long-term strategic thinking – and this also applied to the elements that were later highlighted as its fundamentals, namely that pension insurance was made compulsory for all citizens, that the pension level was set at a high level, or that the rapidly growing pension funds could be used for state-controlled investments.[50] If Gustav Möller had succeeded in implementing his Beveridge-inspired proposal for basic security in health insurance, or the Social Democrats had been more successful in finding compromises on the ATP issue to avoid an expected defeat in the referendum, the foundation on which the coming social reforms were built would have looked very different. And had the party lost government power in any of the elections of the 1950s – something that was perceived as a constant threat by contemporaries – this would also have transformed the outcome.

The Discontent of Great Expectations

In Social Democratic historiography, the 1950s is a period when the party consciously and systematically moved its positions forward, laying the foundations for a strong welfare state. But, as we have seen, and as Tage Erlander has repeatedly confirmed in his diary entries, ideological clarity and combativeness were hardly the hallmarks of the party at this time.

48   Esping-Andersen, 'Making of a Social Democratic Welfare State'.
49   Åmark, *Hundra år av välfärdspolitik*, pp. 280ff.
50   Lewin, *Planhushållningsdebatten*, pp. 411ff.

Eric Hobsbawm's view that the Social Democratic parties in practice lacked their own distinctive economic policy seems to have been confirmed in this case. Or, in the words of the Social Democratic polemicist Roland Pålsson, 'Hopes were high after the war, socialism appeared to be the only and obvious alternative, but after a few years the international climate hardened into a cold war and in that cold post-war radicalism froze, its programmes and slogans were put on ice.'[51]

Even if the Social Democrats had had a programme of radical reformism in their desk drawer, the conditions for implementing it were not ideal. The spirit of the times in the heyday of the Cold War militated against a socialist offensive, and the political balance of power did not facilitate a major expansion of the Folkhem. Between 1951 and 1957, the Social Democrats were in a coalition government with the Farmers' Union – a party with bourgeois values that advocated austerity rather than economic expansion. During this period, the other bourgeois parties also strengthened their parliamentary position, and increasingly opposed the growth of the public sector.[52] After the 1956 parliamentary elections, there was a bourgeois majority among the electorate for the first time since 1930.

The bourgeois advance was particularly troubling for the Social Democrats, because it came at a time when the economy and prosperity were booming as never before. How was it that the bourgeois parties were able to profit from this? For Liberal leader Bertil Ohlin, the reason for the Social Democratic defeat was obvious: 'Socialism and socialist ideas have played out their role. Living standards are rising, people are being *embourgeoisés*. Taxes are growing too fast. Education increases. More and more wage earners are and feel middle class.'[53]

In a draft analysis of the election after the setback in the 1956 parliamentary elections, Tage Erlander and his young assistant Olof Palme noted that the party had done very well among industrial workers. But this was not enough to achieve a majority among voters: 'If we are to retain a dominant influence in Swedish politics, we must be able to win over the middle class to our policies.'[54] Again and again, Erlander and

---

51   Roland Pålsson, ed., *Inför 60-talet: debattbok om socialismens framtid* (Stockholm: Rabén & Sjögren, 1959), pp. 9ff.

52   Emil Uddhammar, *Partierna och den stora staten: en analys av statsteorier och svensk politik under 1900-talet* (Stockholm: City University Press, 1993), pp. 439ff.

53   Bertil Ohlin, 'Socialismens sista chans', *Vecko-Journalen* 39 (1956).

54   Kjell Östberg, *I takt med tiden: Olof Palme 1927–1969* (Stockholm: Leopard, 2008), pp. 136–40.

his young colleagues pondered these questions, which were in some ways quite new. They were about the special problems of the welfare society. Never before had the vast majority of a country been free from want and hunger, able to formulate demands that were not a matter of mere survival, but of building a decent life – indeed, for many a life of modest abundance. At the same time, the people were dissatisfied:

> But it is a different discontent from that which sprang from unemploy-
> ment and mass poverty, from the fear of sickness and old age. We are
> in that small and extremely privileged part of the world where that
> kind of discontent need no longer exist. What, then, are the founda-
> tions of modern discontent? We still have a shortage of housing, our
> hospitals do not have the capacity we want, our schools cannot accom-
> modate all those who seek them. In a society of privilege, no such
> problems arise . . . The discontent that exists is in fact an expression of
> the fact that we live in a democratic society where people demand that
> society be adapted to their needs. And it is those demands, that
> discontent if you like, that drives the transformation of society. Goals
> that were previously distant and unrealistic are now within the reach
> of the majority of the people.[55]

The problem was thus the *failure to satisfy high expectations*. With great clarity, Erlander saw that this could have quite different political impli-cations than the Liberal Ohlin had hoped for:

> People who live in poverty with constant fear of unemployment and
> illness have little ability to plan for anything other than the day. But in
> a welfare society, families would have a very different chance to plan
> for the future. This must have profound implications for politics. Its
> task will be to try to adapt society to people's long-term aspirations. It
> is of extraordinary interest to note that while improved living stand-
> ards have given people much greater freedom of advance, they have
> used this increased freedom to bind themselves more tightly than
> before. Anyone who buys a modern dwelling or a home of his own
> commits himself to a very substantial expense in the form of rent,
> mortgage payments, and whatever else may be involved. Anyone who
> gives their children the opportunity to acquire a longer education

---

55   Ibid., p. 138.

is committing themselves in the same way. More and more people are committing themselves to instalment contracts for consumer durables, with the car and the TV dominating.[56]

And if income were to fall away, the consequences would be severe: 'It is no longer just a question of guaranteeing a minimum standard, freedom from want and hardship, by means of social policy. Increasingly, it has become a question of using social policy to guarantee a reasonably preserved standard of living – a national insurance.' Therefore, society had to enter the world of individual families 'not as an oppressive authority but as an instrument for greater freedom and better living conditions for all'.[57]

What Palme and Erlander succeeded in doing together was to formulate a kind of ideological basis for Social Democracy in a welfare society. By making society responsible for people's basic security, the state ensured that people in a Social Democratic society could *not* afford *not* to show solidarity.

And the idea was also to give the state a broader, more offensive role. State-planning efforts in the economic sphere were becoming *comme il faut* around this time in the Western world, and Sweden was not even a pioneer in this respect.[58] The postwar Fordist project affirmed rationality and state planning to facilitate market forces. The Cold War pushed further the demand for state planning in capitalist economies – and here, of course, armaments and defence planning took a special place. In the second half of the 1950s, this tendency was reinforced. One important reason was the threat from the Soviet Union.

In the autumn of 1957, the Soviet Union launched Sputnik 1 into space – a small satellite, just over half a metre in diameter. A month later, it launched the dog, Laika, into orbit. The conquest of space had begun. The Soviet Union sent shock waves through the Western world. Was communism about to catch up, and even overtake the capitalist economies? And if so, how would the West regain the initiative? The arms race entered a new phase.[59]

During the 1950s, the party's rising star Olof Palme eagerly followed American domestic political discourse. One of the social commentators

---

56 Ibid., p. 139.
57 Ibid.
58 Ekdahl, *Mot en tredje väg*, p. 176.
59 Hobsbawm, *Age of Extremes*, p. 547.

Palme carefully read and discussed was the well-known newspaperman, Walter Lippman. Americans had become accustomed to always being at the forefront of technological and industrial development. It soon became clear to the world that the Russian space satellite was the result not of a lucky accident, but of a strong coordinated effort. Palme referred with interest to Lippman's conclusions:

> Politicians have declared that the private standard of living takes precedence over the common good . . . People have been led to believe that the highest aim of American society is to make possible the greatest possible enjoyment of consumer goods. As a result, our public institutions, particularly those concerned with education and research, have been put on a scandalous starvation diet in relation to population growth.[60]

However, the American commentator who came to mean the most to the Swedish Social Democrats was the economist John Kenneth Galbraith. His 1958 book *The Affluent Society* (translated into Swedish in 1959) had the same triggering effect on the party's debate on ideas as Keynes had had a generation earlier. Once his book was translated, Galbraith was invited to Harpsund to present his ideas.[61] In an almost programmatic article, 'Radical Renewal', in *Tiden* in 1960, Palme referred to his theses with great enthusiasm. Galbraith took as his starting point the imbalance that existed in Western industrial societies between what business produced and the services that society alone could provide. Palme referred to this approvingly:

> As the standard of living rises, people begin to demand more and more things that cannot be obtained on the market . . . This applies to roads, streets, town planning, schools, research, health care.
>
>   The reason for the severe backlog in the public sector is the exaggerated belief in the superiority of the market economy and the scale of values in society that elevates the production and sales of private enterprise, while the actions of the public sector are subjected to judgements such as bureaucracy, wastefulness, exploitation of the taxpayer, etc. . . . A vigorous expansion of the public sector therefore

---

60   Östberg, *I takt med tiden*, p. 142.
61   John Kenneth Galbraith, *The Affluent Society* (Boston: Houghton Mifflin, 1958).

appears to Galbraith to be a most important task in meeting the desires of the people in the rising standard of society.[62]

Thus, somewhat surprisingly, Erlander's – and even more so Palme's – main influence in formulating the party's policy for the 1960s came from American economic liberalism.

Neutrality and the Bomb

After the Second World War and the debate about the Swedish concessions to Nazi Germany, considerable political agreement was reached that Sweden should take a neutral stance. Sweden would not join any military alliance, and in the event of another war, the objective would be for Sweden to remain neutral. This approach enjoyed strong popular support throughout the postwar period. Only small groups, mainly some bourgeois newspapers, advocated open Swedish accession to military cooperation with the Western powers – which, from 1949, meant the North Atlantic Treaty Organization (NATO).[63]

However, the Social Democratic government was willing to envisage some form of organised military cooperation, at least with its neighbours. In 1948, Sweden took the initiative of negotiating a Nordic defence alliance with Denmark and Norway. The proposal failed, mainly because Norway wanted more formal cooperation with the United States. One important consideration was that the Americans had threatened to stop arms exports to a neutral Nordic defence alliance.[64]

Sweden continued to take a formal non-aligned position. One way of doing this was to invest in strong national defence; as a result, Sweden developed into a regional military superpower in the postwar period. At times, only the United States, the Soviet Union, and Israel invested more in defence relative to their size. The Swedish Air Force was among the strongest in the world after those of the two major

---

62 Olof Palme, 'Radikal förnyelse', *Tiden* 7 (1960).

63 For background, see Ulf Bjereld, Alf W. Johansson, and Karl Molin, *Sveriges säkerhet och världens fred: svensk utrikespolitik under kalla kriget* (Stockholm: Santérus, 2008).

64 Alf W. Johansson and Torbjörn Norman, 'Sweden's Security and World Peace', in Misgeld, Molin, and Åmark, *Creating Social Democracy*, pp. 361–3.

powers. Most defence policy decisions could be implemented with a high degree of party-political consensus, and Swedish Social Democracy took a strong pro-defence stance. By arguing vigorously that strong defence was a prerequisite for Swedish non-alignment, it succeeded in gaining support for its line even among those significant groups within the labour movement that traditionally had sympathies for pacifism and disarmament. 'Non-alignment in peace aiming at neutrality in war' was how formal Swedish policy summarised the national position. In reality, however, Swedish foreign policy during the Cold War was much more complicated.

First, there is no doubt that sympathies in Sweden lay with the Western powers. This applied to the political elite, and of course to the business community – not to mention the military. Swedish Social Democracy was distinctly Western-oriented. The Swedish trade union movement played a central role in the pro-Western and CIA-funded International Confederation of Free Trade Unions, which not only made important efforts to spread the trade union movement to the 'Third World', but was also an important cog in the fight against communist influence. For many years, LO chairman Arne Geijer was president of the organisation, and was much appreciated by the US leadership. 'Mr Geijer is without doubt one of the very best friends that the United States has among foreign labour leaders [and] takes a stronger anti-communist and more pro-US position than almost any other labour leader', the US ambassador reported back to the State Department.[65]

However, relations between Sweden and the Western Bloc were not just a matter of ideological affinity. The Swedish government had strong economic reasons for close trade relations with the West. In the late 1940s, cooperation had already developed in several military areas, especially in the fields of war materials and intelligence.[66]

In order to maintain strong military defence, Sweden needed to import modern and technologically advanced weapons from the United States and Great Britain. Initially, the Americans were reluctant to facilitate this, wanting primarily to pressure the Swedes into joining NATO, as they had done with the Norwegians. Soon, however, they changed tactic. The new American line was to ensure that the Swedes were well

---

65   Östberg, *I takt med tiden*, p. 275.
66   Bjereld, Johansson, and Molin, *Sveriges säkerhet*; Robert Dalsjö, *Life-Line Lost: The Rise and Fall of 'Neutral' Sweden's Secret Reserve Option of Wartime Help from the West* (Stockholm: Santérus, 2006), Chapter 5.

equipped and friendly to the West.[67] The stronger Sweden was militarily, the stronger NATO's northern flank would be. Despite the declared Swedish non-alignment, the Americans did not hesitate for a moment to assume where Social Democratic–led Sweden belonged in the event of war. The United States would therefore ensure that Sweden was able to buy the military equipment it needed.[68] But the Americans demanded a quid pro quo: that Sweden participate in the extensive trade embargo that the United States had established against the Eastern Bloc. Sweden would participate in this economic warfare, and commit itself not to export strategically important goods to the Soviet Union and its allies. The Swedish government also undertook to pursue a trade policy along the same lines as that of the NATO allies – something that was not easy to reconcile with a Swedish policy of strict neutrality.[69]

Another important area of collaboration was intelligence. Sweden, in cooperation with the United States and using American equipment, conducted extensive signals intelligence activity against the Soviet Union, as became evident when a Swedish plane conducting reconnaissance was shot down by the Russians.

Despite a growing Swedish military industry, the need for access to advanced American technology increased further towards the end of the 1950s. Target-seeking missiles, and even more advanced radar and signals intelligence equipment, were high on the Swedish wish-list. The United States was still willing to supply the Swedish armed forces with the most modern products – but, again, it demanded something in return. The Americans now asked for guarantees that no workers seen as security risks would come into contact with American military products. In plain language, this meant that Communists and Communist sympathisers would not be allowed to work in the Swedish defence industry, or other sensitive areas of production. This in turn required the Swedes to demonstrate that such security risks were under control. To ensure this, a new organisation was developed within the Swedish military intelligence service, later known as the IB. From the outset, its activities were based on close cooperation with Social Democracy and the trade union movement. Employees of the IB were usually recruited

67   Charles Silva, *Keep Them Strong, Keep Them Friendly: Swedish–American Relations and the Pax Americana, 1948–1952* (Stockholm: Akademitryck, 1999).

68   Dalsjö, *Life-Line Lost*, p. 53.

69   Gunnar Adler-Karlsson, *Western Economic Warfare 1947–1967: A Case Study in Foreign Economic Policy* (Stockholm: Almqvist & Wiksell, 1968).

from the Social Democratic movement. Reliable trade unionists reported their knowledge of the political views of their workmates.[70] The information gathered was used not only to impress the Pentagon, but also by the LO in the fight against communist influence in the trade union movement. Anti-communism, which had been a prominent feature of Social Democracy and the LO since the interwar period, sharpened during the Cold War of the 1950s. Every trade union had to be turned into a battlefield against communism, proclaimed a famous slogan of Prime Minister Erlander.

Of course, the purchase of materials and the exchange of information with other states were not, in themselves, impossible to combine with military non-alignment, even if they were essentially only with a military bloc. But it became more complicated if cooperation was extended to concrete plans for assistance in the event of war. Such plans abounded between Sweden and the NATO countries. The Swedish military was extended to accommodate the take-off and landing of bombers from the West. The Swedish Air Force was coordinated with the Danish and Norwegian NATO allied air forces. Secure supply routes and lines of communication for use in war were established with Scandinavian neighbours. Good contacts were established between the Swedish military command and NATO and there were hard-coded telex lines between Stockholm and the United States NATO headquarters in Wiesbaden.[71]

There is no doubt about how the United States viewed Swedish neutrality. When the Eisenhower administration summarised the security situation in Scandinavia in 1960, it treated Sweden in the same document, and from much the same perspective, as it did NATO members Denmark and Norway. It noted that all three countries were ideologically aligned with the West, and had great strategic importance as NATO's northern flank. Finally, it stated that if the Soviets were to attack Sweden, the United States 'should be prepared to come to the assistance of Sweden' as part of a NATO response to the aggression.[72] The Soviet Union, too, was well aware of the nature of Swedish–Western cooperation. One of

70   Lars Olof Lampers, *Det grå brödraskapet: en berättelse om IB: forskarrapport till Säkerhetstjänstkommissionen* (Stockholm: Fritzes offentliga publikationer, 2002), pp. 119ff.
71   Dalsjö, *Life-Line Lost*, pp. 161ff.
72   Sverige Neutralitetspolitikkommissionen, *Om kriget kommit-: förberedelser för mottagandet av militärt bistånd 1949–1969: betänkande* (Stockholm: Fritze, 1994), appendix 11.

those who handled issues of secret Swedish cooperation with NATO was the air colonel and top Soviet spy Stig Wennerström. Through his strategic positions in the Ministry of Defence and the Foreign Ministry, he was able to follow in detail large parts of Swedish–Western cooperation, and report everything back to his Russian clients.

What was the problem with the double standard implicit in the Swedish policy of neutrality? Was it not in fact a guarantee of peace?

From a security point of view, there is no answer to this question. The Cold War never became hot in Europe. We cannot know whether Swedish neutrality would have been respected. There is much to suggest that Swedish duplicity actually made the situation worse. There was a great risk that the Soviet Union might have treated Sweden as NATO's secret seventeenth member.

What we know, however, are the domestic political consequences of the Swedish policy of neutrality. In the public debate, there was a broad consensus on its stated aim of trying to keep Sweden out of a future war by not joining any of the military alliances of the Cold War. Only minor bourgeois groups argued in favour of joining NATO. But the problem was that there was another part of the policy, based on assurances of tacit cooperation with the Western powers. And this part was kept secret, creating a democratic dilemma. Citizens could not be informed about the full content of one of the most important political issues of the time: conditions for the country's security during the highly uncertain period of the Cold War. Even less could they participate in a real discussion of the policy, or influence its formulation.

This dilemma was given an incoherence by the fact that what was supposed to be a deep secret was in fact widely known. Both West and East were privy to the details of Swedish–Western cooperation. But even in Sweden it was no secret: every young man who did his military service learned that the enemy would come from the East, and help from the West.

During the most intense phase of the Cold War, it was possible for politicians to maintain a façade of unity. Few wanted to risk challenging the official image. The harsh treatment of those who argued for a third position between East and West had a chilling effect. But towards the end of the decade, there was a noticeable upturn in public debate. One important reason for this can be found in the Cold War's own atrocious logic. The threat of the atomic bomb created a reaction against the polarised worldview of the 1950s.

The Bomb

In the 1950s, humanity lived in the shadow of the threat of a devastating nuclear war. Burgeoning stocks of armaments and test explosions kept the threat alive. The issue of the Swedish atomic bomb was one of the biggest domestic political battles of the 1950s.[73] It was given particularly explosive force by the fact that the Social Democratic Party was split down the middle at all levels; even within the cabinet, the prime minister and the foreign minister were on different sides.

In the years after Hiroshima, nuclear weapons were seen primarily as a matter for the major powers, but in the 1950s this picture changed. 'Tactical' nuclear weapons became an increasingly attractive option for the Swedish military leadership.[74] The bourgeois parties also soon came out in favour of a Swedish nuclear bomb, as did large parts of the Social Democratic establishment. In secret, but with the support of the Social Democratic leadership, preparatory research for a Swedish atomic bomb was also begun. In 1957, the commander-in-chief demanded that Sweden acquire nuclear weapons, and the government was now required to give clear answers.

Central parts of the party leadership, including the prime minister and his close associate Olof Palme, had a positive attitude to Swedish nuclear weapons. But in other parts of the party, where pacifist currents persisted, resistance grew. Most important here was the Social Democratic Women's League, which mobilised all its resources to stop the bomb. Many local workers' communes and Social Democratic Youth League clubs agreed. So did key figures from an older generation, including Ernst Wigforss and Rickard Sandler, and the foreign minister, Östen Undén. Action groups against the bomb were also formed, whose membership included prominent cultural figures and the archbishop of Uppsala. Resistance to the bomb was becoming a mass movement. Tage Erlander increasingly feared that the conflict would blow up the party, and frantically sought ways to postpone a decision. Erlander was particularly concerned about the actions of the Women's League. But with

---

73   Karl Molin, 'Party Disputes and Party Responsibility', in Misgeld, Molin, and Åmark, *Creating Social Democracy*, pp. 394–401.

74   For political and military considerations on the atomic bomb, see W. Agrell, *Fred och fruktan: Sveriges säkerhetspolitiska historia 1918–2000* (Lund: Historiska Media, 2000), pp. 132ff.

a vigour and independence that was unusual for a Social Democratic ancillary organisation, the Women's League had stuck to its opposition despite intense pressure to accept a compromise.[75]

In order to find a solution, Erlander appointed a committee that included leading representatives of the various parts of the movement. The resulting compromise was to postpone the decision for a few years. At the same time, the pro-nuclear campaigners made sure that they would be able to continue their research without any transparency, so that any future decision would not be delayed.[76]

Ultimately, Sweden would not develop an atomic bomb. The military leadership began to waver as it became clear how much an atomic bomb would have deducted from defence budgets. For the same reason, the United States opposed a Swedish atomic bomb. The United States, which included the Swedish armed forces under the American defence umbrella, preferred strong Swedish conventional capability on NATO's north-eastern flank. The United States had the nuclear bomb, and that settled the matter to US satisfaction – and a Swedish bomb could not have been constructed without the help of American technology.

---

75   Östberg, *I takt med tiden*, p. 176.
76   Ibid., pp. 179ff.

6

The 1960s: The People's Home and Its Fractures

1960

In 1960, there were few signs that the decade would be the most turbulent of the postwar era. Most observers, at least in the industrialised world, were optimistic about future development. The long postwar boom was to continue. The welfare state seemed not far away. Cars, televisions, and refrigerators – not to mention baths and indoor toilets – which before the Second World War had been unattainable for most people, were now within the reach of hundreds of millions of people in Europe and North America.[1] Unemployment, the great scourge of the interwar years, had been driven back. A slight easing of the Cold War was in sight. The races for social reform and for socially useful technological advances to some extent complemented the arms race.

From the perspective of the Western elites, the storm-clouds were gathering to the south. Across three continents, the colonial liberation struggle entered a more intense phase with many dimensions. In Algeria, the National Liberation Front was pushing the French army towards another defeat. In the Congo, new and old colonial interests were sabotaging the construction of an independent African state. In Cuba, there were signs that Castro was developing the country into the first socialist state in Latin America.[2]

In the 'First World', however, a happy optimism reigned with regard to future progress. And the happiest and most progressive of all were the small Social Democratic countries of northern Europe. The years

---

1   Lennart Schön, *An Economic History of Modern Sweden* (London: Routledge, 2012), pp. 231ff.

2   Tony Judt, *Postwar: A History of Europe since 1945* (New York: Penguin, 2005), Chapter 9.

around 1960 were, in many ways, the strongest period for Swedish Social Democracy.[3] The Swedish economy continued to advance. Together with Switzerland, Sweden topped the international income league table. Industrial production, which had grown by 4 per cent a year during the 1950s, took another leap forward, doubling in the following years. Manufacturing was the big winner, and there was now room to produce consumer goods on a massive scale: vacuum cleaners and washing machines from Electrolux, telephones from LM Ericsson, cars from Volvo and Saab. Unemployment was below 2 per cent.

The 1960 parliamentary elections were a clear Social Democratic success. The decline of the 1950s was a distant memory. Of particular significance was where the new voters came from: the new middle class. In 1956, 31 per cent of white-collar workers had voted Social Democratic; four years later, that had risen to 41 per cent, and the share would continue to grow during the 1960s. With income-based pensions and health insurance, the standard of living of the working class was no longer the norm under the new social policy. The new model also linked the middle class to the Social Democratic project through a strong state, high taxes, and a universal, publicly funded welfare system.

Moreover, this breakthrough had taken place without jeopardising the working-class base. In the 1962 municipal elections, the Social Democrats received more than 50 per cent of the vote. The policy of consensus was deeply rooted, and celebrated triumphs when LO chairman Arne Geijer and the director of the Swedish Employers' Association visited the US Congress in the early 1960s to present the Swedish model. Not least, it was the peaceful labour market that impressed this audience. At least in terms of official statistics, strikes had essentially disappeared.[4]

It was not only the class cooperation and optimism of eternal growth of the Swedish model that had been confirmed. The strong state and the politics of collective solutions had also emerged with enhanced reputations from the ATP struggle. The public sector's share of GDP grew steadily. At the same time, Sweden was evolving from a low-tax to a high-tax country. In 1960 the minister of finance, Gunnar Sträng,

3 Francis Sejersted, *The Age of Social Democracy: Norway and Sweden in the Twentieth Century* (Princeton, NJ: Princeton University Press, 2011), Chapter 8.
4 Stig Hadenius, *Swedish Politics during the 20th Century: Conflict and Consensus* (Stockholm: Svenska Institutet, 1997), pp. 101–4; Yvonne Hirdman, Jenny Björkman, and Urban Lundberg, *Sveriges historia. 1920–1965* (Stockholm: Norstedt, 2012), pp. 562–5.

pushed through his demand for a new sales tax that would quickly generate new resources for the expansion of the welfare state.

In addition to the social security reforms of the 1950s, a fundamental reform of the education system was in the early 1960s. A coherent, compulsory nine-year primary school education was introduced. For those who went on to secondary education, child allowances were extended. And for those who went on to enter the greatly expanded higher education system, a generous regime of student grants was introduced. All education was free.

The Social Democratic movement – comprising the Social Democratic Party, the LO, youth and women's associations, cooperatives, educational activities, and dozens of other organisations closely linked to the party – was stronger than ever. The state bureaucracy gradually became Social Democratic. One factor facilitating this process was, of course, the long period for which the Social Democrats had governed. Another was the social broadening of recruitment into higher education. By 1970, one-third of the civil servants under forty – that is, newly recruited – had working-class backgrounds.

Experience in political work became a significant advantage. Many of the new welfare-state bureaucrats could be defined as movement intellectuals. Their careers had often begun within the Social Democratic Party and Swedish Social Democratic Youth League. Possessing a membership card for the Social Democratic Party was also considered an important advantage in securing higher positions inside the state bureaucracy. The directors-general of almost all important national boards were now Social Democrats. In 1975, when Sweden acquired a Social Democratic commander-in-chief, the last conservative bastion had fallen.[5]

The Gospel of Eternal Growth

It was hardly a time that called for internal re-examination and soul-searching within the Social Democratic Party. The powerful labour movement was characterised by strong self-awareness.

5   Kjell Östberg, 'The Swedish Social Democracy: Civil Servants, Social Engineers and Welfare Bureaucrats', in Mathieu Fulla and Marc Lazar, eds, *European Socialists and the State in the Twentieth and Twenty-First Centuries* (Cham: Palgrave Macmillan, 2020), pp. 212ff.

In 1961, the LO Congress endorsed a report titled *Samordnad närings politik* (Coordinated industrial policy), which was markedly pro-business. In it, the optimism and unlimited faith in economic growth of the Rehn–Meidner model celebrated its greatest triumphs. The quest for efficiency as a means of driving economic development was its overriding objective. The role of the state was important, but within the framework of a market economy and free competition. Indeed, the state's task was above all to remove all obstacles through a coordinated economic policy, so that the liberal market economy of the textbooks could also become a practical reality, according to Rudolf Meidner's biographer Lars Ekdahl. In the report, the trade unions were portrayed as important instruments for removing obstacles to a further increase in the rate of economic growth.[6]

In 1960, the Social Democrats adopted a new party programme. The party magazine *Tiden* summed up its analysis a year later in the following clarifying lines: 'The new party programme . . . did not imply a reorientation of the party's policy. It purged certain Marxist language . . . and increased attention was given to new areas of active intervention such as economic and labour market policy. Otherwise, the position which the party has long represented was codified.'[7] Some critical voices were nevertheless heard from within the party. Oppositional tendencies were evident within the Student Union. The Social Democrats had had to 'buy the great self-proclaimed social security reforms . . . in return for refraining from more radical interventions in economic life that would have changed the balance of power, equalised incomes and wealth and created better scope for investment in public activities.'[8]

A class compromise during the boom years was all Social Democracy could deliver, others muttered. There was no master plan for the development of a fundamentally different, perhaps socialist, Sweden. And despite the high tone from party leaders, the Swedish welfare state in the mid-1960s was quantitatively no different from that of other countries with advanced welfare systems. In 1965, the social spending as percentage of GDP of Belgium, France, the Netherlands, and West Germany

---

6 Lars Ekdahl, *Mot en tredje väg: en biografi över Rudolf Meidner*, vol. 2, *Facklig expert och demokratisk socialist* (Lund: Arkiv, 2001), pp. 112ff; Landsorganisationen i Sverige, *Samordnad näringspolitik* (Stockholm: LO, 1961).

7 *Tiden* 5 (May 1961), p. 257.

8 Roland Pålsson, ed., *Inför 60-talet: debattbok om socialismens framtid* (Stockholm: Rabén & Sjögren, 1959).

was around 16 per cent, while Sweden's was 13.5 per cent. Swedish taxes were still at the average level for Europe.[9]

Moreover, the high Swedish standard of living was mainly the result of the head start that Swedish industry gained after the Second World War, and the ability of the Swedish export industry to assert itself on the international market – even though the extremely pro-business policies of the Swedish Social Democrats had facilitated this development.

The Cracks in Welfare

In the mid-1960s, the minister of finance, Gunnar Sträng, could look back with contentment and declare that the welfare state was almost complete, with only a little plastering needed on its façade. But no sooner had the words been uttered than widespread criticism of the cracks in the welfare state broke out within the Social Democratic movement. Class divisions existed between blue- and white-collar workers: one-third of workers were low-paid, queues for housing were long, the working environment was miserable in many places, and childcare was lacking.

The criticism was supported by research. In 1966, the sociological study *Den ofärdiga välfärden* (Unfinished welfare) attracted a lot of attention. Inequalities in living conditions are enormous and privileges persist, the authors claimed. One finds differences in economic standards, in education, in cultural life, in the legal system, in the range of illnesses, in the treatment of the sick and disadvantaged. 'Class society continues to shape individual values and social attitudes.'[10]

Attention was also paid to the upper part of the social pyramid. Communist leader C. H. Hermansson, who was also an economist, in his book *Monopol och storfinans* (Monopoly and big finance) demonstrated an increasing concentration of power in business.[11] He coined the term 'the fifteen families', which for a long time thereafter denoted the narrow ownership of Swedish business. A government inquiry on economic concentration set up shortly afterwards largely confirmed this picture.

---

9   Göran Therborn, 'Arbetarrörelsen och välfärdsstaten', in *Klass, allianser och välfärdsstat: analys och teori i arbete 1967–2021* (Lund: Arkiv, 2021), p. 242.

10   Gunnar Inghe and Maj-Britt Inghe, *Den ofärdiga välfärden* (Stockholm: Tiden/ Folksam, 1967).

11   C. H. Hermansson, *Monopol och storfinans* (Stockholm: Arbetarkultur, 1962).

Other areas were soon to become salient as well. During the 1960s, the environment in the broad sense became a political priority. Rachel Carson's book *Silent Spring*, first published in English in 1963, served as an international wake-up call. In Sweden, the chemist and environmental commentator Hans Palmstierna's *Plundring, svält, förgiftning* (Plundering, starving, poisoning), published a few years later, had a similar impact.[12] The dangers of DDT and mercury attracted considerable attention. The debate on the construction of electric power stations in the still-untouched Vindel River accentuated a Social Democratic dilemma with major implications for the future: the trade-off between the environment and employment. The working environment also came under fire. The curse of silicosis, a form of occupational lung disease, was placed under the spotlight, and triggered an intensive discussion on working conditions and co-determination.

Urbanisation and the closely related phenomenon of sparsely populated rural areas came to be discussed in increasing detail in the shadow of the record years of economic growth of the 1950s and 1960s and the labour relocation policy, a consequence of the Rehn–Meidner model. Large parts of northern Sweden, in particular, were being stripped of jobs and social services. The other side of the coin was the impact of urbanisation, in relation to which the housing shortage was at the centre of the debate: where would all the newly arrived workers live? The solution was the million-dweller programme, adopted by parliament in 1965. A million apartments were to be built over a ten-year period. However, the problems associated with the programme were soon recognised – in particular, the tendency towards social segregation in large, newly built areas with sterile environments. Developments in the old city centres also became subject to heated debate, at the centre of which were two interrelated issues: the increase in car use in inner cities, which had promoted a growth in the construction of large roads and car parks in the inner city, and the mass demolition of older houses. A large part of Stockholm's city centre was torn down in the 1960s.[13]

Not surprisingly, it was the Social Democrats who were caught in the crossfire of the increasingly intense debate about the cracks in the Folkhem. After all, the party had held government power for over thirty

---

12 Hans Palmstierna and Lena Palmstierna, *Plundring, svält, förgiftning* (Stockholm: Rabén & Sjögren, 1967).

13 Kjell Östberg and Jenny Andersson, *Sveriges historia. 1965–2012* (Stockholm: Norstedt, 2013), pp. 126–30.

years. Criticism of bureaucracy and abuse of power grew from both the right and the left. In the municipalities, which were often presented as the cradle of Swedish democracy, a process of centralisation was taking place. This was partly due to the role of the municipalities in the provision of the central parts of the welfare state, and the parts that were growing fastest: schools, social care, and perhaps most crucially housing construction were mainly municipal affairs. In order to cope with the expansion of activity, extensive municipal mergers were required. By the early 1970s, over 2,000 municipalities had been consolidated down to 278.

The results of the 1966 municipal elections were a major wake-up call for the Social Democrats. Their 42.2 per cent share of the vote – which would be a dream today – was the worst result the party had achieved since 1934. Many wanted to explain the setback by means of Prime Minister Tage Erlander's inability to answer a question on television concerning what a young homeless couple in Stockholm could do to find somewhere to live. Referring, as Erlander did, to the public housing agency, where waiting times could be as long as ten years, was widely considered unacceptable. The Social Democrats had failed in one of their core areas, housing policy, and television had become a force that could sway election outcomes.[14]

When the party board made its evaluation, Erlander claimed that it was the most serious setback to hit Social Democracy in the generation of which he was a part: 'Let us cold-bloodedly admit that we have suffered a crisis of confidence, especially among young voters.'[15] Erlander felt the chilly wind of a dawning radicalisation among young people. But it was not only young people who were pushing back. There was also growing radicalisation within the labour movement.

Social Democratic Counter-offensive

The Social Democrats tried to capture and channel these currents. They decided to convene an extraordinary Party Congress in 1967 – a rare event in the party's history. At this meeting, LO chairman Arne Geijer

14 Thord Strömberg, 'The Politicization of the Housing Market: The Social Democrats and the Housing Question', in Klaus Misgeld, Karl Molin, and Klas Åmark, eds, *Creating Social Democracy: A Century of the Social Democratic Labor Party in Sweden* (University Park: Pennsylvania State University Press, 1992), pp. 260ff.
15 Kjell Östberg, *I takt med tiden: Olof Palme 1927–1969* (Stockholm: Leopard, 2008), p. 370.

gave a high-profile speech in which he directed unusually harsh criticism at the shortcomings of the welfare system.[16]

Most striking, however, was Geijer's rejection of the uncritical optimism about economic growth that had long been one of the LO's hallmarks. As we have seen, the 1961 LO report *Samordnad näringspolitik* had unequivocally stated that economic policy should be focused even more concertedly towards economic expansion and increased productivity, and that it was the task of the trade unions to work towards this end. By now, dissatisfaction with the downsides of growth policy had reached into the LO castle, and Geijer warned Congress: 'Listening to the debate today, one has been left with the impression that our problems will be solved if we have rapid economic development . . . This may be true in general, but for the individual this development means increased risks of widening the gap in the distribution of income and wealth.'[17]

Geijer's words of warning by no means meant that the growth ideology had been abandoned; economic expansion was still the overarching goal. But, in the period that followed, the contradiction between growth and increased productivity, on the one hand, and exclusion, low incomes, and widening social inequality, on the other, would become the focus of social debate. Geijer's speech resulted in an appeal for greater equality. Instead of words like '[social] security', which had long dominated Social Democratic election posters, it was the very concept of equality that became the symbol of an effort to counteract and abolish class and gender differences. A historian has counted the occurrence of the word 'equality' in Social Democratic congress documents in the postwar period. The results are unequivocal: in 1960 it appeared 530 times; in 1969, 4,682 times.[18] Congress also appointed a special Equality Commission, headed by the grand old lady of welfare policy, Alva Myrdal. The more concrete results of this new orientation were delayed, however. First, policy had to be worked out through inquiries and within ministries.

More important in the short term was the economic policy offensive. The party wanted at all costs to shed its reputation as a tired caretaker party that accepted the consequences of structural change for ordinary

---

16   Ibid., pp. 374ff.
17   [SAP,] *Protokoll. Extra kongress, 21–23 oktober 1967* (Stockholm: Partiet, 1968).
18   Bo Stråth, *Mellan två fonder: LO och den svenska modellen* (Stockholm: Atlas, 1998), pp. 95–7.

people without any alternatives. Many motions called for strong government action, and the call for an 'active industrial policy' was to be a beacon for these endeavours. A special Ministry of Economic Affairs was set up, while more active use was to be made of state-owned enterprises and the Investment Bank.[19]

But the results proved to be limited. State-owned enterprises have never been particularly extensive in Sweden, the number of people employed in state-owned industries never having risen above 10 per cent – lower than in many other capitalist countries. This proportion also decreased between 1950 and 1970, the golden years of Social Democracy. But the initiative gave the impression that Social Democracy was committed to this new path.

By the 1968 elections, the Social Democrats were to reap the harvest. The party received 50.1 per cent of the vote – and, for the first time since the war, majorities in both the First and Second Chambers. This result can be explained partly by the fact that the election took place in the weeks following the Soviet invasion of Czechoslovakia, which undermined support for the Left Party in particular. But the Social Democrats had now been given a clear mandate to pursue a more active welfare policy.

---

19   Jonas Pontusson, *The Limits of Social Democracy: Investment Politics in Sweden* (Ithaca, NY: Cornell University Press, 1992), pp. 127–34.

7

The 1970s: A Socialist Sweden?

A Perfect Storm

By the end of the 1960s, Sweden was seen as an exceptional country. Living standards were among the highest in the world and social safety nets were well developed. The country had been governed by the same party for a third of a century, and, at the same time, there was a deep sense of social peace. The economy was booming, corporate structures were working well, and strikes had virtually disappeared. The country had just gained a young prime minister with a radical image, Olof Palme, who was happy to talk about the Social Democratic ambitions of Swedish society, and had the audacity to criticise the US war in Vietnam in front of the world. And behind the headlines about Swedish promiscuity was a secularised and liberated society.

To some extent, the image was a bit excessive. We have seen the discussions about the cracks in the Folkhem, and the extent of Swedish welfare was by no means unique. And talk of the socialist country finding a happy medium between capitalism and communism had little support in a country with a government as pro-business as Sweden's.

It was in the 1970s that the big changes took place. The scale of the social and political reforms introduced in this period was unprecedented, even by international standards. In retrospect, the period has been presented as the high point of democratic socialism. Was Sweden about to become another country? What happened was the result of a perfect storm, in which a series of political, social, structural, and cyclical factors interacted. Since the mid 1960s, Sweden had been undergoing an extensive and profound youth radicalisation, stimulated mainly by solidarity with Vietnam. It quickly spread to large numbers of leading intellectuals. Unlike in many other countries, radicalisation broadened and deepened in the 1970s. Of great significance was the widespread radicalisation of women, which included both the new-wave women's movement and traditional women's associations. A broad environmental movement with opposition to nuclear power at its centre widened the social base for radicalisation.

Most important, however, was the wave of wildcat strikes that broke out in 1969–70, challenging thirty years of corporate class collaboration. The question of workers' power in the workplace suddenly became central for the labour movement once again. The traditionally class-collaborationist LO was influenced to the point of accepting the Meidner Funds – which if implemented would have meant that trade unions would today control most of Swedish business.

The Social Democratic movement was organisationally stronger than ever. It had been in government for two generations, and could rely on a local and national welfare bureaucracy with wide-ranging ambitions for social transformation. Radicalisation spread throughout the Social Democratic movement, with youth and women's associations adopting extensive socialist programmes. In addition, the downturn that followed the international postwar boom was delayed in Sweden, and a section of the bourgeoisie was also swept along in the radical spirit of the times, while employers were for a time uncertain about what tactics they should use.

The greatest impact of the deepening radicalisation was the development of the solidarity-based welfare state. In a few years, the most comprehensive social reforms ever undertaken were implemented. The public sector's share of GDP increased by 50 per cent in a single decade. Virtually all social reforms were carried out in the public sector. With few exceptions, all schools, universities, hospitals, health centres, nursing homes, and day care centres were publicly financed, owned, and operated. Municipal housing companies were the country's largest landlords. The question was now raised of whether a public sector outside the direct control of the market could be used as a lever for wider attacks on capitalist structures – whether a reformist Social Democracy had the potential to transcend the boundaries of capitalism.

But the 1970s had barely elapsed before hopes of a reformist path to socialism faded and the Social Democrats lost government power. What happened?

The Radicalisation of the 1960s

The development of Social Democracy from the mid-1960s onwards cannot be understood in isolation from the influence of the deep and widespread international radicalisation that swept the world at that time. The radicalisation has often come to be equated with the youth revolt that was one of the main expressions. This is a gross oversimplification. The roots of radicalisation lie mainly in the anticolonial struggle in Africa, Asia, and Latin America.[1]

In Indochina, on the Indian subcontinent, and in Africa, political advocacy and civil disobedience had long been combined with insurrection and guerrilla warfare. In the mid-1950s, the struggle in Algeria became emblematic of the determined, protracted, armed war of liberation led by Marxist-oriented liberation movements. It is difficult to overestimate the importance of developments in the Third World, which so sharply highlighted the unequal distribution of the earth's resources, for the initial phase of 1960s radicalisation. The fight against apartheid was another early cause in this broad struggle. South Africa played a central role in shaping public opinion, and the Sharpeville massacre of 1960 brought racism to the world's attention, as did the nascent civil rights movement in the United States. These developments complicated the clear-cut picture of international politics. Countries that presented themselves as champions of democracy and human rights in the US-dominated West during the ideological struggle of the Cold War did not hesitate to voice their support for dictatorships in Asia and Latin America – or indeed apartheid in southern Africa.

The 20th Congress of the Soviet Communist Party in 1956, with its criticism of some of the crimes of Stalinism, was a significant event in opening up a discussion that had begun tentatively within the traditionally monolithic communist parties. At the same time, the limitations of the reforms were demonstrated when the Soviet Union crushed the 1956 uprising in Hungary, leading to widespread defections – especially by intellectuals in western European communist parties.

---

1   Geoff Eley, *Forging Democracy: The History of the Left in Europe, 1850–2000* (Oxford: Oxford University Press, 2002), Chapter 21; Tony Judt, *Postwar: A History of Europe since 1945* (New York: Penguin, 2005), Chapter 9.

This facilitated a development in which protests against the Cold War and its own self-annihilating logic became an important part of young people's radicalisation. The threat of the bomb became a starting point for worldwide protest movements. The 1962 Cuban Missile Crisis, in which the entire world feared the onset of final nuclear war, also marked the beginning of a political rapprochement between East and West – a period of détente.

The postwar youth generation certainly played a decisive role in the radicalisation of the 1960s. In 1964, there were more teenagers than ever before in the industrialised world. Working youth shared in the prosperity, and for the first time large groups of young people became economically independent. The market was not slow to take advantage of this opening. Teenage clothes, music, and magazines became big business.[2] A few years later, radicalisation began to flood the universities. The 1960s saw a significant broadening of recruitment to universities and colleges, consisting largely of students whose backgrounds and prospects looked nothing like those of previous graduates. Many lacked natural loyalties to the old upper class – and they quickly became the bearers of growing radicalisation. In Sweden, too, Algeria and the fight against apartheid became important causes. The fight against the bomb took on a special prominence, because a Swedish atomic bomb was a major domestic political issue around 1960.[3]

In 1965 the first Vietnam demonstrations took place, and the Vietnam solidarity movement United NLF Groups (De förenade FNL-grupperna), the main symbol of the new social movements of the 1960s, grew at a furious pace. But the Vietnam movement was by no means alone in attracting a responsive youth generation. The new social movements had a strong impact in Sweden.[4]

A large number of international solidarity groups emerged, working in support of liberation movements in South Africa and the Portuguese colonies, in solidarity with underground movements in Spain, Portugal, and Greece, or with guerrilla movements in Latin America. The black Civil Rights movement in the United States had received early Swedish support and, when parts of it were radicalised in the form of the Black

2 Judt, *Postwar*, Chapter 12.
3 On Sweden and 1968, see Kjell Östberg, *1968 – när allting var i rörelse* (Johanneshov: Bokförläggarna Röda Rummet, 2018); Kjell Östberg, 'Sweden and the Long "1968": Break or Continuity?', *Scandinavian Journal of History* 33, no. 4 (2008).
4 Östberg, *1968*, pp. 59–66.

Panthers and Black Power, support groups were soon formed in Sweden. The charismatic leader Stokely Carmichael made several acclaimed visits to the country, including a meeting with Olof Palme. And the list of new movements was even longer. The environmental movement got its first boost when protests against the frenzy of demolition taking place in city centres began to gain momentum.

What these new movements had in common was that they consciously sought new forms of engagement. The organisational forms of the 1960s were clearly designed for action: independent grassroots groups and propaganda teams.

A crucial reason for the rapid impact of 1960s radicalisation in Sweden was the role of intellectuals and the importance of the politicisation of culture.[5] An increasing number of leading intellectuals connected with the radical ideas of the time – not least by often actively supporting and participating in the new social movements. Most had an explicitly socialist point of view, many with party-political affiliations, ranging from the left wing of Social Democracy to Maoist groups of various shades.

Cultural workers – as writers, actors, filmmakers, and artists now liked to call themselves – developed their own structures to make it easier to get their message across. Meanwhile, several of the leading representatives of the new wave in cinema that reached Sweden in the mid 1960s were drawn into the same process of radicalisation. Vilgot Sjöman's diptych *I Am Curious (Yellow/Blue)* was a congenial and at times ingenious blend of the political and sexual-liberation currents of the time.

Although students were a central part of the 1960s radicalisation in Sweden, student struggle in the narrower sense was not a very prominent part of it. Students were more involved with Vietnam, or supporting striking workers. A spectacular highlight, however, was when students, inspired by their comrades in Paris, occupied their own union hall in protest against a university reform. The fact that the then minister of education, Olof Palme, came and spent a night speaking with the revolutionary students added to the sense of spectacle.

---

5   Ron Eyerman and Andrew Jamison, *Social Movements: A Cognitive Approach* (Cambridge: Polity Press/Blackwell, 1991), Chapter 4; Östberg, *1968*, pp. 67–76.

A New Left

Just as important for the new social movements as the new forms of action, however, was rapid political radicalisation in which the New Left played a decisive role.[6] This was also an international phenomenon. It is clear that by the mid 1960s, there was a growing influence of critical, Marxist-influenced political thought in conscious opposition both to the fossilised Marxism that characterised the Soviet Union and to the ideologically impoverished parties that Social Democracy was thought to have spawned.

Young people were now looking to thinkers who could renew Marxism. For them, it was easy to find the link between theory and practice. After all, Che and Castro, Ho Chi Minh and Mao, Ben Bella and Hugo Blanco, Angela Davis and Bernadette Devlin, Rudi Dutschke and Tariq Ali – and all the radical politicians, and student and guerrilla leaders of the time – were also Marxists of one kind or another.

In 1966, a few young Lund academics, including Göran Therborn, published the book *En ny vänster* (A new left). They were deeply influenced by the international debate, especially by the British New Left, and argued for a free and humanist socialism.[7] In Sweden, many of the New Left's supporters initially came from Social Democracy and its student unions. Their primary concern was therefore to influence their own party in a more radical direction. But interest from the party was weak, and when the representatives of the New Left formed their own organisation, they were simply expelled from their mother party. Instead, the Left Party – communists – as the Communist Party was now called, was able to capture many of them.

Credit for this went mainly to the new party leader, C. H. Hermansson, who was himself strongly influenced by the new currents. He was elected party chairman in 1964 on a programme that represented a break with the party's Stalinist past, and he managed to win over the leaders of the New Left. In his book *Vänstens väg* (The road for the left), he linked up with the international New Left, and in particular promoted the demand for democracy in the workplace. He was also

---

6   Perry Anderson, *Considerations on Western Marxism* (London: Verso, 1979).
7   Göran Therborn, ed., *En ny vänster: en debattbok* (Stockholm: Rabén & Sjögren, 1966).

influenced by discussions of structural reforms, as developed at the time by André Gorz and Ernest Mandel.[8]

Marxism also became a powerful influence in the academic world. Students and scholars formed groups like Young Philosophers, and published influential journals. Towards the end of the decade, the open and searching New Left faced competition from its more traditional and orthodox counterparts – chief among them, the Maoists. An important reason for the strength of Maoism was that it controlled the leadership of the powerful Vietnam solidarity movement.[9]

Unlike in many other countries, radicalisation did not die out in Sweden as the 1960s gave way to the 1970s, but broadened and deepened. The new women's movement had a strong impact, and built important alliances with its predecessors. In the environmental movement, radical sixty-eighters worked side by side with older generations, including those with bourgeois values, to stop nuclear power. Crucially, however, the Social Democratic movement itself, and the trade union movement in particular, also became part of the deep wave of radicalisation.

The Workers Fight Back

In the autumn of 1968, the author Sara Lidman, who together with Jan Myrdal was the main public face of the Swedish Vietnam solidarity movement, published the book *Gruva* (Mine), a series of interviews with miners from the northern ore fields.[10] It was a fierce attack on the poor working conditions, hard piecework, and hierarchical work organisation of the state-owned mining company Luossavaara-Kiirunavaara Aktiebolag (LKAB). In many ways, it was in line with the discussion about the working environment that was developing in the trade union movement at the time, and which was also expressed at the Social Democratic Party Congresses in the late 1960s. However, the book was criticised by the Social Democratic establishment, and in November 1969 the minister of finance, Gunnar Sträng, launched a strong public outburst against Sara Lidman. Her book was exaggerated and biased,

---

8   C. H. Hermansson, *Vänsterns väg: ett debattinlägg* (Stockholm: Rabén & Sjögren, 1965).

9   Kim Salomon, *Rebeller i takt med tiden: FNL-rörelsen och 60-talets politiska ritualer* (Stockholm: Rabén Prisma, 1996).

10   Sara Lidman, *Gruva* (Stockholm: Bonnier, 1968).

Sträng argued, insisting that mine workers were in fact content and upset by the book's claims. A month later, the 'great miners' strike' paralysed the iron fields, and the Swedish labour market model was shaken to its foundations.

Until December 1969, the Social Democrats and other political and industrial leaders could claim that the ongoing radicalisation was only a youth phenomenon, with some support from a group of writers and other intellectuals. But on the morning of 9 December 1969, thirty-five miners put down their tools in the small village of Svappavaara, fourteen miles north of the Arctic Circle. Soon the strike had reached the much larger mines of Kiruna and Malmberget. For fifty-seven days, 5,000 workers were on strike. The reaction was strong in the Social Democratic Party headquarters, among leaders from the LO and the Employers' Association (SAF), and in the chancellery. If the political unrest spread to the rest of the working class, the consequences would be much more far-reaching.[11]

The strike began as a wage dispute, but its demands soon broadened considerably. In eighteen points, a programme was formulated that summed up many of the issues that had been at the heart of the trade union and political struggles of recent years. The miners demanded substantial wage increases, but also the abolition of piecework pay, the same benefits as white-collar workers, a wage supplement for everyone over fifty, and a reduction in the retirement age from sixty-seven to sixty. Several demands related to the working environment. Noise, silicon dust, and toxic diesel fumes were well-known problems that workers claimed had not been addressed. The time study system was strongly criticised. Particular attention was drawn to LKAB's decision to hire an American management consultant. The consultant had presented thirty-one theses for more effective management, which were used in the company's management training.[12] It is no exaggeration to say that these theses were on a collision course with the dominant anti-hierarchical, egalitarian ideals of the time.

The strike was also directed against the workers' own union, which called on them to return to work. It was led by a directly elected strike committee, and regular strike meetings were held with several thousand

11 Kjell Östberg, *När vinden vände: Olof Palme 1969–1986* (Stockholm: Leopard, 2009), pp. 31–7.
12 *Pappren på bordet: protokoll och dokument från den stora gruvstrejken i Malmfälten 1969/70. D. 1* (Stockholm: Ordfront, 1972), pp. 22ff.

participants. It was not difficult to see how strongly all of this contrasted with the centralism and bureaucracy that characterised the Swedish trade union movement at the time.[13]

The miners' strike became a mass-media event of huge proportions. Radio and TV channels broadcast live from strike meetings and demonstrations. The miners traditionally had a reputation for radicalism, and the workers were able to express themselves well, often in heated terms. Many journalists were present, and representatives from left-wing groups, cultural workers, and radical scientists also went up to the ore fields. Around the country, left-wing groups and trade unions organised demonstrations and meetings, and large sums of money were raised. Sara Lidman was invited to speak at a strike meeting, and was received with loud cheers. Lidman also initiated a strike fund, using seed capital from the proceeds of the new paperback edition of *Gruva*. The effort to build alliances between radicalised youth and intellectuals and some of the core groups of the Swedish working class could hardly have been more clearly on display.[14]

But even more disconcerting for the trade union and political establishment was the massive public support for the illegal strike. In a poll, 80 per cent of the population said that they supported the strikers' demands, only 13 per cent rejecting the wildcat strike. Much more than a simple wage struggle, the miners' strike came to symbolise the demand of the working class for a dignified life in general. It managed, not least, to incorporate some of the central critiques of 1960s radicalisation – of capitalist predation and tendencies towards authoritarianism – while voicing a clear demand for a deepening of democracy.

The Swedish labour market model would never return to its former shape. Before the miners' strike was over, a wave of wildcat strikes broke out across the country, apparently inspired by it. In particular, the Swedish engineering industry – a national flagship – suffered widespread work stoppages. Around the country, workers at Volvo, Saab, Electrolux, and LM Ericsson went on strike. This first wave was broadly successful for the strikers, delivering substantial pay rises. After a few weeks, the SAF was forced to issue directives aimed at preventing local employers from raising wages in response to wildcat strikes.[15]

---

13 Östberg, *När vinden vände*, p. 33.
14 Ibid.
15 Christer Thörnqvist, *Arbetarna lämnar fabriken: strejkrörelser i Sverige under efterkrigstiden, deras bakgrund, förlopp och följder* (Gothenburg: HIstoriska Institutionen, 1994).

The wave of strikes proved to be the beginning of a new trend in which Sweden quickly lost its special position at the bottom of the international league table of strike activity. Another round of strikes followed in the spring of 1971. The mid-1970s saw a new peak in high-profile strikes. The biggest was the forest workers' strike, which surpassed the miners' strike in both length and the number of individual strikers. The central demand was for a monthly wage. A series of women's strikes involving cleaners and seamstresses took place in 1974–75. For most of the cleaners, the strikes were at least partially successful, but a total of thirty women were dismissed and not subsequently reinstated.[16]

There were several reasons for this long wave of strikes starting at the beginning of the decade. It was an international phenomenon driven by the economic downturn that beset the turn of the decade, of which the events of May 1968 in France, and Italy's 'Creeping May' a few years later were two other effects.[17] Behind several of the most high-profile strikes in Sweden were groups of workers traditionally characterised by political radicalism: miners in Malmfälten, dockers in Gothenburg and Ådalen, and forestry workers in Norrland.[18]

The strike wave confirmed and deepened the leftist currents. It was thus of decisive importance for the continued radicalisation of the LO and parts of Social Democracy. The strikes coincided with demands for greater equality and increased public influence over business that, as we have seen, were being pursued within the labour movement at this time. The radicalisation of the trade union movement had roots of its own, fed by the concrete problems its members were confronted with on a daily basis.[19] Arne Geijer's high-profile criticism of the labour movement's failures to abolish inequalities in working life at the Party Congress of 1967 would hardly have been developed if it had not reflected discontent from below in the trade union movement. Although one of the main arguments of this book has been that the LO, through the corporatist Saltsjöbaden Agreement, has pursued a trade union policy that has largely demobilised the unions, and above all has tried to take away their

---

16   Eva Schmitz, *Systerskap som politisk handling: kvinnors organisering i Sverige 1968 till 1982* (Lund: Media-Tryck, 2007).

17   Thörnqvist, *Arbetarna lämnar fabriken*, p. 294.

18   Ibid., pp. 104ff.

19   Lars Ekdahl, *Mot en tredje väg: en biografi över Rudolf Meidner*, vol. 1, *Tysk flykting och svensk modell* (Lund: Arkiv, 2001), pp. 232ff.

best weapon, the strike, this does not mean that the trade unions completely ceased to function as fighting class organisations. Local grievances over the working environment, influence over working conditions, redundancies, and pay progression were constant. Moreover, although they were rarely recorded in official strike statistics, short, spontaneous strikes were not uncommon in the context of local wage bargaining and, particularly in profitable companies, contributed to 'wage creep' – wage increases outside the centrally negotiated agreements.

Power over Work

Towards the end of the 1960s, the question of power in the workplace returned, after a long absence, as an important issue in the trade union movement. The 1969 Metalworkers' Congress called for action on the contested Section 32 of the contracts, 'the right of employers to manage and distribute work and freely to employ and dismiss workers' – the provision that employers had been demanding be respected in all collective agreements since 1906. But what signalled a new direction was that the trade union movement was calling for a political solution. Attempts to abolish Section 32 by negotiation with employers had come to an end after seventy-five years of trying.

The wave of wildcat strikes pushed developments further. The radicalisation within the LO was profound. Already during the miners' strike, the LO-owned daily *Aftonbladet* had written that the party had not 'sufficiently succeeded in understanding and channelling dissatisfaction with the existing society . . . Unconsidered, unthinking statements by prominent party members about the convergence of interests between employers and employees have aroused dissatisfaction and justified indignation. The party should not seek to conceal class differences. It must clarify the conflicts of interest.'[20]

The 1971 LO Congress was the most radical in several decades. The issue that dominated a record number of motions was working conditions. Demands for socialisation and workers' democracy were also discussed intensively.[21] Rudolf Meidner, who had just been commissioned

---

20   Editorial, *Aftonbladet*, 21 December 1969.
21   Anders L. Johansson and Lars Magnusson, *LO: 1900-talet och ett nytt millennium* (Stockholm: Atlas, 2019), p. 132.

by the 1971 LO Congress to conduct the inquiry that would, a few years later, result in the proposal for wage-earner funds, argued that the LO's radicalisation had to be seen as the result of both 'a growing discontent in the workplace and a wave of radicalisation in society as a whole'.[22]

The Social Democratic government showed great sensitivity to the demands of the LO. In the first half of the 1970s, a series of labour-law reforms were implemented that shifted the rules of the game in the labour market in favour of the trade unions. But, more than that, they helped to secure fundamental change to one of the historic cornerstones of the Swedish model: that labour market conditions were mainly regulated by the parties themselves.

In 1971, parliament passed a law strengthening the position of older workers in the labour market; in 1972, it was decided that employees would have board-level representation; in 1973, a revision of occupational health and safety regulations began, and was completed with the 1978 Work Environment Act, which gave workers the power to stop dangerous production; in 1974, employees were given the right to study leave without employers being able to influence what they wanted to study. At the same time, a Shop Stewards' Act was introduced, giving union representatives extensive rights to carry out union work during paid working hours.

Symbolically, the most important of the laws passed in the first round was the Employment Protection Act 1974, which repealed part of Section 32. The law did not prevent employers from dismissing employees in the event of a work shortage, but they had to follow a formula that gave those with the longest tenure the strongest employment protection. And in 1976, the Co-determination Act was passed with the aim of abolishing the traditional right of employers to manage and distribute work. According to one history of the LO, it is only a mild exaggeration to say that this series of laws represented a union triumph of unparalleled proportions.[23]

What most of the reforms had in common was that issues that had previously been dealt with mainly through agreements between unions and employers were now regulated by legislation. Since the laws also

---

22   Lars Ekdahl, *Mot en tredje väg: en biografi över Rudolf Meidner*, vol. 2, *Facklig expert och demokratisk socialist* (Lund: Arkiv, 2001), p. 233.

23   Johansson and Magnusson, *LO: 1900-talet och ett nytt millennium*, p. 165.

took away a number of employers' established rights, they were naturally seen as important successes for the trade unions.

To put it a little more bluntly, the LO and the Social Democratic government, under the pressure of extensive radicalisation of the trade union movement, in effect cancelled key parts of the Swedish labour market model. At the same time, the decisions came into direct conflict with fundamental aspects of employers' decision-making power over production.

The New Women's Movement: Group 8

Thus, as we have seen, unlike in many other countries, the radicalisation that began in the 1960s broadened and deepened in the 1970s. The new social movements continued to grow while increasingly influencing the old ones. The women's movement is perhaps the clearest example.

At least since the 1960s, Sweden had been regarded as one of the world's most gender-equal countries, and had frequently been at the top of the regular UN rankings. Historians can debate how long Sweden has held such a position, but it is clear that development during the 1960s and '70s was spectacular. This was for structural reasons, as well as being the result of the efforts of particular individuals; old and new social movements were involved in an interesting and complex interplay.

The 1950s were generally regarded as a period of backlash for Swedish women. The ideal, supported by tax legislation and the welfare system, was a gender division of labour in which men 'were responsible for the big household and women for the small'. In politics, too, men were responsible for the big household: as late as the mid-1960s, they accounted for 90 per cent of MPs.[24]

In the early 1960s, this ideal came into conflict with a strong countervailing factor: the shortage of labour. A first step in response was to recruit workers from other countries – but the government and labour market partners also began a determined effort to facilitate women's employment, not least as industrial workers. This required a change in the view of women's place in work and society. Existing gender roles

---

24 Yvonne Hirdman, 'Genussystemet: reflexioner kring kvinnors sociala underordning', *Kvinnovetenskaplig tidskrift* 3 (1988).

became subject to challenge, including the model of the male bread-winner associated with Keynesianism.[25]

The extensive debate in the 1960s on a new division of labour between men and women was mainly conducted by Liberal and Social Democratic student unions. But in 1970 Group 8 was formed, marking the arrival of the new women's liberation movement in Sweden.[26] The women who initiated Group 8 had themselves participated in the various expressions of 1960s radicalisation, and many also had links to Maoism, Trotskyism, and other left-wing groups. But they were dissatisfied with the inflexible treatment of women's issues in those quarters, and the subordination that they often reproduced.

Group 8 saw itself as a revolutionary movement with a socialist perspective. It essentially took a traditional Marxist view of the origins and causes of class society and gender oppression. The subordination of women was built into capitalism. Group 8 made a rapid breakthrough in public opinion and membership; the influx soon outstripped the organisation's capacity to absorb it. The movement's spectacular activities also attracted considerable media attention.

The Group 8 action programme focused on concrete demands related to work, study, children, and sexuality, with the issue of women's situation in the labour market at its centre. The right to work was the foundation that would give women economic independence, and thus the possibility of political and social equality. Group 8, like much of the rest of the left, placed great emphasis on getting its message out to the workers, some of whom took jobs in typically female industrial workplaces.[27]

But a truly novel dynamic emerged when the new women's movement built alliances with its predecessors. The traditional women's associations, especially those linked to the political parties, were also radicalised. The influence of the new wave of feminists was significant. On a range of important issues, such as the expansion of day care centres and legislation against sexual abuse, the breadth of women's

---

25 Christina Florin and Bengt Nilsson, "'Something in the Nature of a Bloodless Revolution': How New Gender Relations Became Gender Equality Policy in Sweden in the Nineteen-Sixties and Seventies', in Rolf Torstendahl, ed., *State Policy and Gender System in the Two German States and Sweden 1945–1989* (Uppsala: Historiska institutionen, Uppsala University, 1999).

26 Schmitz, *Systerskap som politisk handling*.

27 Ibid., pp. 133ff.

mobilisation was stunning. Women belonging to revolutionary women's groups such as Group 8 and Lesbian Front could be seen demonstrating and holding opinion meetings together with women from the House-wives' League and the Conservative Women's League. As we have seen, the Swedish women's movement already had a long tradition of success-ful cooperation across class and social boundaries, ever since the suffrage struggle at the beginning of the century.[28]

The 1970s are probably the most important decade ever in relation to women's policy and gender-equality reforms. In a short time, reforms included seven months of paid parental leave, new marriage laws strengthening the position of women, improved support for single parents with children (mainly women), free abortion, and the decision to give all children the right to day care. The position of women was also strengthened through an increase in their representation in political decision-making bodies.

Growth, the Environment, and Nuclear Power

During the 1960s, the broad topic of the environment emerged as an important social issue and quickly gathered political salience: environ-mental pollutants, working conditions, and the consequences of urbanisation – housing shortages and traffic problems – were all hotly contested.[29] Around 1970, the environmental debate entered a new phase. A new independent environmental movement emerged in a variety of incarnations. In the big cities, for example, action groups were set up to prevent the demolition of old buildings and the spread of car driving.

Environmental action groups were by no means just a metropolitan phenomenon. Protests against the curbing of waterfalls for hydroelectric power plants, and against forest pollution, were among the more high-profile actions. In 1976 there were nearly a thousand local action groups across the country, an estimated two-thirds of them having environmental issues on their agenda. The aim of virtually all of these

---

28 Emma Isaksson, *Kvinnokamp: synen på underordning och motstånd i den nya kvinnorörelsen* (Stockholm: Atlas, 2007); Östberg, *1968*, pp. 93–6.

29 Andrew Jamison, Ron Eyerman, and Jacqueline Cramer, *The Making of the New Environmental Consciousness: A Comparative Study of the Environmental Movements in Sweden, Denmark and the Netherlands* (Edinburgh: Edinburgh University Press, 1990).

groups was to influence political, usually municipal, decisions through a combination of parliamentary and non-parliamentary action.

An important feature of the environmental groups of the 1970s was that they managed to attract a much broader range of activists, socially and in terms of age, than the social movements of the 1960s.[30] In many groups, there was a pronounced scepticism towards contemporary forms of civilisation, which focused on the downsides of rapid economic growth.

But this criticism had much broader support among both radical social commentators and the general population.[31] These ideas came to challenge one of the mainstays of Social Democracy: faith in growth. The Social Democrats were critical of radical environmental movements, whose ideas were alien to the party's basic social vision.

Olof Palme was not insensitive to the discussion of the downsides of growth. He carefully read the Club of Rome's well-received *Limits to Growth*, which warned against unbridled growth and emphasised the relationship between growth and climate. He also initiated the first major UN conference on environmental protection, held in Stockholm in 1972. When asked by a journalist in 1974 which threat worried him most, he did not identify the atomic bomb or world hunger – the issues he usually raised in his major speeches. With surprising prescience, he said instead, 'The risk of climate change as a result of human activity.'[32]

But a few years later, with Swedish industrial production hitting rock bottom, it was equally obvious to him that the solution was, after all, industrial development. Society should improve, but this could only be achieved through growth in production. When a journalist reminded Palme in an interview of his earlier criticism of the 'idiocy of the gadget society' and pointed out that he now seemed to be saying the exact opposite, Palme responded with a strikingly forceful outburst against those who did not acknowledge the importance of growth.[33] Palme never abandoned his bedrock conviction that growth – and a Social Democratic government – could solve the fundamental problems of society.

---

30   Ulf Stahre, *Den alternativa staden: Stockholms stadsomvandling och byalagsrörelsen* (Stockholm: Stockholmia, 1999); Janerik Gidlund, *Aktionsgrupper och lokala partier: temporära politiska organisationer i Sverige 1965–1975* (Lund: LiberLäromedel, 1978).

31   Carl Holmberg, *Längtan till landet: civilisationskritik och framtidsvisioner i 1970-talets regionalpolitiska debatt* (Gothenburg: Historiska Institutionen, 1998).

32   Östberg, *När vinden vände*, p. 246 – see also pp. 228–30.

33   Ibid., p. 230.

And growth required energy. In the 1950s and '60s, hydroelectric power was being developed in northern Sweden, and cheap oil could be imported from seemingly inexhaustible and constantly emerging sources. But this situation changed drastically around 1970. Only a few large, untamed waterfalls remained in Sweden, and environmentalists demanded that these be protected from further development. For a long time, the government took the line that employment – for those who built the power plants and in industry – should be given priority. But a broad alliance of environmentalists, intellectuals, and media personalities mobilised in support of environmental interests, and in the Riksdag the bourgeois and radical socialist currents were united in their opposition. In the end, the government withdrew its proposal for further expansion. The environmental movement had become a formidable political force.

The 1973 oil crisis accentuated the problem of Sweden's heavy dependence on oil. The sharp rise in prices, combined with criticism of the environmental problems associated with oil use, prompted a debate on alternative energy sources. For the Social Democrats, the solution was a major expansion of nuclear power. Little did they know that the battle over nuclear power would become the most important political issue of the 1970s, leading to the party's first loss of government in forty-four years.[34]

A crucial event was when respected physicist and Nobel laureate Hannes Alfvén appealed to the government to reconsider its commitment to nuclear power. His criticism was quickly taken up by the non-parliamentary environmental movement, which formed the People's Campaign against Nuclear Power. But nuclear power became a truly incendiary issue only when the main opposition party, the Centre Party, committed fully to opposing it.

What gave the party's position added weight was that it had been pushed by the party leader, Thorbjörn Fälldin, himself. The latter described nuclear power as a fateful risk, and declared that he could not imagine participating in a government that built more nuclear power plants.

Over the next few years, the nuclear debate raged on. Supporters of nuclear power in industry and technology argued that critics were

---

34   Jonas Anshelm, *Socialdemokraterna och miljöfrågan: en studie av framstegstankens paradoxer* (Stockholm: Symposion, 1995).

greatly exaggerating its risks. In the labour movement, the benefits of the employment the industry provided were repeatedly stressed. A majority in parliament advocated the construction of dozens of reactors.[35] Meanwhile, the People's Campaign against Nuclear Power became by far the largest social movement of the mid-1970s. It brought together the broad spectrum of movements that had formed the backbone of the radicalisation of the 1960s and '70s, but also the Swedish Christian Democrats and, as we have seen, the largest bourgeois party, the Centre Party. The movement carried out a series of high-profile demonstrations, and gathered its members together in impressive study activities. Criticism of growth dominated the discussion in these circles. 'Sun, wind and water' became the movement's main slogan.[36]

Although the leaderships of both the Social Democratic Party and the LO were warm supporters of nuclear power, the party membership was divided. Again, it was within the Women's League that opposition was strongest. Many leading women, among them Alva Myrdal, took part in the campaign against nuclear power. When the party gathered its members for local consultations, only 16 per cent were explicitly in favour of the continued expansion of nuclear power. A larger proportion were against, while most members had not made up their mind.

The issue of nuclear power came to dominate the 1976 election campaign.[37] In high-profile debates, the two main candidates for prime minister, Olof Palme and Thorbjörn Fälldin of the Centre Party, clashed repeatedly. It is clear that Fälldin's principled opposition made a greater impression on the audience than Palme's pro-nuclear stance.

The Social Democrats lost the elections, and thus the government, after forty-four years of rule. Paradoxically, a number of voters with roots in radical movements, and often with explicit left-wing sympathies, voted for the Centre Party to stop nuclear power – thereby contributing to the emergence of a bourgeois government. At the same time, the Social Democrats' unquestioning belief in growth, which had been the party's central credo for half a century, was a key reason for its historic electoral loss.

---

35   Östberg, *När vinden vände*, p. 224.

36   Abby Peterson, Håkan Thörn, and Mattias Wahlström, 'Sweden 1950–2015: Contentious Politics and Social Movements between Confrontation and Political Cooperation', in Flemming Mikkelsen, Knut Kjeldstadli, and Stefan Nyzell, eds, *Popular Struggle and Democracy in Scandinavia: 1700–Present* (London: Palgrave Macmillan, 2018).

37   Östberg, *När vinden vände*, pp. 186–91.

International Solidarity

In the 1970s, Sweden was not only known for its advanced welfare state. It also sought to take its place in international politics by pursuing a more active foreign policy. A frequent criticism from the right was that Sweden wanted to present itself as a 'moral superpower'. These ambitions were closely linked to Olof Palme's first term as prime minister, in 1969–76.[38]

As a young minister of education, Palme had already attracted international attention by publicly criticising the United States, and the Vietnam War in particular. At the time, it was extraordinarily unusual for a leading politician in a Western country to attack the United States and its foreign policy in such forceful terms. To claim, as Palme did, that South Vietnam's National Liberation Front (FNL) represented democracy in Vietnam more than the United States was extremely controversial. The radio address Palme gave after the United States carried out the terror bombing of Hanoi at Christmas 1972 deserves to be reproduced in full:

> We should call things by their proper names. What is going on in Vietnam today is a form of torture. There cannot be any military justification for the bombings. Military spokesmen in Saigon have denied that there is any evidence of North Vietnamese escalation.
>
> Nor can the bombings be a response to Vietnamese obstinacy at the negotiating table. The resistance to the October agreement in Paris comes – as the *New York Times* has pointed out – mainly from President Thieu in Saigon. People are being punished, a nation is being punished in order to humiliate it, to force it to submit to force.
>
> That is why the bombings are despicable. Many such atrocities have been perpetrated in recent history. They are often associated with a name: Guernica, Oradour, Babi Yar, Katyn, Lidice, Sharpeville, Treblinka. Violence has triumphed. But posterity has condemned the perpetrators. Now a new name will be added to the list: Hanoi, Christmas 1972.[39]

---

38 For this section, see ibid., pp. 102–47.
39 Kjell Östberg, *I takt med tiden: Olof Palme 1927–1969* (Stockholm: Leopard, 2008), p. 304.

Not surprisingly, Palme's address aroused great wrath in Washington. 'That Swedish asshole' was said to have been President Nixon's classy description of the Swedish prime minister. For several years, there was no American ambassador in Stockholm.

At the same time, Palme's irreverent statements aroused the interest and approval of many Third World leaders. Sweden was a non-aligned country, albeit with close ties to NATO. This meant that it could sometimes openly criticise the great powers, not least the United States. At the same time, it consciously sought to act as a bridge-builder between the non-aligned states of the North and South. In this endeavour, Sweden and Palme benefited from the decreasing tension between the great powers. The 1960s and '70s were characterised by détente in the Cold War. It was a period when the major powers had extensive problems in their own spheres of interest – the United States in Indochina, the Soviet Union in eastern Europe and its relations with China – and they both had every reason to try to maintain the status quo in the international balance of power. Growing economic problems for both powers increased their interest in limiting the arms race, including through the first round of Strategic Arms Limitation Talks in 1972. The German question was temporarily resolved, not least through the efforts of German Social Democratic prime minister Willy Brandt, but also by de facto recognition of its existing borders. Détente reached something of a climax with the European Security Conference in Helsinki in 1975.[40] This temporary pause in the Cold War, and the relative weakening of the great powers, gave Olof Palme greater room for manoeuvre.

The UN helped to fulfil Palme's – and Sweden's – ambitions to play a role on the world stage.[41] Between 1960 and 1980, the UN added fifty-five new members – most of them from the Third World, and many with left-leaning governments. Palme made some of his most important international speeches under the auspices of the UN: at the Stockholm Environment Conference in 1972; at the General Assembly sessions on the New World Economic Order in 1974; at the Women's Conference in Mexico in 1975; and at the Conference on Apartheid in 1977. These speeches were often delivered before an audience including Third World

40   Judt, *Postwar*, pp. 496–500.
41   Alf W. Johansson and Torbjörn Norman, 'Sweden's Security and World Peace', in Klaus Misgeld, Karl Molin, and Klas Åmark, eds, *Creating Social Democracy: A Century of the Social Democratic Labor Party in Sweden* (University Park: Pennsylvania State University Press, 1992), pp. 366ff.

leaders, in gatherings that often featured Palme as the only statesman from the First World. His eloquent and pointed language when expressing his solidarity with the African and Asian delegates naturally contributed greatly to the image of Olof Palme as a radical politician, ever ready to take the side of poor countries.[42]

Sweden's and Palme's contribution to discussions on a new world economic order attracted particular attention. The background was a growing dissatisfaction with the fact that the gaps between the rich and poor countries of the world were tending to widen. The 1973–74 oil crisis highlighted how the rich world had systematically exploited the disposal of cheap raw materials from the Third World. In the spring of 1974, the non-aligned states called for the UN General Assembly to be convened to discuss the need for a new, fairer international economic system. At the sixth special session of the UN in April 1974, resolutions and programmes of action were adopted with the aim of changing the balance of economic power between rich and poor countries. Sweden was one of the few Western countries to vote consistently in favour of the resolutions, and Palme was once again under the international spotlight.

This period reached its peak in 1975–76. It coincided with Sweden's tenure of one of the fifteen seats on the UN Security Council. On many controversial issues, Sweden voted with the non-aligned countries of the Third World, and the Swedish vote was often decisive for the outcome. This was the case for several votes on Israel–Palestine, such as the vote on the right of the Palestine Liberation Organization to participate in Security Council debates on the Middle East, and a series of decisions on boycott actions against South Africa. To the explicit displeasure of the United States, Sweden repeatedly broke 'the Western Front'.

Sweden's position on South Africa was particularly important, and reflected the deep commitment that Sweden had demonstrated since the 1950s to the fight against apartheid.[43] In 1969, Sweden was the first Western country to provide aid directly to a number of African liberation movements: FRELIMO in Mozambique, the MPLA in Angola, SWAPO in Namibia, ZANU and ZAPU in Zimbabwe, and the PAIGC in

---

42   Östberg, *När vinden vände*, p. 111.
43   Tor Sellström, *Sweden and National Liberation in Southern Africa*, vol. 1, *Formation of a Popular Opinion (1950–1970)* (Uppsala: Nordic Africa Institute, 1999); Tor Sellström, *Sweden and National Liberation in Southern Africa*, vol. 2, *Solidarity and Assistance (1970–1994)* (Uppsala: Nordic Africa Institute, 2002).

Guinea-Bissau. This decision was highly controversial. Three of the movements were active in the colonies of Portugal – a country with which Sweden had diplomatic relations and had cooperated closely in the European Free Trade Association.[44] Although the sums involved were relatively small and it was explicitly stated that the aid could not be used for military purposes, the decision attracted considerable international attention.

During this time, Sweden's policy towards Israel and Palestine also changed. From an early date, Swedish Social Democracy, like most Social Democratic movements, had had a pronounced pro-Israel policy, and close contacts with the Israeli Labour Party. Sweden now openly criticised Israel's occupation policy, and took an unequivocal stand in favour of an independent Palestinian state in the occupied territories. Palme also met Yasser Arafat on several occasions, which was highly controversial in the 1970s.[45]

In 1975, Palme made a very successful visit to Cuba.[46] The highlight of the trip was the speeches that Castro and Palme made at the military barracks in Moncada, the cradle of the Cuban Revolution, to an audience of 100,000. Palme's speech largely consisted of a tribute to the Cuban Revolution:

> Yesterday, Moncada was a bastion of oppression. Here they tortured. Here human dignity was trampled. It was a place of murder . . . Today, Moncada has a school. Here children learn to read and write. Here the foundations of the future are laid. That's why Moncada today is also a symbol of Cuba's peaceful progress . . .
>
> The demands of the people cannot be suppressed. Neither terror nor incessant oppression can defeat demands for freedom, social justice, and national independence. That was the case in Cuba yesterday. So it is in Vietnam and Portugal today. It will be the same in Chile tomorrow.

At a subsequent press conference, Palme strongly criticised the US blockade against Cuba. He also pointed out that the democratic process in Cuba had made significant progress, and highlighted local people's

---

44   Ann-Marie Ekengren, *Olof Palme och utrikespolitiken: Europa och tredje världen* (Umeå: Boréa, 2005), pp. 204ff.

45   Östberg, *När vinden vände*, pp. 121–6.

46   Ibid.

representative bodies. A joint communiqué stressed that 'relations between the two countries have developed very favourably and are characterised by great sympathy and mutual understanding'. Palme underlined that, for Sweden, cooperation with Cuba was an example of how aid became meaningful when the recipient country made conscious efforts towards development for the benefit of the vast majority of the population.[47]

Although Palme was often outspoken in his support for radical movements, his efforts should be seen above all as those of a bridge-builder. There is no reason to question the sincerity of Palme's support for the colonial liberation struggle, or for the radical regimes that came to power after independence. But an important reason for his dialogue with Third World leaders was to persuade them to maintain their non-alignment and not be drawn closer to the Eastern Bloc.

In Swedish domestic politics, Palme was often portrayed by his political opponents on the right as an accomplice of communism. Nothing could have been further from the truth. Palme began his political career as a kind of intellectual soldier in the Cold War when he led the building of an international anti-communist student movement, and he maintained his anti-communism for life. Likewise, he retained his fundamental pro-Western values. An important motivation for his criticism of the Vietnam War was that he believed the United States had betrayed its original liberal and anticolonial values. He also supported Sweden's secret close cooperation with NATO. 'For God's sake, make sure that our military cooperation with the Americans continues now that I'm messing with their government', he told the Swedish defence leadership in the middle of the Vietnam War.[48]

At the same time, Palme, together with West German prime minister Willy Brandt and Austria's Bruno Kreisky, was part of the triumvirate that took over the leadership of the Socialist International in the mid-1970s. The Socialist International had long been a largely insignificant gentleman's club – with fewer resources than a German district association, as Willy Brandt liked to say. It was also a product of the Cold War, and reflected a time when the labour movement was divided into communist and pro-Western organisations.

---

47   Ibid., pp. 126–30.
48   Östberg, *I takt med tiden*, p. 311; state public investigation SOU 2002:108, pp. 108, 271ff, 286, 289, 325, 692.

The exceedingly proactive Brandt, Kreisky, and Palme decided to give the Socialist International a thorough shake-up, and they divided up the work among themselves: Brandt took charge of its Latin American operations; Kreisky broke with its traditionally pro-Israeli line and established important contacts in the Arab world; and Palme turned to Africa, and southern Africa in particular. Without doubt, Social Democracy managed over the coming decade to assert its international role in a way that it had never been able to before – or since.

Its first main test was Portugal.[49] In 1974, revolution erupted in Portugal – between Europe and the Third World.[50] Power was placed in the hands of the Armed Forces Movement (MFA), which declared its intention to implement a process of democratisation and find a solution to the colonial question. Among the younger generation of officers that had planned and executed the coup were a great many who wished to see a much more radical social revolution.

The revolt garnered immediate and strong public support. Thousands of workers' committees were formed around the country, and in rural areas – especially in the south – there were widespread land occupations. The MFA's mission to lead Portugal's transition to socialism was formally established, and an extensive programme of nationalisation of banks and industry was launched. These events were a great source of international unease among Western governments, whose principal response was to bring Portugal into the western European fold and keep it in NATO.

Olof Palme and the Swedish Social Democrats were also part of this international effort.[51] In the autumn of 1974, Palme became the first foreign premier to visit the country after the revolution, and he was warmly received. Palme was clearly an interesting discussion partner for the radical officers. At the same time, he gave his unconditional support to the efforts of the Socialist Party to institutionalise democracy and tie Portugal closer to the West. He and Willy Brandt were the most talked-about speakers at the Socialist Party's election meetings, and their contributions were considered fundamental to the successes of the socialists. The result of the elections in April 1975 was a great victory for the Socialist Party. It was obvious that the European Social Democrats

---

49   Ibid., p. 115.
50   Raquel Varela, *A People's History of the Portuguese Revolution* (London: Pluto, 2019).
51   Östberg, *När vinden vände*, pp. 131–9.

had helped by steering the Portuguese revolution onto less radical tracks. Portugal kept its close relations with both the West in general and NATO in particular.

When Palme met Henry Kissinger in person for the first time a few weeks later, in Helsinki in the summer of 1975, it was Portugal that dominated their exchange. The conversation between the old sparring partners reflected a deep mutual respect. Kissinger was clearly interested in burying the hatchet, and began by saying how nice it was for them finally to meet: 'We have been fencing for so long . . . Since we are out of Indochina, what should we quarrel about? Actually, I think our relations have been improving.' He then cut straight to the point: 'What is your view about Portugal?'[52]

Palme talked about the Swedish Social Democrats' tactic of supporting the Socialist Party but maintaining good relations for the time being with the sitting MFA government. 'Our analysis is not very different from yours', Kissinger replied. 'We believe it is also important to keep contact with the moderate elements in the military group . . . My feeling is there is a possibility of the right-wing coup.'

'You know more', said Palme, who had urged caution about the danger of a new Chile, and was well aware of the freely flowing rumours of a CIA-backed intervention in Portugal too. Kissinger's laconic 'We don't know' seems hardly to have convinced him.

Palme received the closest thing to confirmation that his actions were appreciated when, in the spring of 1976, Kissinger spent a few days in Stockholm to meet with him. The old conflicts over Vietnam were a thing of the past, and Kissinger expressed his satisfaction with Sweden's international actions.[53] 'Of course, we have had differences of opinion earlier', said Kissinger, 'and no doubt will continue to do so in the future. But we are mature enough to get over our differences.'

Palme and Kissinger then went systematically through a number of important hotspots of international conflict. They dwelled on the situation in southern Africa, while Palme tried to persuade the United States to increase its commitment to Angola and Mozambique without necessarily accepting governments led by the MPLA or FRELIMO. Kissinger asked Palme to keep him informed of power developments in Angola.

52　White House Memorandum of conversation, 30 July 1975, *Arkiv* 86–87 (2002), pp. 35–43.

53　Östberg, *När vinden vände*, pp. 138ff.

It was clear that Palme's role had changed, now in US eyes as well, from one of troublesome Vietnam critic to that of an important go-between keeping lines of communication open between the Western powers and the Third World. Nonetheless, this does not mean that Palme's role can be reduced to that of a henchman for the West. The significance of a leading politician from the First World siding with, and giving voice to, radical regimes from the Third World on crucial issues was considerable.

Completing the Welfare State

Ruling for forty years had given the Social Democrats unique know-ledge and skills. The leading figures in the government had long experience of rule. Tage Erlander had been prime minister for twenty-three years; Gunnar Sträng had been in government for thirty-one years, and had been minister of finance for twenty-one years when he resigned in 1976. At the local level, it was easy to find leading municipal politicians who had held office for the same length of time.

The gradual strengthening of the Social Democrats' grip on the state bureaucracy also opened up the possibility of reforming parts of it. Moreover, it provided space for improvisation. The institutionalisation of gender politics is a good example.[54] During the 1970s, an impressive number of reforms were presented in the field of gender equality. There were some concerns among women inside the party that the reforms would be delayed or blocked by hesitant men. They encour-aged Olof Palme to form a new Council on Equality between Men and Women, connected directly to his own chancellery. The council had the power to promote political proposals and bills in many different fields. It cooperated with other parts of government, with governmen-tal boards, with parliament, and with all of corporatist Sweden: the trade unions and employers' associations, popular movements, and – of course – feminist organisations.[55] It is of course difficult to measure the concrete impact of the work of the Council. Anyway, the women who ran its daily work constituted the first generation of Swedish femocrats.

---

54   Ibid., pp. 214ff.
55   Florin and Nilsson, '"Something in the Nature of a Bloodless Revolution"'.

The combination of the long boom, the strong Social Democratic state, and the powerful radicalisation of the time created a political climate with few precedents in modern Swedish history. It fundamentally transformed prevailing values in areas such as culture, gender equality, and sexuality. But perhaps the most visible results were in terms of social and political change.[56] The reforms carried out during this time were the most comprehensive ever undertaken in Sweden – or, perhaps, anywhere. Most of the characteristics that we associate with the Swedish welfare society were implemented or reformed during a few intense years in the early and mid-1970s. The share of the public sector in GDP increased from 26 to 38 per cent during the 1970s. To this should be added all the reforms of the labour market that were agreed during a few hectic years.

The way in which the welfare state was organised was of utmost importance. The move away from market dependency towards an increasingly decommodified system was striking.[57] Everything from schools and preschools to elderly care was publicly funded, owned, and operated. Municipalities were the country's largest house-builders and landlords, and infrastructure such as telecommunications and railways was, of course, state-owned. A rapidly growing welfare bureaucracy with a strong ideological drive formed the backbone of the institutional structure. The public sector became the spearhead of social transformation. Would it also become the lever in a process that would replace capitalism with a socialist system?

The reforms that had already been carried out were of such magnitude that many, both inside and outside the country, asked how far Social Democracy was prepared to go.[58] The Swedish health care system had been fundamentally reformed. All citizens had access to health centres run by the county councils. Each visit would cost SEK 7 (about US$1). Hospital care was free. In order to strengthen a unified public health service, pharmacies were nationalised – one of the few proactive nationalisations carried out by the Social Democratic government. The

---

56   Kjell Östberg and Jenny Andersson, *Sveriges historia. 1965–2012* (Stockholm: Norstedt, 2013), pp. 214ff

57   Gøsta Esping-Andersen, 'The Making of a Social Democratic Welfare State', in Misgeld, Molin, and Åmark, *Creating Social Democracy*.

58   Sven E. O. Hort, *Social Policy, Welfare State, and Civil Society in Sweden*, vol. 1, *History, Policies, and Institutions 1884–1988* (Lund: Arkiv, 2014); Östberg and Andersson, *Sveriges historia*, pp. 218–20.

state also took over a significant part of the Swedish pharmaceutical industry, with the aim of achieving a health service free from private profit.

The universal health insurance guaranteed sick pay in the amount of 90 per cent of a person's salary from the first day of illness. Unemployment insurance levels were raised along the same lines. At the same time, working hours were gradually reduced. In 1971, the forty-hour week was passed into law. In 1976, the retirement age was reduced from sixty-seven to sixty-five, and in 1977 a five-week paid holiday was introduced.

A significant part of the reforms implemented had a clear gender dimension. The most important were parental insurance and the expansion of day care centres. The 1974 decision on parental insurance gave parents the right to stay at home for six months, with compensation based on health insurance. This insurance was quickly extended in several stages; it now stands at sixteen months, for thirteen of which full compensation is payable. From the outset, most of the leave could be taken by either the mother or the father.

In 1974, municipalities were also obliged to plan for full-time childcare for all children, while the state undertook to contribute substantial subsidies. The fees were income-related; for low-income families, they were almost symbolic, but high-income families also paid only a moderate fee. The reform attached great importance to the quality of the day care centres, and paid close attention to the educational and developmental importance of the activities it provided. It also laid down clear recommendations on staffing levels in each centre.

Support for families with children was expanded to include a means-tested housing allowance, designed so that middle-income families with high rents and/or many children could also benefit. During the 1970s, the child allowance was increased several times. Many important reforms were also carried out in the area of sexuality and family life. Free abortion was implemented from 1975. A new marriage law made divorce easier, while tax reform made it easier for women to earn a living. By the end of the decade, men and women were working at almost the same rate.

Nine years of primary schooling had been made compulsory in the 1960s. Upper secondary education was now greatly expanded, covering between 80 and 90 per cent of young people up to the age of nineteen. Teaching, learning materials, and school lunches were free of charge, and child allowances were paid through all years of schooling. Schools were run by municipalities, with only a few private schools remaining. The result was an internationally unique uniform school system. Colleges and universities expanded rapidly. All students were entitled to state subsidies, including loans with long repayment periods and low interest rates. Social exclusion from higher education was greatly reduced.

At the same time, the education explosion created educational gaps between generations. Substantial resources were therefore invested in adult education, providing entitlement to student grants. Employers were also obliged to give employees time off work to study. All tuition was free of charge.[59]

The ambition to suppress the market was perhaps particularly noticeable in housing policy – long one of the spearheads of Social Democratic welfare policy.[60] Housing construction became one of the sectors most heavily regulated by public planning; extensive housing construction was delayed. Long-standing economic prosperity meant that construction had to take a back seat to other investments in order not to drive up inflation. The high influx of people to the big cities and the large numbers of children who now wanted to leave home made the housing shortage one of the most hotly debated issues of the time – contributing, as we have seen, to the defeat of the Social Democrats in the 1966 municipal elections.

All of this represented a new start. A government inquiry proposed the building of a million new apartments over the next ten years, and the 'Million Programme' became one of the most high-profile projects in Swedish welfare policy. Financing could now be provided mainly through loans from the rapidly growing ATP pension funds. Construction would be facilitated by a far-reaching rationalisation of production. Meanwhile, the role of municipalities was further strengthened. They were given greater responsibility for public land policy, and municipal housing companies became by far the dominant developers.

As non-profit municipal construction companies enjoyed more favourable lending conditions, the scope for profit in this part of the housing market was limited. Rents were to be set following negotiations between landlords and the tenants' association, and were to be aligned with rents of non-profit municipal housing companies.

---

59 Östberg and Andersson, *Sveriges historia*, pp. 287–9.
60 Thord Strömberg, 'The Politicization of the Housing Market: The Social Democrats and the Housing Question', in Misgeld, Molin, and Åmark, *Creating Social Democracy*.

In 1974, parliament adopted guidelines governing state support for culture.[61] They largely repeated the ideas about democratic culture dating from the 1960s, and this was no accident. The proposal had been drawn up by a committee appointed by Olof Palme, and consisting largely of the leading radical writers and artists of the time. A central objective of state cultural policy would be to counteract the negative effects of commercialism. The aim was to provide opportunities for creative activity that should be designed with the needs of 'disadvantaged groups' in mind. Above all, the 1974 decision meant that politics at various levels – not least local and regional – assumed overall responsibility for bringing cultural activities to citizens. Financial support also increased significantly. As a result, radical troubadours and theatre groups with subversive ambitions were, for a time, able to spread their messages with the help of subsidies from the state they wanted to overthrow.

All these reforms, of course, had to be paid for. When economic growth started slowing, an active fiscal policy was therefore required. Well into the 1960s, Sweden was not a particularly high-tax country. However, the introduction of a sales tax – converted into Value Added Tax in 1968 – provided the minister of finance, Gunnar Sträng, with an important tool for financing the expansion of the welfare state. Rising real wages and progressive income tax scales also tightened the tax burden for many wage-earners.

The Social Democrats, as we have seen, had a fundamentally statist perspective early on, without advocating nationalisations. The state became an instrument of social and political reform, and from the 1930s onwards the building of the welfare state was the party's central task. This perspective was shared by the social movements of the 1960s and '70s: Their demands for reform were mainly addressed to the state – and state expansion and increased state intervention were in many cases unproblematic, as long as they were in the service of strengthening the welfare state, implementing social reforms, pursuing economic and gender-equality policies, or legislating for enhancing the rights and power of labour.[62]

More evidence of the impact of the statist perspective, and of the breadth of social radicalisation, is that the vast majority of decisions on

---

61   Carl-Johan Kleberg, *Expenditure on Culture in Sweden: Memorandum Prepared within the Secretariat of the Swedish National Council for Cultural Affairs* (Stockholm: Statens kulturråd, 1973).

62   Östberg, *1968*, pp. 119ff.

the expansion of the public sector were taken with a high degree of political consensus, including the support of the bourgeois parties.[63] The Conservatives, now called the Moderates, might occasionally think the pace of reform was too fast and advocate private alternatives; but the party's support for the welfare system as it was designed at the time was total, according to Hans Zetterberg, a political scientist specialising in conservative politics. Instead, criticism could be heard from the liberals that the refurbishment of the welfare sector was not going fast enough.[64]

Strong support for the welfare sector is also confirmed by the fact that when a bourgeois government took office in 1976, there was no immediate end to social reforms. The bourgeois government initially pursued much the same Keynesian policy as its predecessors, and during its term the bourgeois tripartite coalition nationalised significant parts of the Swedish shipbuilding and steel industries. Only around 1980 did it become possible to see the first signs of social cutbacks.

Building Socialism?

But what was the potential of the reforms that were implemented? And what was the pressure to move forward? The French political scientist Maurice Duverger saw a society where the forces of capitalism were already partly offset by those of socialism.[65] Was Sweden, at last, on the road to socialism?

The dramatic events of 1968, centred on Paris, provided the New Left with new theoretical ammunition. Out of the factory and student occupations emerged new forms of action that tore down authoritarian structures, built strike committees, and revived ideas of workers' self-management.[66] In Sweden, too, socialism became an obvious point

63 Emil Uddhammar, *Partierna och den stora staten: en analys av statsteorier och svensk politik under 1900-talet* (Stockholm: City University Press, 1993); Emil Uddhammar, 'Conflict, Consensus and the Influence of Political Parties: The Swedish Case 1900–1999, with a Reference to the United Kingdom', working paper, City University of Stockholm, 2000.

64 Carl Tham, *Jämlikheten som försvann: socialdemokratin efter Erlander: en debattskrift* (Stockholm: Folk och samhälle, 1973).-

65 Maurice Duverger, interview, *Il Giorno*, 16 May 1970; Östberg, *När vinden vände*, p. 139.

66 Tariq Ali, *Street-Fighting Years: An Autobiography of the Sixties* (London: Verso, 2018 [2005]).

of reference for the new movements. Many, including Social Democrats, actively supported the socialist struggle in the Third World, from Cuba to Vietnam. Group 8 declared in its programme statement that it was a socialist organisation whose aim was to work for the abolition of women's oppression and the overthrow of capitalism, while Maoist and Trotskyist groups promoted their socialist alternatives energetically.[67] But, even for Social Democrats, socialism suddenly became something more than only a word to adorn triumphant speeches, or the symbolic demand for the nationalisation of banks and insurance companies that had routinely been rejected by Party Congresses since the 1930s.

In the 1970s a lively discussion also arose within Social Democracy about a socialism built from below. Members of the party's Youth League had often belonged to Social Democracy's right wing. But in the early 1970s the Youth League adopted a radical programme for transition to a socialist economy, presenting a number of concrete proposals on how to implement economic democracy. Nationalisation was not the main way forward; on the contrary, a counterweight to central government was needed. Employees should have a say in all the important decisions taken by companies – in relation to the direction of production, the organisation of work, the working environment, and profits. Power and ownership should be transferred from private capital to elected bodies, trade unions, and cooperatives.[68]

The Social Democratic Women's League demanded that all housing production be placed under democratic control, that property ownership be socialised, and that all new construction take place on socially owned land. Housing should not be used for speculative purposes: increases in value must be passed on to society. Housing policy would be a bridge to another, socialist society.[69] Women's campaigns for gender equality also took on a clear socialist perspective. Full equality and security for children were only possible if economic power relations were changed. People's entire existence depended on the conditions established in productive life.

---

67   Östberg, *1968*, pp. 76ff, 101ff.
68   Sveriges socialdemokratiska ungdomsförbund, *Program för socialistisk ekonomi* (Johanneshov: Frihet, 1973).
69   *Kvarteret Framtiden: bostadspolitiskt program* (Stockholm: Sveriges socialdemokratiska kvinnoförbund, 1978).

The Christian Social Democrats were the most committed environ
mentalists in the party. To save the environment, they demanded an
ecological socialism that could crush capitalism.[70]

The party was also influenced by the newly awakened socialist ideas.
A new party programme was presented for the 1975 Party Congress.
More than 500 motions had been submitted, most of them seeking to
tighten up the programme in a more radical, often socialist direction.
They contained frequent demands for state ownership of 'natural
resources, credit institutions and enterprises to such an extent that the
decisive power over them is placed under the control of the citizens', or
that 'the present mixed economy is replaced by a socialist economy in
which economic democracy is included as a means of control'.[71]

In particular, criticism was directed at the gap that existed between
the party programme and the party's practical policies. A party that
wanted fundamentally to transform the current society could not be
content with a vague account of what it should not look like – it also had
to be able to show how it intended to achieve its goal, many insisted. The
road to a socialist society had to be concrete – and to begin immediately.
Progress in this direction had already begun, insisted the party board:
'The measures and instruments previously presented by the party
board show that we are gradually moving from a predominantly
mixed economy to a society in which the decision-making power over
the means of production is increasingly transferred to society and the
employees.'[72]

It is obvious that for some years during the 1970s, the hope of
expanding the limits of democracy also persisted within Social
Democracy – as did the realisation that this would probably require a
society other than the capitalist one.

Olof Palme was swept along with the socialist euphoria. Palme's
ambitions to test the limits of reformism are perhaps most clearly
illustrated in his correspondence in the early 1970s with his German
and Austrian party friends, Willy Brandt and Bruno Kreisky.[73] Palme

---

70   Sveriges kristna socialdemokraters förbund, *Socialistisk miljöpolitik för 80-talet*
(Stockholm: Sveriges kristna socialdemokraters förbund, 1980).

71   Sveriges socialdemokratiska arbetareparti, Kongress, *Motioner D. 1*, Socialdemokratiska partistyrelsen, 1975 (minutes from SAP congress).

72   Ibid.

73   Willy Brandt, Bruno Kreisky, and Olof Palme, *Letters and Conversations* (Stockholm: Tiden, 1976), pp. 28–30, 76, 121–2.

painted a dystopian picture. Capitalist society was in crisis; its fundamental values were being questioned; many rejected capitalism, morally and ideologically. Income inequality threatened to widen. There was a huge concentration of capital. Employees were being pushed out of a harsh production process, and losing their jobs. The environment was threatened by rapid poisoning. Fear was spreading through society, and there was an obvious risk that this fear might create a kind of fascist development, Palme claimed in the correspondence, in tones that are strikingly familiar in the present. The market could not solve these problems:

> It is not possible to leave decisions to private economic interests and let profit motives and competition be the deciding factors in shaping the environment, using land, safeguarding employment or managing technological development . . . The question must not be whether we should have more planned management and whether we should have more democracy in economic life, but rather how this planned management should be built up and how democratic influence should be organised.[74]

Palme showed no reticence in describing the ambitions – and successes – of the Swedish Social Democrats: 'We have come further in realising socialism than the countries that usually call themselves socialist.'[75]

Wage-Earner Funds

But the most radical demand for movement in a socialist direction came from the LO. The background was a growing dissatisfaction with the consequences of the solidarity wage policy. Critics argued that successful companies were able to make unfairly high profits by not allowing unions to extract the wage increases that would have been possible.

The LO decided to set up an inquiry headed by Rudolf Meidner. The result was a proposal for wage-earner funds.[76] Few Swedish books have

---

74 Ibid., p. 30.
75 Ibid., p. 29.
76 Ekdahl, *Mot en tredje väg*, vol. 2; Ilkka Kärrylä, 'The Contested Relationship of Democracy and the Economy: Debates on Economic and Industrial Democracy in Finland and Sweden, 1960s–1990s', PhD diss., University of Helsinki, 2019; Ilja Viktorov, *Fordismens kris och löntagarfonder i Sverige* (Stockholm: Acta Universitatis Stockholmiensis, 2006).

influenced the social debate more than the modest 120-page document that the committee subsequently published, in the autumn of 1975.[77] The basic thrust of the text was that employees should be given a share of the profits of the large and medium-sized companies. Every year, a proportion of a company's profits – in the form of shares – would be transferred to funds controlled by the unions. It was apparent from a table in the document that Meidner expected the system to give employees control of a majority of the shares in most companies after a period of between twenty and seventy-five years. In advancing this proposal, Meidner had three objectives in mind: to give employees a stake in company profits; to attack the growing concentration of power and ownership by creating a new ownership group; and to find a workable form of employee influence through ownership.

The proposal would prove to be explosive stuff. In two important respects, it was in clear contravention of Social Democracy's fundamental commitment to a reformist strategy. It acknowledged ownership as a central factor, and channelled welfare funds through union-led bodies rather than the state. The radical tone of the proposal did not frighten the LO, however. On the contrary, it was received with warm enthusiasm. Seen in the longer perspective, it might seem inconceivable that the LO, a bastion of reformist inertia and sobriety within the labour movement, would so readily give its backing to a proposal of such inherent dynamism. The only explanation is that the radicalism that characterised Swedish society at this time had also taken a firm grip on the labour movement.

For the Social Democratic Party leadership, the question was not so simple. The very idea that employees would have a stake in the profits of a company was not that controversial per se. It was in fact a classic liberal demand – the Liberal Party being particularly vocal advocates of individual stake-holding during the postwar period. Nor did Palme have any principled objections to employees sharing in company profits. But Meidner's proposal on wage-earner funds was something completely different.

And so it was for Swedish capital. As Jonas Pontusson has shown, the radicalisation of the 1970s pushed through decisions that directly interfered with the right of companies to determine the conditions of

77   Rudolf Meidner, *Employee Investment Funds: An Approach to Collective Capital Formation* (London: George Allen & Unwin, 1976).

production themselves.[78] The Employment Protection Act and the Working Environment Act were two examples of this. But now the unions wanted to pose an open challenge to the power of employers.

Social Democracy and the Intellectuals

The extensive social and political reforms that characterised Sweden in the 1970s – and which led many to ask whether Sweden was becoming a different country – have been described here as a symbiosis between radical social movements, not least trade union movements, and a competent, responsive, and decisive Social Democracy. But it was not a love story. In reality, the mistrust between the actors often ran deep. Many of the social movements were represented by intellectuals with political sympathies far to the left of the Social Democrats, and viewed the party's double message with suspicion.[79] And the Social Democrats' distrust of the young radicals, who so harshly criticised the party for abandoning its ambitions of social transformation, was hardly less extensive.

During the 1970s, additional issues complicated the relationship between Social Democracy, the intellectuals, and the new social movements. The distrust was so profound that a huge part of the left was unwilling to support the Meidner Funds, suspecting that they would be hijacked by the trade union bureaucrats. As we have seen, in the eyes of the environmental movement's activists, Social Democracy soon came to seem like a smug, self-sufficient party fixated on economic growth. Tensions culminated around the question of building nuclear power plants.

The single issue that most damaged the position of Social Democracy among intellectuals was, however, the so-called *IB-affären*. A group of journalists who were tied to the journal *Folket i Bild/Kulturfront* – a cultural flagship of the left wing in the 1970s – revealed the existence of a secret military intelligence agency whose task it was to watch over and maintain registers of Swedish radicals. The exposé also showed that secret agents were functioning in left-wing groups as provocateurs.

---

78   Jonas Pontusson, *The Limits of Social Democracy: Investment Politics in Sweden* (Ithaca, NY: Cornell University Press, 1992), Chapter 7.

79   Östberg, *När vinden vände*, pp. 260–74.

It documented direct links between the Social Democratic Party, with Olof Palme as a key figure, and the surveillance activities – carried out, among other means, by a large number of workplace informants. The fact that the party's representatives falsely denied all knowledge of the surveillance only increased the general indignation. When the responsible journalists were sentenced to jail for spying, the limit was felt to have been reached.[80] Subsequent government investigations have shown that the newspaper's claims were essentially correct.[81]

The deepening rift between the New Left and Social Democracy is a phenomenon familiar from many national contexts. But in other countries it proved possible, to some degree, to rebuild a relationship that was more permanently broken in Sweden. At the congress in Épinay in 1971, the French Socialist Party was reformed and renewed, and left radicals closely involved in this effort. The victory of the Union of the Left ten years later can be seen as a belated success of the radicalisation of 1968 – and important groups from the radicalised generation were linked during this process to the project of the Socialist Party.[82] In the Federal Republic of Germany, the country's Social Democratic Party managed during the 1970s to repair its relations with a part of the lost generation.[83] Significant parts of the generation of 1968 were to be found in leading political positions in these countries.

But Swedish Social Democrats lost most of the intellectuals who were radicalised during the 1960s and '70s. In only a few cases were sixty-eighters to be found in leading positions in the ministries and chancellery, and few became active Social Democrats. On the whole, the movement intellectuals of the 1960s and '70s chose other career paths – the media, universities, schools, health care, and other aspects of welfare-state administration rather than the civil service or the chancellery. This has had significant consequences for the political landscape of the late twentieth century, and especially for the Social Democratic Party.[84]

---

80   Ibid., pp. 156ff.
81   Säkerhetstjänstkommissionen, state public investigation SOU 2002:92.
82   Michel Winock, *Le Siècle des intellectuels* (Paris: Seuil, 1997).
83   Peter Merseburger, *Willy Brandt 1913–1992: Visionär und Realist* (Munich: Deutsche Verlags-Anstalt, 2002).
84   Östberg, *När vinden vände*, pp. 270ff.

Electoral Losses

Voters certainly did not give the Social Democrats their uncritical support. In the 1970 parliamentary elections, the party's share of the vote fell by almost 5 percentage points to 45.3 per cent, though this was enough to retain government power with the help of the Left Party communists. The decline was partly explained by the fact that Sweden was hit by the deepening recession that swept the world in the wake of the end of the long postwar boom.[85] Inflation increased and unemployment rose to over 2 per cent – a shock to the country that had become accustomed to labour shortages as the major problem in the labour market. In the run-up to the 1973 elections, for the first time in half a century, the three bourgeois parties had managed to unite to challenge the Social Democrats for government.

The economy was still much worse than the Swedes were used to, and for the strong social movements, such as women's liberation and the environmental movement, the Social Democratic government was a brake. Liberals thought the pace of social reforms was too slow, and the Centre Party criticised the downsides of growth and the government's lack of environmental commitment. The world's most successful reform government was losing support.[86]

The government was saved by a confluence of circumstances, with some dramatic external events making a contribution. The king died in the middle of the election campaign at the same moment as the internationally renowned Norrmalmstorg bank robbery of Kreditbanken took place (hostages held during the robbery would later be the first to display symptoms of 'Stockholm syndrome'). The prime minister, Palme, skilfully used these events to call for national unity. But the party still lost another 2 percentage points of the vote. The outcome created a deadlock situation (175:175 seats).

A closer analysis of the election results suggests two worrying trends. The Social Democratic Party declined sharply among youth voters, while the Centre Party, with its environmental profile, made strong gains, and the Moderates had strong success in the growing residential

85   Lennart Schön, *An Economic History of Modern Sweden* (London: Routledge, 2012), pp. 299–304.
86   Östberg, *När vinden vände*, pp. 215ff.

areas around the big cities, where the new middle class lived. This did not bode well for the future of the alliance between the Social Democrats and these groups, which had hitherto been a major factor in the party's electoral success.

The Social Democrats remained in office, and managed to manoeuvre their way through compromises with the bourgeois parties. This tactic was facilitated by strong support for welfare programmes. It was during this 'equilibrium parliament' that important reforms, such as the Co-determination Act, free abortion, and the expansion of day care centres, were decided.[87]

Olof Palme put a lot of effort into trying to secure closer parliamentary cooperation with the Liberals. One motive, of course, was that the Social Democrats realised that, sooner or later, they would need the support of another party in order to retain power. Another motive was probably that cooperation with a bourgeois party would make it easier for Palme to resist overly radical demands from within his own movement.

The international economic downturn continued in the wake of the first oil crisis, and pressure on the Swedish economy increased. The costs of the extensive social reforms that were implemented thus became greater. Pressure from below and the threat of further strikes created pressure for significant wage increases – not least in the public sector, which was growing rapidly at the time.

The government met the continuing downturn with a traditional countercyclical policy. VAT was reduced, child allowances were increased, and food subsidies were introduced. There was widespread talk of a bridging policy that would help Sweden past the international recession. The leading Swedish economists applauded. In retrospect, the policy has been seen as a failure. Bourgeois economists have said that Sweden was trying to 'escape the consequences of the oil crisis'.[88] But in the eyes of those observing at the time, the policy seemed a great success. 'One Nation Creates a Miracle Despite the World Recession', read the international press.

The temporary boom strengthened the Social Democrats in the run-up to the 1976 elections. Nevertheless, the party lost both the elections and their place in government. The decline in their vote was

---

87   Ibid.
88   Schön, *Economic History of Modern Sweden*, pp. 301ff.

moderate, at only 0.9 percentage points; but as the Left Party vote also declined slightly, the three bourgeois parties were able to gain a majority in parliament, with 180 seats against 169 for the left bloc.

What was the reason for the loss? In retrospect, many have wanted to interpret the result as a reaction against excessive radicalisation, a bloated welfare state, and high taxes. It was Pomperipossa's fault.[89] It is now a widespread belief that the loss was determined by a newspaper article by the beloved children's author Astrid Lindgren, in which she told the story of the witch Pomperipossa, who, like Lindgren herself, had to pay a marginal tax rate of 102 per cent. She was brusquely reprimanded by the minister of finance, Gunnar Sträng, who claimed that she was a good storyteller but less successful with figures. She must have miscalculated. But it turned out that Lindgren was indeed paying 102 per cent tax on part of her income – as a result of a tax proposal from the Liberal Party.

But there is very little empirical support for the idea that the election loss was a tax revolt. Despite the extensive media campaign in bourgeois newspapers against high taxes, it is striking how little dissatisfaction with taxes was raised by voters. Only 13 per cent explicitly mentioned the tax burden as an important election issue, according to a poll conducted by a leading Conservative sociologist. Instead, unemployment and nuclear power dominated voters' concerns.[90]

On the contrary, support for the solidarity-based financing of the welfare state commanded an impressive degree of consensus at the time, even in the bourgeois circles – so much so, in fact, that the tax burden rose even further when the new bourgeois government took office, from 45 to 47 per cent.

Why Did the Social Democrats Lose the 1976 Elections?

However, the Pomperipossa debate probably reflected – not least in the way Sträng had tried to belittle Lindgren's claims – a typical example of what we would today call 'mansplaining'. It would prove an issue of considerable significance for the election loss, and central to criticism of the power-hungry Social Democrats.

---

89 Östberg and Andersson, *Sveriges historia*, pp. 248ff.
90 Östberg, *När vinden vände*, pp. 186–91.

The deep distrust of authority, and the related lively discussion of how democracy could be deepened and extended to other parts of society, was central to the agenda of the new social movements. These rebounded sharply against the party that had ruled the country for almost half a century. But the decisive reason for the election loss was undoubtedly the issue of nuclear power. Among the electorate, 3–4 per cent switched from the Social Democrats to the anti–nuclear power Centre Party in the final stages of the election campaign.[91] The deep social radicalisation broke forty-four years of Social Democratic rule. A significant number of people who had been radicalised in the 1970s chose to vote for a bourgeois party, contributing to the change of government. The fact that their votes did not halt the expansion of nuclear power made the paradox no less remarkable.

The nuclear issue continued to dominate Swedish domestic politics throughout the rest of the 1970s. The government formed between the three bourgeois parties threatened to unravel even before it took office. The anti–nuclear power Centre Party was by far the largest, with almost 25 per cent of the vote. In the election campaign, party leader Thorbjörn Fälldin had 'put his honour on the line' by not helping to bring more reactors online. The other two parties, the Liberals and the conservative Moderates, called for further expansion. One of the first decisions of the incoming government was to approve another reactor. Fälldin fell by the wayside and accepted the start of new reactors. It is easy to imagine the outrage felt by the Social Democrats, having lost the election on the issue of nuclear power expansion, when the election victor promptly reneged on his promise.

After a few more years, the bourgeois government broke down. Fälldin now refused starting new nuclear power plants. To the surprise of many, the Social Democrats supported the advent of a Liberal minority government. The idea was probably to test the ground for a coalition government between Social Democrats and the Liberals after the 1979 elections. Social Democratic Party strategists believed that the split in the bourgeois parties would make a new bourgeois majority government impossible.[92]

But the issue of nuclear power again helped to block the Social Democrats' return to government. The accident at Pennsylvania's Three Mile

---

91   Sören Holmberg, 'Kärnkraften och vänster-högerdimensionen: konfliktlinjer i svensk politik', *Statsvetenskaplig tidskrift* 81, no. 2 (1978).
92   Östberg and Andersson, *Sveriges historia*, p. 260.

Island power plant in 1979, when nuclear material was released into the environment, increased opposition to nuclear power once again. The Social Democrats quickly proposed a referendum. This was an unexpected initiative – the demand for a referendum had long been driven by the anti-nuclear movement, strengthened by the recent public support it had enjoyed. It had been firmly rejected by the Social Democrats, who had traditionally taken a sceptical view of referenda. But the hope now was to postpone discussion of nuclear power until a post-election referendum. The Social Democrats wanted to avoid at all costs losing another election on the issue of nuclear power.

But the party's calculations were wrong. The attempt to defuse the nuclear issue in the election campaign benefited the bourgeoisie more than it did the Social Democrats. After all, it was for the latter that the nuclear issue was the real scourge. At that point, the issue of nuclear power could no longer prevent the formation of a new bourgeois government. The election was another narrow victory for the bourgeois parties. Many Social Democrats abstained from voting, partly because they disliked the fact that the party had allowed a liberal government to emerge.

The referendum took place in March 1980. Everyone had expected a choice between the two clear alternatives that had dominated the debate since the mid-1970s – the 'Yes' line of Social Democrats, Liberals, and Moderates, backed by business and large parts of the trade union movement, against the 'No' line of the Centre Party, Left Party, and the anti-nuclear movement. But the Social Democrats did not want to make things that easy. They wanted to avoid being on the same side as the Moderates, and pushed for the 'Yes' line to be split in two, even though the parties had the same programme: a maximum of twelve reactors would be built, and nuclear power would be abolished in thirty years at the latest.

In order to encourage the Moderates to refuse to go along with a joint election ballot, the Social Democrats demanded a rather extensive printed backside itemising a series of energy policy demands that had nothing to do with the nuclear reactors themselves. The result was three options on the ballot: Line 1, backed by the Moderates, and Line 2, backed by the Liberals and the Social Democrats, with both lines accepting twelve reactors in total, and Line 3, backed by opponents of nuclear power, who wanted to stop new reactors and close already active plants.

For a long time, polling indicated that Line 3 would win a majority of the vote. But a number of events soon took place that changed the balance of opinion. In the autumn of 1979, the second oil crisis erupted. Attention suddenly turned to the problem of oil dependency; the oil crisis was followed by an economic recession. The referendum result produced success for Line 2, which outnumbered the anti-nuclear Line 3 by 39.3 to 38.6 per cent, while Line 1 received 18.7 per cent.[93]

More than forty years have now passed since the referendum. Six reactors have been decommissioned so far. And recently the Social Democrats have approved construction of a new generation of nuclear plants.

Changing Winds

Towards the end of the 1970s, the spirit of the times was shifting. In Sweden, the left-wing wave was being overpowered by currents from the right. The outcome of the nuclear referendum also symbolised the weakening of many of the social movements that had sustained the radicalisation of the 1960s and '70s. The Social Democrats failed to regain power in the 1979 elections, and the economic crisis saw the bourgeois government begin to implement severe austerity policies for the first time. The neoliberal counter-revolution had now reached Sweden.

International developments were mixed, but increasingly pointed to a retreat of progressive forces.[94] Certainly, the United States had been defeated by the FNL and other liberation movements in Indochina in 1975. In Portugal, the fascist dictatorship fell in the Carnation Revolution of 1974, as did Franco's regime in Spain a few years later. The last African colonies finally won their independence. In 1979, the shah of Iran was deposed by a popular uprising, while a left-wing regime came to power in Afghanistan.

But a development in another direction could also be discerned. A US-backed military coup in Chile in 1973 had toppled the leftist regime of Socialist Salvador Allende, confirming that Latin America remained the backyard of the United States. Similar developments in countries including Argentina, Bolivia, and Uruguay also suggested that guerrilla

---

93   Ibid., pp. 262ff.
94   Judt, *Postwar*, Chapter 16.

movements had reached an impasse. Victories for liberation movements in Indochina were followed by wars between China and Vietnam, and by Pol Pot's terror in Cambodia. In Iran, the people's revolution soon became the preserve of the mullahs, while in Afghanistan the arrival of Russian troops marked not the progress but the death-knell of progressive developments in that country. Proxy wars in the Horn of Africa hinted at the reinvigoration of the Cold War.

The economic situation continued to deteriorate. It was clear that the long boom that had governed economic development since the end of the Second World War had now entered a much more turbulent phase. The welfare state seemed to have reached its limits. The growth that had formed the social basis of the postwar political compromises on welfare was soon a thing of the past. The Fordist world order was coming to an end. Keynesian economic policy no longer worked, bourgeois economists argued. Those countries that pursued policies of expansion financed by international borrowing risked a protracted debt crisis as economic upturns were delayed. Stagflation – a combination of the two economic blights of inflation and economic stagnation – entered the world economy for the first time.[95]

The result was economic and political regime change.[96] In 1976, the Swedish Academy of Sciences awarded the American economist Milton Friedman the Economics Prize in memory of Alfred Nobel. A fundamental idea of Friedman's monetarist theory was that government attempts to stimulate the economy were ineffective in the long run, only driving up inflation. Instead, Friedman advocated that interventions in market forces should be as small and as predictable as possible. Friedman's ideas soon came to function as a cornerstone of the ideological rebirth that has come to be known as neoliberalism – although the novelty of the ideas it espoused is debatable, since they were largely ideas that had lain dormant for some decades.[97]

The rapid international spread of neoliberal ideas contributed to the discrediting of Keynesianism. The new currents in science, politics, and the media successfully framed the crisis as a result of 'over-regulation', which necessitated extensive deregulation and a 'slimmed-down' state. This did not mean a smaller state in general, but only a dismantling of

---

95   Schön, *Economic History of Modern Sweden*, pp. 278ff.
96   David Harvey, *A Brief History of Neoliberalism* (Oxford: Oxford University Press, 2007); Judt, *Postwar*, Chapter 17.
97   Harvey, *Brief History of Neoliberalism*, pp. 22ff.

the state's welfare functions. The liberal state still had an important role to play in guaranteeing private ownership, enforcing laws, and ensuring the proper functioning of free markets and free trade.[98]

The central task of economic policy became that of creating a good climate for investment, stimulated by increased profits. It also became important to widen the market to include sectors not previously exposed to capital accumulation. The privatisation of public services, especially in the welfare sector, thus became a key item on the neoliberal policy menu.

Other institutional changes included the liberalisation of financial and other economic activities: banking and currency regulations, and trade policy. Fiscal reforms to reduce marginal taxes were also included, as were demands for a politically independent central bank.

The importance of institutional frameworks had not diminished as a result of the neoliberal shift in power. On the contrary, there was a very strong will to achieve international harmonisation in a market-oriented direction. Moreover, in the context of a more globalised economy, one can point to the importance of international bodies such as the International Monetary Fund, the World Trade Organization, the World Bank, the G8 and G20 meetings, and the EU in implementing and maintaining the new regime.

As intended, neoliberal policies led to a massive redistribution of resources from labour to capital. While the final phase of the Fordist era in particular had seen a substantial reduction in social and economic disparities, since 1980 the trend has been in the opposite direction. Increased corporate profits were combined with slower wage growth and periodic real-wage reductions, tax reforms with sharply reduced wealth and marginal taxes. Public-sector savings and efficiency gains, as well as widening gaps in education, pointed unequivocally in the same direction.[99] On the other hand, the impact of policies on overall economic growth was limited.

In Sweden, neoliberal ideas prompted an ideological rebirth of the economic and political bourgeoisie. Deep and widespread radicalisation had for some time put employers on the defensive. I have already noted the support that the expansion of the universal welfare state had received

---

98 Ibid., Chapter 3.
99 Wolfgang Streeck, *Buying Time: The Delayed Crisis of Democratic Capitalism* (London: Verso, 2014), Chapter 2.

even from the bourgeois parties. The Conservative leader, Gösta Bohman, could be heard speaking positively about the Swedish mixed economy, with its strong state influence.

The combination of a radical LO pushing for pro-union legislation and the wave of strikes further contributed to the pushing back of employers. But the union offensive only became truly threatening when the LO endorsed the proposal for wage-earner funds. Suddenly, the survival of private enterprise itself was at stake.[100]

A few key figures began to prepare for a counter-offensive. In the early 1970s, the SAF's information director, Sture Eskilsson, had already studied the left wave with interest. He had been impressed by its high theoretical level, and noted the importance of the left's intellectual think tanks. Inspired by what he saw, he led the SAF to develop an extensive information and propaganda operation to push back the leftists. When the wage-earner fund became a real threat, these plans were put into action.

But the financial resources available to him were quite different from those of left-wing activists. Hundreds of millions of kronor were pumped into a sprawling network that, in addition to the traditional employers' organisations, eventually came to include the Industrial Institute for Economic and Social Research, the Centre for Business and Policy Studies, the think tank Timbro, and several book publishers, newspapers such as the *SAF Magazine* and the daily *Svenska Dagbladet*. Ad hoc business-funded organisations and pressure groups also sprang up, ranging from 'Taxpayers Union' and 'People against Wage Earner Funds' to 'Women in Favour of a Bourgeois Government'.[101]

These networks were not just empty shells. An alternative vision of society was consciously being formulated. These organisations placed themselves at the centre of the international debate. Several of neo-liberalism's American figureheads, such as Robert Nozick, Ayn Rand, and Milton Friedman, were translated into Swedish, and the Frenchman Henri Lepage's *Demain le capitalisme* (*Tomorrow, Capitalism*) was widely distributed. Special efforts were made to attract the young generation. Using NHL hockey star Ulf Nilsson and ABBA singer Anni-Frid Lyngstad as figureheads, the SAF successfully sold the message 'Invest in

---

100 Kristina Boréus, *Högervåg: nyliberalismen och kampen om språket i svensk debatt 1969–1989* (Stockholm: Tiden, 1994), Chapter 3.
101 Ibid., pp. 103–13.

yourself!' A massive lockout in 1980 was not a decisive victory for employers, but it was a way to demonstrate their muscle, and was seen by SAF chair Curt Nicolin as 'an investment for the future'.

An important background to the rapid adoption of neoliberal ideas was the deteriorating economic landscape. When the Social Democrats handed over government power in 1976, the Swedish economy seemed to be at its strongest for some years. However, just as the country had managed to escape the international recession of 1974–75, it was now missing the international boom of 1977–78.[102] Swedish export industry was hit hard. In particular, key parts of Sweden's core industries were knocked out by the restructuring crisis that was ravaging the world in shipyards, steel, mining, and textiles. Warnings of industrial closures and redundancies poured in to the new government. The dilemma for the bourgeois government was substantial. It had pledged not to interfere with the Swedish welfare model. Initially, no one knew any medicine against economic crises other than the Keynesian one introduced by the Social Democrats forty years earlier. As a result, huge state resources were deployed to try to save the threatened industries, the minister of industry's 'emergency department' injecting SEK 30 billion in industrial aid over just a few years. Important parts of the industries in crisis were transferred to state-owned groups such as Swedish Steel and Swedish Shipyards. It was an irony of fate that, during its first years, the bourgeois government carried out the largest nationalisations ever seen in Sweden.[103] Moreover, as social spending continued to rise as a result of both earlier decisions and a number of new reforms, the Swedish budget deficit increased sharply.

Few foresaw then that Sweden was rapidly entering a situation in which growth would be slower and income development more sluggish than in most comparable countries for a long time to come – or that the country would lose its cherished place among the most successful industrial nations.

Bourgeois economists have been keen to explain this development in terms of the negative consequences of the Swedish model: high taxes, a large public sector, low labour market mobility, and the expansionary economic policies pursued by both Social Democratic and bourgeois

---

102 Schön, *Economic History of Modern Sweden*, pp. 468, 475; Lars Jonung, *Med backspegeln som kompass: om stabiliseringspolitiken som läroprocess* (Stockholm: Fakta Info Direkt, 1999), pp. 164ff.

103 Östberg and Andersson, *Sveriges historia*, p. 254.

governments in an attempt to overcome and counteract the economic crisis. But it is more fruitful to point to causes linked to structural problems of the capitalist economy. In particular, from the mid-1970s onwards, profits for Swedish industry fell – a reflection of a declining rate of profit. At the same time, investment fell sharply. The sharp rise in wages in 1975–76, due in no small part to the increased militancy of the working class, and a simultaneous decline in productivity, left Sweden unusually ill-prepared for the international economic downturn, which therefore hit key Swedish industries particularly hard.[104] After the second oil crisis, in 1979, growth ceased, and inflation reached double digits. In the spring of 1980 the bourgeois government changed course. In the midst of a deepening recession, economic policy was tightened. For the first time in several decades, the government presented a programme of cuts to the public sector.

Keynes was dead – and Sweden had taken its first steps towards a supply-oriented economic policy.

The Retreat

At the same time, the social movements and social mobilisation that had been the driving force behind radicalisation slowed down. There were many reasons for this. The dreams of the left faded with the withering carnations of the Portuguese struggle, the implosion of the Maoist project, and the age of suspended revolutions. The sixty-eighters were starting families and making careers; for many, the activist period was over. The economic crisis put a dampener on strike movements.

Social Democracy began its retreat, starting with the wage-earner funds. The proposal had aroused great enthusiasm, and not only within the LO. For the party leadership, the issue was more complicated.[105] Its scepticism had many causes. For one, there was the problem of public opinion and the escalating antagonism of the business sector and the right-wing parties, both of which were conspiring to make attacks on the funds one of the key issues in the election. Above all, however, those at the top of the party had important ideological objections. Olof Palme had invested a great deal of effort in developing and updating the party's

---

104 Pontusson, *Limits of Social Democracy*, pp. 99–103.
105 Viktorov, *Fordismens kris och löntagarfonder*.

traditional reformist line to meet the demands of the 1970s. The far-reaching reform of labour law that culminated in the Co-determination Act was about to bring a third stage of democratisation to fruition in the economic sphere. But the red line was drawn at ownership.

Without doubt, the issue of wage-earner funds became one of the thorniest political problems that Palme had had to deal with, perhaps the thorniest. His first reaction was therefore to try to strike the issue off the political agenda.[106] However, the most important task was reach agreement on a proposal between the party and the LO, and so a joint taskforce was set up. The contribution of the party executive, particularly that of Palme and its new economic spokesperson Kjell-Olof Feldt, to making the proposal less provocative was to add a fourth objective to the three originally formulated by the LO and Meidner: to provide capital for industrial investment. Their aim in setting out this objective was to win over parts of the right-wing camp, and ideally employers as well. The issue of capital formation, investments, and savings might be fundamental to the economic policies of the 1980s, said Feldt: 'We have tried to combine the different kinds of funds that we have been discussing into one system that will benefit both corporate growth and economic democracy.'[107]

But it was not the role of wage-earner funds as suppliers of venture capital to businesses that fired the enthusiasm of LO members – nor that of active party members. What the 65,000 members of the various discussion groups held ahead of the 1978 Party Congress were primarily interested in was a proposal that gave employees power over companies. Moreover, almost all responses to the circulated proposal were critical of the rosy picture that the briefing material painted of the market economy. Not unreasonably, Palme was worried that the members of the groups would arrive at the 'wrong' conclusion. It would be 'a fundamental misunderstanding in the study-circles if they equate economic democracy with wage-earner funds . . . The constant risk, for our members as well as us, is that we say that we are implementing economic democracy.'[108]

Irritation mounted, within the union movement most of all, over how the party executive was dealing with the issue of wage-earner funds.

---

106 Östberg, *När vinden vände*, pp. 254ff.
107 Ibid., p. 253.
108 Ibid.

Thus, in 1981, the LO and the Social Democratic Party presented another joint document, 'Arbetarrörelsen och löntagarfonderna' (The labour movement and wage-earner funds). In the discussions leading up to it, Palme describes how the proposal had been continually adjusted:

> We have removed some things that have caused the greatest upset in some quarters, things that were perceived as the confiscation of private property. We have a market economy and will continue to do so. We have to change it from the inside.
>
> Putting it simply, I would like to say that I do not think that this proposal is decisive for socialism, but I *do* think that it is critical to our ability to bring Swedish industrial society through the 1980s and '90s in a way that conforms reasonably well to our values. This is not exactly the same but it is important enough. This is why I believe that capital formation, employment and democracy are closely related.
>
> And then to some members of our party, the fight against the concentration of power is the most important thing. This latitude we need to have in a large party so that different members can push different aspects of policy.[109]

A few months later, Palme declared that the proposal had been extensively tweaked: 'I can understand if the Meidner proposal upset business people, but I would be very surprised if this current proposal did so.'[110] A radical political programme had once again been transformed into a harmless proposal aimed primarily at stimulating and strengthening industrial growth.

The turnaround did not escape internal protest. At the party executive meeting, held in the autumn of 1980 to draft 'The Labour Movement and Wage-Earner Funds, leading members warned of the risk that a debate would erupt on broken promises and on whether the idea could be sold to the wider party'. But the disappointment felt by many led not to revolt but to passivity. Enthusiasm for wage-earner funds in this new form was dramatically deflated.

If Palme had thought that a watered-down fund proposal would have been easier for employers to accept at this stage, he was very much mistaken. They rejected out of hand every invitation to hammer out a

---

109   Ibid., p. 256.
110   Ibid.

compromise. For them, the campaign against the funds — regardless of their form – was the perfect departure point for a mobilisation of pro-market forces. Not since the Farmers' March of 1914 had so many right-leaning demonstrators gathered on the streets as at the 4 October 1983 anti-fund demonstrations.

When the Social Democratic Party returned to government in the autumn of 1982, work began immediately on drafting a bill – at which point more limitations were added to the proposal: union ownership was restricted to 10 per cent; the boards of the funds would be appointed by the government, and capital added for seven years only, and that was all that would be. At last, the proposal was ready to put before the Riksdag.

This is how Meidner's biographer Lars Ekdahl sums up the result of eight years of toil:

> The . . . implemented wage-earner funds, in other words, can hardly be compared with Meidner's then eight-year-old proposal. Gone was the profit distribution that, through obligatory targeted employee share issues, would increase the union-controlled funds' holdings in the companies. Gone was almost all union power over industry, at a local and sector level; gone was the return from the funds that would strengthen democracy and knowledge formation within the union movement; gone was the determination to break the solid concentration of power and wealth once and for all; gone was the self-evident objective to make the funds a democratic component of a class society; gone was the attempt to fundamentally reform the capitalist class society; gone was the idea of the funds as an element of a democratic socialist strategy.[111]

When, on 21 December 1983, the Riksdag finally made its decision, the Social Democratic minister of finance, Kjell-Olof Feldt, penned one of the most-quoted lines of contemporary Swedish poetry: 'Wage-earner funds are a pile of shit, but see how far we've shovelled it.'[112] Regardless of the circumstances surrounding the inception of this little ditty, it accurately expresses the party leadership's attitude to what had originally been the LO's fund proposal. It was not something they had wished

---

111 Ekdahl, *Mot en tredje väg*, vol. 2, p. 294.
112 Östberg, *När vinden vände*, p. 258.

for, let alone felt passionate about. Pressure from the members – not only within the LO, but also many active Social Democrats from other parts of the movement – to bring about a fundamental shift in workplace hierarchies was, for a time, so strong that it was impossible to ignore; and here, of course, we cannot overlook party leader Olof Palme's powerful rhetoric about economic democracy and labour reform, which had actively contributed to firing these expectations.

A crucial problem with the proposal for wage-earner funds was thus that it challenged private ownership, breaking with the party's functional socialist credo. In the tradition of Karleby and functional socialism, Olof Palme instead advocated legislation. When it came to workers' demands for real influence, his alternative was the proposal of a co-determination law. Thus, one of the central demands of the trade union movement was to abolish the right of employers to 'manage and distribute work' themselves: the hated 'Section 32'.

When the Co-determination Act (Lag om medbestämmande i arbetslivet, or MBL) was adopted in 1976, it was, according to Palme, 'the greatest distribution of power and influence that has taken place in our country since universal suffrage was implemented'. This was a gross exaggeration. The law was quickly renamed 'the horn': the employers now only had to honk before they overran the unions.[113]

The MBL gave unions the right to negotiate with employers on all important workplace issues – but virtually no power to prevent decisions they opposed. The intention was that unions and employers would reach agreements that would give employees real influence; but no such agreements were ever reached. Employers, whose power to decide had been curtailed by the laws already in place, notably the Employment Protection Act, saw no reason to give up more power voluntarily. In practice, these laws meant that the LO and the Social Democratic government broke with one of the pillars of the Saltsjöbaden Agreement: that labour relations should be regulated by the labour market parties themselves, without state intervention. The Co-determination Act was an attempt to re-establish the route of negotiation. But if the spirit of Saltsjöbaden was first challenged from the left, it was now from the right – from the employers – that the death blow would come.

From a longer-term perspective, it seems clear that the Social Democratic leadership was not prepared to provide the conditions for real

113   Ibid., pp. 42ff.

workers' influence. The neutering of the wage-earner funds is just one illustration of this fact. But the Social Democrats were not prepared to use MBL for this purpose either. In the public sector, there would have been good opportunities for the national government, as well as those of regions and municipalities run by the Social Democrats, to act as model employers, and sign agreements on far-reaching powers for employees to determine working hours and other working conditions.

But no such agreements were introduced. Instead, the LO and the employers' association signed a 'Development Agreement' in 1982. The agreement represented a retreat from everything the LO had fought for over more than a decade.[114] There was no mention of workers' democracy within corporations, or of co-determination. In the same spirit as the earlier toothless agreements on enterprise works councils, the main aim was to make production more efficient.[115]

The retreat from wage-earner funds and their replacement by the toothless Co-determination Act symbolised the end of the short period in which the party, under the pressure of a wave of social mobilisation and extensive demands to challenge the unlimited power of capital, tested the potential of Social Democracy. It took place during a period when the Fordist model was facing its dissolution and neoliberalism was eagerly waiting in the wings.

I have pointed to several factors that undermined the conditions for a continued offensive: the change in the global balance of power; the economic crisis, which also affected the willingness of the workers to fight; the powerful mobilisation of employers; the slowdown of the activities of social movements; tensions between the LO and the party leadership. But, above all, challenging capital's power over production would have required a party that was prepared to make full use of the enthusiasm of workers and their trade unions in a fight for real workers' democracy. But the Social Democratic leadership drew back. It was not prepared to step beyond the limits of reformism.

---

114 Kärrylä, 'Contested Relationship of Democracy and the Economy', p. 424.
115 Bernt Schiller, '*Det förödande 70-talet*': *SAF och medbestämmandet 1965–1982* (Stockholm: Arbetsmiljöfonden, 1988), pp. 203ff.

8

Social Democracy under Neoliberalism

The Turn

The Social Democrats' loss of the 1976 elections was not unexpected. After forty-four years in power, many voters probably thought it was time for a change – especially as the electoral programme of the bourgeois parties also endorsed the social reforms of the preceding decade, and a vote for the Centre Party seemed like a guarantee against the expansion of nuclear power.

But the party's failure to come back in 1979 was much more difficult to explain. The bourgeois government had collapsed after only two years, and the Centre Party had failed in its promise to halt the expansion of nuclear power. For a year, the country had been governed by a minority Liberal government with little over 10 per cent support in parliament.

In a memo written just a few months after the 1979 elections, the Social Democrats' senior economist, Carl Johan Åberg, argued that the party was having problems formulating its economic policies – something that had been considered the party's strength since the 1930s. This was partly due to the bourgeois dominance of the profession of economics. Åberg suggested that the party cultivate a group of economists closely allied with the party who could bring ideas and expertise – even if they might deliver some 'bitter truths'.[1] A direct result of Åberg's memorandum was the formation of the Social Democratic Economic Association, which developed connections with leading economists in the party and trade union movement. After a few years, it had well over a hundred members. The membership list included veteran fighters from the old Keynesian school, such as Gösta Rehn and

---

1 Hans Bergström, *Rivstart? Om övergången från opposition till regering* (Stockholm: Tiden, 1987), p. 94.

Rudolf Meidner, and several economists from within the trade union movement. Central to future developments, however, was the recruitment of a group of young economists from the Stockholm School of Economics, all of whom were well versed in the neoliberal ethos now gaining ground among economists. One of its leading figures, Klas Eklund, made it clear that its aim was to form 'a pool of brain power' that could liberate the party from its traditional economic thinking.[2] This group of economists quickly became highly active, hosting regular seminars. From the outset, it paid particular attention to critical examination of the size and efficiency of the public sector, and to the need for a market-oriented approach to economic policy.

In the autumn of 1980, the party set up a 'Crisis Group' led by Palme's closest associate, Ingvar Carlsson, with the aim of drawing up a programme to rescue Sweden from its current economic crisis. Some of the leading young economists were also associated with this group. Kjell-Olof Feldt, who was slated to be minister of finance in a new Social Democratic government, played a decisive role.

The result was a new shift in direction for the party. Private enterprise would now become the engine of the Swedish economy's recovery, while state intervention would be limited. 'An upturn in industrial production must lead to an improvement in industry's profit situation. At the same time, overall savings in the country must be increased by restraining consumption', was the harsh message.[3] The fight against inflation was given priority. The party now proposed drastic curbs in the growth of the public sector and a freeze in government reforms. In short, the public sector was to be squeezed.

Growth was still an overriding goal, but the relationship between growth and welfare shifted decisively. Growth could no longer be used for social reforms, as it had been in the past, because the government claimed that there was no room for reforms. As Jenny Andersson has shown, the idea of a zero-sum relationship between growth and welfare sharpened when growth stagnated. Increasingly, social spending became something that was seen as costing resources. The welfare society was now framed as a burden that had to be reformed.[4]

---

2 Jenny Andersson, *Between Growth and Security: Swedish Social Democracy from a Strong Society to a Third Way* (Manchester: Manchester University Press, 2006), Chapter 6.

3 Ibid.

4 Ibid.

When the Crisis Group sent out a questionnaire in the spring of 1981 to test what the views of the party membership were on proposals such as reintroducing unpaid days into health insurance, or extending the working week by a few hours, the reactions were trenchant. This was certainly not the Social Democratic policy that members had expected after six years of bourgeois party rule. Scepticism was also evident higher up the party hierarchy. When the party executive discussed the survey, several heavyweights, including the former minister of finance, Gunnar Sträng, declared that he and many others 'were very critical of the proposals of the Crisis Group', and that it was almost like SAF propaganda. LO chair Gunnar Nilsson thought the questions were stupid. Olof Palme, on the other hand, was quick to pick up on the new ideas. He was clearly in favour of trying out the new course, even if he admitted that he had not grasped all of its aspects.[5]

The debate about this policy and its consequences came to play a prominent role within Social Democracy for years to come. And the result of the debate was a fundamental transformation of the entire Social Democratic project. The 1982 elections were a great success for the Social Democrats: 45.6 per cent was a vote share that the party has never surpassed since. Although the party leadership had already decided on its new policy, austerity was hardly the order of the day in the election campaign. With the slogan 'Room to manoeuvre, not a straitjacket!', it criticised the cuts made by the bourgeois government, and suggested that a new government would pursue a much more expansionary policy. It quickly became clear that this was not true.[6]

1982: The Return

The change in the Social Democrats' economic policy after the change of government in 1982 is a dramatic event in contemporary Swedish history. It is universally agreed that there was a sharp reversal of the economic policy pursued by the Social Democrats until the 1970s. Instead of preserving its 'room to manoeuvre', the government continued and deepened the cuts initiated by the bourgeois parties.

---

5 Kjell Östberg, *När vinden vände: Olof Palme 1969–1986* (Stockholm: Leopard, 2009), pp. 285ff.
6 Ibid., pp. 287ff.

The government had not even taken office when it decided to start with a shock devaluation of 16 per cent. The stated aim of this move was to try to increase the competitiveness of Swedish industry in one fell swoop. The price was largely paid by the party's voters in the form of inflation, lower living standards, and increased unemployment. Ten years earlier, Palme had argued that the question should not be whether Sweden should have 'a more planned economy . . . but rather how this planning should be built up'. In the 1980s, all talk of a planned economy disappeared, in word and deed. Instead, the overriding aim was to guarantee higher profits for industry.

Soon came the first really tough austerity measures. The fight against inflation was given top priority also in Sweden, even if it meant increased unemployment. At the same time, the public sector had to be reduced, and tax increases were out of the question. Cuts were made that affected pensioners, medical aid, student grants, housing subsidies, and financial support to municipalities. The incoming minister of finance, Kjell-Olof Feldt, was pleased.[7]

The next step was to liberalise state control over the economy. The big symbolic decision was the abolition of most detailed credit-market regulations, including bank lending limits, in November 1985. Soon afterwards, currency regulations began to be relaxed. By the early 1990s, Sweden was one of the most deregulated countries in these areas. Following neoliberal doctrine, the Social Democratic government removed a number of key tools for controlling and regulating the flow of capital.[8]

This drastic turnaround in economic policy implemented by the Social Democrats in the 1980s was orchestrated from above. The policy had first been developed by a small group of economists inspired by the neoliberal ideas of the time, and backed by Feldt, who had a background as an economist. This group, known colloquially as the 'chancellery right', quickly answered the need for intellectuals that arose when a significant proportion of young intellectuals radicalised in the 1960s and '70s, unlike previous generations, chose other career paths than as social engineers in the Social Democratic administration. The fact that the

---

7   Kjell-Olof Feldt, *Alla dessa dagar-: i regeringen 1982–1990* (Stockholm: Norstedt, 1991), pp. 117ff.

8   Torsten Svensson, *Marknadsanpassningens politik: den svenska modellens förändring 1980–2000: en bok från PISA-projektet* (Uppsala: Acta Universitatis Upsaliensis, 2001); J. Magnus Ryner, *Capitalist Restructuring, Globalisation and the Third Way: Lessons from the Swedish Model* (London: Routledge, 2002), pp. 148–52.

intellectual leaders of the Social Democratic movement were economists was a new phenomenon. None of the previous ministers of finance
had been economists: Hjalmar Branting had studied astronomy, F. W.
Thorsson was originally a shoemaker, Ernst Wigforss was a philologist,
Per Edvin Sköld studied history of religions, and Gunnar Sträng had
been a garden worker before making a career in the LO. Previous social
engineers consisted of a rich mix of economists, sociologists, historians,
physicians, and architects. But now it was the economists who set the
tone. To the surprise of many, they were backed by Palme.

In the division of labour that developed, Feldt was responsible for the
concrete design of policy, tough messaging, and battles with disgruntled
ministers. Palme's most important role was to provide ideological
backing by arguing that the new economic policy was a prerequisite for
the later pursuit of a classic Social Democratic welfare policy.

Nothing in the party's 1982 election campaign had signalled any
dramatic change of course. The massive social cuts therefore came as a
surprise not only to the party's voters, but also to many leading Social
Democrats themselves. A new generation making their parliamentary
debut at this time, including future party leader Mona Sahlin, as well as
Anna Lindh and Margot Wallström, both later ministers of foreign
affairs, expressed their disappointment at the severe austerity measures.
The strongest protest came from Stig Malm, the chair of the LO, and
there was widespread talk of a 'War of the Roses' – the roses being the
symbol of Social Democracy. Malm, in turn, was under great pressure
from his members, who were the hardest hit by the cuts.[9]

The trade union movement had suffered several defeats since the
late 1970s. The wage-earner fund proposal had been derailed, the Co-
Determination Act had proved a disappointment, unemployment had
risen, and real wages had fallen in the wake of the economic crisis. By
the mid-1980s, workers' annual income had fallen by a month's salary
since the late 1970s, while share prices had trebled and bank profits
had mushroomed as a result of the pro-business policies of the Social
Democratic government, the left-wing press reported.

The protests were not long in coming.[10] A series of wildcat strikes
broke out around the country. Then, in January 1986, when the government presented its budget without delivering on promises to restore

---

9 Östberg, *När vinden vände*, pp. 301ff.
10 Ibid., pp. 375–82.

unemployment benefits, while demanding that the unions sign a three-year agreement with low wage increases, tempers flared. Criticism of the budget kicked off two months of protests and demonstrations of discontent that shook the government to its core. The revolt spread far into the centre of the Social Democratic movement.

'Something is wrong', read the LO magazine *LO-Tidningen*. 'While the unemployed are now trudging to the unemployment office, the stock market is rolling in billions with great vigour. We see on TV sweaty stock-brokers and happy millionaires who have become multi-millionaires.' The loudest rumblings came from the county of Dalarna, where car workers were fined for participating in wildcat strikes that autumn, and striking cleaners were dismissed. In a statement, the unions called for a fight against 'speculation, unreasonable profits, tax breaks, wealth growth and luxury consumption, as well as executive perks and political privileges that are eroding Sweden's economy'. Instead, they called for mobilisation for substantial wage increases in that spring's contract negotiations.

The statement, which quickly became known as the Dala Appeal, had an immediate impact, and attracted considerable media attention. A number of large and small trade union organisations across the country quickly endorsed the call, several of them traditional Social Democratic strongholds. Soon it had brought together organisations representing some 100,000 members, and the leaders called a national meeting in the spring. The party was deeply shaken, and in a meeting with the party's executive committee, LO chair Stig Malm spoke plainly:

> Tell me how to deal with the opinion of 100,000 of our members who work full time, but who need economic relief to get by, when I have to tell them that you can't get a real-wage increase . . . What trade union movement on this globe stands up after a devaluation and does not bother to compensate itself because it feels responsible for a crisis policy to increase the level of profits? . . . Instead, it is others who are hijacking it.[11]

The depth of the concern became clear when one of Palme's most loyal associates, the industry minister Thage G. Peterson, also agreed: 'Many party members do not understand the party's line on distribution

---

11   Ibid., p. 379.

policy . . . there is concern about jobs . . . I know of no time in the past when the debate has been as tricky as it is now.'[12] But the hard core of the leadership, Palme and Feldt, remained unmoved. Criticism of the injustices created by the policy was dismissed with surprisingly little empathy. 'Populist arguments are used. It creates chauvinistic moods', Palme argued. Instead, they focused on identifying the leftist groups believed to be behind the actions and discussing how to fight them.

How successful the Dala Appeal might have been, and how deeply divided the Social Democratic Party was, we will never know. Without doubt, it was a genuine protest movement, based in the trade union movement, and marshalling support on a scale rarely seen in Sweden. Moreover, opinion polls showed that the Social Democrats had lost up to 10 per cent of their support during the period of the protests.

The Murder of Olof Palme

The assassination of Olof Palme on 28 February 1986 changed everything. The domestic political debate came to a standstill. The Social Democrats' opinion ratings soared, and a new low-wage agreement was quickly concluded between the LO and the SAF. Although the protests later resumed, the momentum of the Dala Appeal had died down. For many, the murder of Palme also symbolises the death of the Swedish model. Palme was perhaps the leading Swedish statesman of the twentieth century, and, together with Hjalmar Branting, the foremost social democratic leader. Palme was only fifty-nine when he was murdered. Still, he had been at the centre of Swedish politics for more than thirty years. During these years, the economic conditions as well as the spirit of the times had changed many times. So did politics – and Palme's political profile.

Palme's background was unusual for a Social Democrat. The party was proletarian through and through, including most of the leadership. Palme, however, was born into a family that had an undisputed place within the country's economic elite, and he had a traditional upper-class education.[13] He had started his career as a combatant in the Cold War.

---

12   Ibid.
13   Kjell Östberg, *I takt med tiden: Olof Palme 1927–1969* (Stockholm: Leopard, 2008), pp. 38ff.

In the early 1950s Palme was the central international actor in the task of building the pro-West International Student Conference, a project financed by the CIA with the main purpose of preventing students from the Third World gravitating towards communism.

But one thing that Palme learned from his international student assignment was the absurdity of the colonial system. He was firmly convinced that the destructiveness of the colonial wars, and of colonialism itself, was also politically counter-productive from the perspective of the West.[14] In domestic matters, the young Olof Palme was positioned securely in the middle of the party, and on some issues even somewhat to its right.[15]

In the 1960s, however, Palme noted the burgeoning radicalism of the time with interest. By virtue of his convictions, he found it easier than many other established politicians to understand the dynamism of the liberation struggles of the Third World. His receptiveness, curiosity, and good relations with influential intellectuals allowed him to grasp the importance of the new social movements. Palme's vociferous opposition to the US war in Vietnam made him a unique figure in international politics.

When demands for more profound reforms found their way into Social Democracy, not least through the voices of the union and women's movements, Palme was often the one able to transform the demands raised into the most eloquent and emphatic words.[16] As prime minister from 1969, he was ultimately responsible for the unique reform wave of the 1970s that encompassed fundamental aspects of social, equality, and labour policy.

Palme was a controversial politician. His apparent radicalism and facility with sharp polemical formulations made him unpopular among bourgeois opponents – not least the police and the military, where an open hatred of Palme developed.[17]

The idea of a connection between Palme's murder and the death of the Swedish model is easy to understand. Palme was the leader of Social Democracy during the period when the Swedish welfare state was at its peak. A number of years after he was killed, large parts of it had been eroded. Palme had endorsed the neoliberal turn that was the central

14   Ibid., pp. 79ff, 106.
15   Ibid., pp. 128ff.
16   Ibid., Section III.
17   Östberg, *När vinden vände*, pp. 362–5.

reason for this development – but there was an important difference between Palme and the architects of the new policy. For Kjell-Olof Feldt, it was necessary to give the party a permanent new direction, breaking with the previous economic policy. For Palme, the new policy was a necessary but temporary evil to bring order to the economy. Or, in Feldt's own words: for people like Palme, it was 'more a question of giving the party the opportunity to return to its old policy by uncomfortable means. We would crawl through a tunnel. On the other side, the light was waiting.'[18]

When Feldt wanted to go further, privatising parts of the welfare system – he specifically proposed childcare centres – Palme balked. He decried the prospect of 'Kentucky fried children' in Sweden, as he put it, playing with the name of the US fast-food chain just introduced in Sweden. In his very last interview, just hours before he was assassinated, he argued forcefully that the solidaristic public sector was an 'essential expression of a society's degree of civilisation. Education, postal and telecommunications services, care for children, health care on equal terms for all, that is a measure of how civilised a society is.'[19]

Yet there is little to suggest that developments would have been different if Palme had survived to continue leading the government. One important reason for this is that the light at the end of the tunnel did not appear. Among other things, the consequences of the economic policies that Palme had advocated so intensely led to a new serious crisis in the early 1990s, which, in turn, ushered in a new wave of austerity, deregulation, and now also extensive privatisation. His successor saw no room for traditional Social Democratic policy.

The murder remains unsolved after almost forty years. The police investigation was handled very poorly from the beginning, often afflicted by profound incompetence. Several government inquiries have criticised the fact that the police refused to investigate relevant international connections, or evidence that pointed to police involvement and associated hatred of Palme within the force. Instead, their investigation targeted individual perpetrators, sometimes on flimsy grounds. The fact that leading politicians interfered in the investigation further contributed to the emergence of more or less well-founded conspiracy theories and a growing lack of trust in basic social functions.[20]

---

18 Feldt, *Alla dessa dagar*, p. 25.
19 Östberg, *I takt med tiden*, pp. 9ff.
20 Gunnar Wall, *Mörkläggning: statsmakten och Palmemordet* (Gothenburg: Bokförlaget Kärret, 2020).

The Crisis of the 1990s

In the 1990s, further decisive steps were taken in the erosion of Sweden's traditional Social Democratic model – and they were advanced by the party itself.

The crisis of the 1990s hit the Swedish economy hard. By the end of the 1980s, there were hopes that the Social Democratic government's cocktail of deregulation, austerity, and pro-business policies had paid off. The devaluation contributed to the transformation of the trade deficit into a surplus, as Sweden became able to take advantage of the international boom. There were signs that investment was picking up and inflation falling as the budget deficit began to narrow. Instead the country was slipping into one of the deepest economic crises of the twentieth century.[21] Its direct cause was the combination of a boom with economic deregulation. Banking and currency liberalisation had created opportunities for banks to increase their lending significantly. High inflation, combined with relatively low interest rates and favourable tax deductions, made borrowing very cheap – for many, real interest rates were below zero. Loans were largely used to buy property and shares, while share prices rose sharply, as did house prices. The stage was set for a major credit bubble.

The Social Democratic government, in which Ingvar Carlsson had now succeeded Olof Palme as prime minister, was squeezed by conflicting interests.[22] Wage-earners, and especially core Social Democratic voters, were demanding compensation for a decade of real-wage cuts and social retrenchment. At the same time, there were increasing calls from economists, not least those in the minister of finance's own department, for economic tightening to address problems of overheating. And these austerity measures would primarily be at the expense of these very wage-earners, through reform freezes and tax increases.

The government chose to follow the economists' advice. In a high-profile move in the spring of 1990, it proposed a two-year wage and price freeze combined with a strike ban. In addition, fines for wildcat strikes would be raised sharply. It was unprecedented for a Social

---

21   Lennart Schön, *An Economic History of Modern Sweden* (London: Routledge, 2012), pp. 324ff.

22   Kjell Östberg and Jenny Andersson, *Sveriges historia. 1965–2012* (Stockholm: Norstedt, 2013), pp. 361ff.

Democratic government to put forward such an openly anti-union request. But the proposal was defeated in the Riksdag when the Left Party, for once, voted with the bourgeois parties.

Instead, the government took two other symbolic decisions with far-reaching consequences for the future. First, it now formally attached itself to the neoliberal norm, stating that the fight against inflation would henceforth take precedence over the fight against unemployment. The consequences were soon vividly apparent in the spiralling unemployment rate.

Second, the government decided to apply for membership of the EEC/EU. In the early 1990s, the European Community was in the process of codifying a neoliberal economic approach as a common platform for the members of the Union, which was introduced as a central part of the Maastricht Treaty in 1993. This came to bind the hands of the Swedish government in relation to economic policy in several areas.

The price of its inability to deal with the economic crisis was paid in the 1991 elections. It was a great success for the right-wing Moderates, who, for the first time in over sixty years, were able to fill the post of prime minister.[23] But the traditional bourgeois parties failed to achieve a majority of their own, and became dependent on the votes of the xenophobic right-wing populist New Democracy. The new government was able to build on the Social Democrats' economic liberalisation, but at the same time vigorously pursued privatisation of the public sector – something the Social Democrats had hitherto been reluctant to do. The consequences were particularly far-reaching in the areas of health care, schools, and housing. Generous opportunities to set up private, for-profit schools with the same level of state subsidies as municipal schools had the effect, after some years, of transforming the Swedish school system into one of the most commercialised in the world. At the same time, the government allowed a very large part of the publicly owned housing stock to be sold into private hands, which contributed to widespread housing segregation.

Moreover, the bourgeois government failed to address the failure of the Swedish economy, which was exacerbated by a concurrent international crisis. It was triggered by sharp fluctuations in credit and financial markets. Currency speculation became a particular problem. The Swedish krona soon became vulnerable to attacks from international

---

23   Ibid., pp. 376ff.

currency traders. Sweden's high inflation and its tradition of strengthening its competitiveness through repeated devaluations increased the
pressure on the krona.[24] The market took its assets home, and the currency flowed out of the country. In September 1992, the Riksbank's
repurchase rate reached a staggering 500 per cent. Its drastic action was
aimed at convincing the finance market that the krona would hold.

When these measures failed, the Social Democrats agreed to help the
right-wing government deliver two comprehensive austerity packages.
Public spending was to be cut by SEK 28 billion, including reduced
levels of health insurance and unemployment benefits, lower pensions,
shorter holidays, an increase in the retirement age, further reductions in
housing subsidies, and cuts in overseas aid. In addition, employers'
social security contributions were reduced. But even these measures did
not help; the Swedish krona was devalued anyway. But the result was a
new intensification of the trend towards public-sector cuts – a move that
included the full participation of the Social Democrats.

In 1994 the Social Democrats were able to form a government again.
The failed crisis policy had created a large budget deficit, and the new
government pursued further social cuts.[25] A new pension system was
introduced in 1994. The ATP, the General Supplementary Pension
system it replaced, had often been described as the jewel in the crown
of the Social Democratic welfare system. When fully developed, this
system had guaranteed employees pensions in the amount of two-thirds
of their final salary. The new pension system would no longer guarantee
a certain size of future pension, but would instead allow the amount to
vary in response to what the economy and demographic developments
would permit. In practice, it turned out to provide between 40 and 50
per cent of the previous income. The new system was also adapted to the
market by enabling the investment of an increasing share of public
pension funds in equities, as well as by requiring individuals to invest
part of their pension in funds, and thereby to become familiar with
investment in shares more generally.[26]

The effects of the 1990s crisis on Swedish society were extensive.
Unemployment, which until 1990 had rarely exceeded 2 per cent, rose
rapidly to between 10 and 12 per cent, and has since rarely fallen below

---

24   Ibid., pp. 357–62.
25   Ibid., pp. 392ff.
26   Urban Lundberg, *Juvelen i kronan: Socialdemokraterna och den allmänna
pensionen* (Stockholm: Hjalmarson & Högberg, 2003).

8 per cent. A balance sheet commissioned by the government showed that the severe cuts fell mainly upon economically weaker groups – not least single parents.[27]

The Changing Boundaries of Politics

The transfer of power from politics to the market that began in Sweden in the 1980s was very much an international phenomenon. The process was underpinned by a transformation of the state and state decision-making processes in ways that made them more amenable to the global neoliberal regime.[28]

Despite their intense and concerted criticism of the strong state, the neoliberals by no means sought a minimal and passive night-watchman state. Above all, the state was to be streamlined in such a way as to safeguard economic growth, competitiveness, and credit-worthiness, while at the same time delivering reduced democratic oversight. The idea that an excess of democracy would lead inevitably to irrational economic decisions that produced waste and debt was central to the thought of Friedrich Hayek. Given the chance, voters could not resist the temptation to grab as much for themselves as they could.

An important safeguard against too much popular influence was increased regulatory control of political activity, combined with greater power for a number of bodies that were not under political control, such as the European Central Bank, the International Monetary Fund, and the World Bank.[29]

The tendencies that brought Hayek's ideas to fruition, shaping the space in which politics was able to operate, had a deep impact in Sweden. They were captured by the so-called Lindbeck Commission, established in 1992. Its aim was to 'identify fundamental weaknesses and propose improvements in the functioning of the Swedish *economic system*', but also 'to propose changes in the *political system* in order to achieve stable

---

27   Östberg and Andersson, *Sveriges historia*, pp. 366ff.

28   Wendy Brown, *Undoing the Demos: Neoliberalism's Stealth Revolution* (New York: Zone, 2015); Colin Crouch, *Post-democracy* (Cambridge: Polity, 2004); Wolfgang Streeck, *Buying Time: The Delayed Crisis of Democratic Capitalism* (London: Verso, 2014).

29   Streeck, *Buying Time*, Chapter 3.

ιules of the game for the economy'.[30] The chairman of the Commission, Assar Lindbeck, had for many years been a Social Democrat and one of Olof Palme's closest economic advisers, but had left the party in protest against the LO's plan for wage-earner funds.

Although the Commission's task was to propose far-reaching changes to the political system, it was entirely made up of economists. The leading function of economics could hardly have been expressed more clearly. And the Commission had no problem identifying where the problem lay: the economic crisis was due not to weaknesses in economic policy, but to 'weaknesses in the general functioning of the political system'.

A common theme in the proposals was to centralise political power while reducing the influence of democratic structures. Within government, more power should be shifted to the prime minister and the minister of finance, and they should rely more on economic expertise. The central bank of Sweden (the Riksbank) was to be guaranteed independence from politicians, and the parliament's ability to influence the national budget was to be curtailed through a strict budgetary process.

Centralised political power would be used to privatise and implement cuts in the public sector. All public production that was not the exercise of public authority should eventually be opened up to competition. The housing markets were to be deregulated. The labour market should be liberalised, for example by relaxing the Employment Protection Act and reducing unemployment benefits. Trade union rights should be restricted, and penalties for taking part in wildcat strikes increased. Social security benefits should be reduced and supplemented by private insurance. Taxes should be reduced, and increased wage differentials encouraged.

Most of its proposals were implemented in the following years – often by Social Democratic governments. It is obvious that these developments in Sweden followed a general European trend in all its main features. The changes in the domestic policy framework took place in close harmony with corresponding developments internationally, which were largely driven and implemented by the EU and its various agencies.

In 1991, the Social Democratic government applied for accession to the EC/EU. The Swedish Social Democrats had long rejected joining the EC/EU and its predecessor, the EEC. Interestingly, an argument was that the EEC, especially through Catholic influence, would pose a threat to the Swedish model, including its social policy. When the party hastily

30 Ekonomikommissionen, state public investigation SOU 1993:16, emphasis in original.

changed its mind, a key argument used by the party leadership to persuade its reluctant membership was that Sweden had a special responsibility to participate in the work of creating a social EU.[31] But this has not been possible given the complex organisational structure of the EU.

Greek political scientist Gerassimos Moschonas has explained why. If you test the idea that the European Social Democrats would unite around an actively expansionary economic policy that, for example, limited the power of the market and made the banks, not the people, pay for the economic crisis, and if they also managed to secure a majority in the politically constituted bodies – the Council of Ministers and the European Parliament – while also, somewhat implausibly, bringing the Commission and the powerful EU bureaucracy on board, could such an expansionary policy be implemented? Moschonas quotes the leading EU expert at the European University Institute in Florence, political scientist Stefano Bartolini, who answers unequivocally: 'Such a policy change would be hindered by the independence of the European Central Bank, by EC law and by the European Court of Justice.' A democratic decision-making process incorporating majority decisions in politically elected and appointed assemblies does not exist within the EU.[32]

Even when the EU's governing body, at the turn of the century, included a robust Social Democratic majority, it was not feasible to pilot the rather modest proposal to combat unemployment that the Swedish Social Democrat Allan Larsson had managed to shepherd through the EU's bureaucratic minefield.

The design of the EU is thus at odds with the kind of parliamentary democracy that has long been the ideal of liberal democracy. The political parties that have traditionally been the basis of national democracies have no obvious position of power in this conglomeration of institutions. They are certainly represented, directly or indirectly, in many EU bodies, but not in a coordinated way. Moreover, the political parties in the EU have to act through its various party groups. In the case of the Social Democrats, this means that the influence of the right-wing German SPD – which has long been deeply embedded in a political

---

31   Östberg and Andersson, *Sveriges historia*, p. 400.

32   Gerassimos Moschonas, 'Reformism in a "Conservative" System: The European Union and Social-Democratic Identity', in John Callaghan, ed., *In Search of Social Democracy: Responses to Crisis and Modernisation* (Manchester: Manchester University Press, 2009), p. 177.

coalition with the conservative Christian Democrats – has been very tangible.

The EU project thus undermines three of the fundamental features of classical Social Democracy, Moschonas notes: faith in the state, faith in the primacy of politics, and a welfare policy linked to the working class.[33]

The Third Way

The crisis of Social Democracy was an international phenomenon. In country after country, Social Democrats chose more or less voluntarily to adapt to new conditions, usually as a direct result of acute political and/or economic crises.[34]

In some cases, resistance was marked. One of the most telling – and dramatic – examples occurred was that of France. François Mitterrand was elected president in 1981 on an advanced reformist programme designed to combat the crisis: raising the minimum wage; introducing a thirty-five-hour week and longer holidays; increasing the retirement age. This programme was strongly supported by the electorate. At the same time, a series of other measures were introduced to intervene in market forces: nationalisation of banks and central industrial concerns; strengthening of state industrial policy and major investment in public-sector jobs; improvement of health insurance; increased financial support for the unemployed. But this effort was half-hearted. After a year, the government slammed on the brakes and implemented a harsh austerity programme with a monetarist-inspired deflationary policy at its core.

This failure alarmed an already shaken Social Democracy. It was not possible to restore Keynes – at least, not in just one country. But whether it would have been possible to mount a more concerted Social Democratic offensive to challenge neoliberalism, we will never know – no further attempts were ever made.[35] Instead, the parties gradually adapted to the new conditions. First was perhaps West Germany, under Helmut Schmidt. Sweden soon followed.

---

33 Ibid.

34 Ingo Schmidt, 'It's the Economy, Stupid', in Ingo Schmidt and Bryan Evans, eds, *Social Democracy after the Cold War* (Edmonton, AB: AU Press, 2012).

35 Ryner, *Capitalist Restructuring*, pp. 125ff.

But the new policy met with widespread resistance; it was not only in Sweden that the War of the Roses was raging. This split existed in most parties until a young, energetic leader of the venerable British Labour Party gave what appeared to be a series of ill-conceived retreats a fresh new face – New Labour – and a new unifying slogan – the Third Way.[36] As Jenny Andersson has ably shown, instead of looking back nostalgically at the politics of another era, New Labour wanted to engage in dialogue on the issues of the new age, such as globalisation, information technology, and individualism.[37] The starting point for engaging in that conversation was acceptance of some basic terms: monetarism, deregulated markets, balanced budgets, the prioritisation of low inflation over fighting unemployment, reduced income transfers (hence increased inequality), and privatisation. Strengthening the competitiveness of the country – or the EU – became a priority. Welfare systems and the public sector would be streamlined, slimmed down, shrunk – but not abolished. Capitalism would not be reined in, but made more efficient. Above all, through the policy of the Third Way, Social Democracy would once again become the main bearer of modernisation. The old Social Democracy had nothing to say about the important issues of the new age.

The primary task of politics would now be to unleash the inherent potential and creativity of individuals, writes Andersson.[38] Behind this fundamentally economic view was the notion that it was knowledge, creativity, and entrepreneurship that drove society forward. The idea of the knowledge society led to a hope for a new golden era of growth and social harmony. The premise was Social Democracy's embrace of growth, the market, and free enterprise.[39] This version of the Third Way quickly became an international hit. Schröder in Germany and Göran Persson in Sweden quickly signed up.

At the end of the 1990s, the European Social Democrats had a somewhat unexpected opportunity to show what the Third Way had to offer. In the years around the turn of the century, after many years of decline, it was suddenly enjoying significant electoral success. At its height, twelve

36   Alex Callinicos, *Against the Third Way* (Cambridge: Polity, 2001).
37   Jenny Andersson, *The Library and the Workshop: Social Democracy and Capitalism in the Knowledge Age* (Stanford, CA: Stanford University Press, 2010).
38   Jenny Andersson, *När framtiden redan hänt: socialdemokratin och folkhemsnostalgin* (Stockholm: Ordfront, 2009), p. 28.
39   Ibid., p. 138.

of the then fifteen member-states had Social Democratic prime ministers, including Germany, France, and Britain. A temporary international
boom seemed to be creating economic space for more expansionary
policies. Surely, the movement towards a 'social Europe' would now be
able to gather real momentum?[40]

But the German and British party leaders, Schröder and Blair, effectively put an end to any 'Euro-Keynesian' deviations. Investment in
'human capital', improved competition, and structural reforms were the
path they pointed to – and here the successes were great. Few periods in
EU history have seen liberalisation and market reform implemented
with such a frenzy as during the unique period of Social Democratic
power between 1997 and 2002. It was then that the foundations were
laid for the EEA and Lisbon agreements, which codified in clearer terms
than before the EU's neoliberal policies – albeit partly dressed up in the
language of 'knowledge society' and 'social partnership'.[41]

The Consequences for the Welfare State

The overriding objective of Social Democratic policy since the democratic breakthrough a hundred years ago has been to make an active
contribution to the growth of the economy in order to create space for
social reforms favouring the working class, and to combat unemployment. The neoliberal shift fundamentally changed the conditions for
pursuing this policy.

The government's task now became to let the market try to solve the
crisis.[42] But perhaps the deepest shift was the change in the view of
the welfare state. Instead of an engine of growth, it came to be seen as a
problem. Criticism of the public sector as bloated, bureaucratic, and
inefficient was a central feature of employers' campaigns in the 1980s.
Unproductive welfare payments, they argued, were taking resources that
should instead have been used to boost production.[43]

This perspective also gradually became that of the Social Democrats.
The idea of the welfare state was not abandoned, but if welfare was to
be saved, it had to be subjected to market adaptation. Far-reaching

---

40   Ingo Schmidt, 'It's the Economy, Stupid'.
41   Andersson, *The Library and the Workshop*, pp. 15ff.
42   Östberg and Andersson, *Sveriges historia*, pp. 357–67.
43   Andersson, *Between Growth and Security*, Chapter 6.

rationalisations and efficiency improvements were therefore advocated. Privatisation was justified on grounds of efficiency, but also because freedom of choice between public and private services would make citizens more satisfied with welfare systems. Cuts in welfare were also justified as necessary in order not to threaten growth – which in turn was a prerequisite for saving welfare in the long run.[44]

All of this would have major consequences for the Swedish welfare state. In an opinion piece in the leading Swedish morning newspaper *Dagens Nyheter* in the autumn of 2020 – under the headline 'No One Is Talking about Sweden No Longer Being a Welfare State' – the authors, including Joakim Palme, argued that representatives of Sweden like to describe their country as a welfare state of the Nordic model.[45] (Joakim Palme is the son of Olof Palme, and one of the foremost experts on the development of the Swedish welfare system.) In reality, however, Sweden has gradually moved away from this model in recent decades. The authors state that the core of the Nordic welfare model is usually considered to be a comprehensive social security system that includes insurance against sickness and unemployment, as well as old-age pensions. The systems are financed by contributions linked to income levels, and benefits are expected to follow the same principle. Except for the highest wage-earners, all citizens should be fully covered by social security.

But this no longer applies, Palme and his co-authors claimed. Politicians have failed to raise benefit levels at the same rate as nominal wages have risen. As a result, a growing number of people do not receive full compensation under the public welfare system. In health insurance, this applies to almost half of wage-earners; but the trend is the same in the pension and unemployment systems. As a result, an increasing proportion of high- and middle-income earners are taking out supplementary insurance on the private market.

A key idea behind the model, these authors wrote, was that it would be easier to gain democratic support for schemes that insured everyone, or at least the majority of the population. If current trends continue, there is a risk that democratic support for universal social security will

---

44 Jenny Andersson and Kjell Östberg, 'The Swedish Social Democrats, Reform Socialism and the State after the Golden Era', in Mathieu Fulla and Marc Lazar, eds, *European Socialists and the State in the Twentieth and Twenty-First Centuries* (Cham: Palgrave Macmillan, 2020).

45 Daniel Barr and Joakim Palme, 'Ingen talar om att Sverige inte längre är en välfärdsstat', *Dagens Nyheter*, 20 December 2020.

decline. It should be added that the levels of compensation in public insurance have also fallen. When they were introduced, the idea was that they would be paid at 100 per cent of income. They have since been gradually reduced, and now usually represent 80 per cent of earnings, or even less – as in the case of unemployment benefit.

The article reflects insightfully on the consequences of thirty years of deregulation, cuts, and privatisation of the public sector, carried out by both Social Democratic and right-wing governments. It is clear that bourgeois governments, and bourgeois-run municipalities, have been the driving force of the changes identified. But, almost without exception, the Social Democrats have accepted them when they have returned to power. Indeed, in some cases their actions have been decisive. Until 1990, as we have seen, the Social Democratic welfare state was almost entirely financed, owned, and operated using public funds. The right wing of the party wanted to open up to privatisation as early as the 1980s – Kjell-Olof Feldt wanted to start with day care centres. But resistance was intense, and there were legislative obstacles to this idea.

But in 1990, on the initiative of the Social Democratic government, a new law was adopted that allowed municipalities to transfer certain welfare services, such as health care and day care centres, into private hands, including those of profit-making companies. The previous year, the Social Democratic government had set up an inquiry to examine the benefits of competition in the municipal sector. One stated aim was to see whether this might enable cuts in public spending.[46]

The right-wing government that took office in 1991 was quick to seize this new opportunity, and decided that private companies in the welfare sector should be given the opportunity to have their activities financed with public funds on the same terms as publicly owned institutions. Reforms of great importance for the future were now being implemented in several areas. Profit-making health centres and schools would be financed as publicly run activities. These decisions had immediate and far-reaching consequences.[47]

---

46   Marta Szebehely and Gabrielle Maegher, 'Vinster i välfärden. En historia om näringslivslobbyism och socialdemokratisk ambivalens', in Lennart Erixon et al., eds, *Politik och marknad: kritiska studier av kapitalismens utveckling* (Stockholm: Dialogos, 2020).

47   Ibid.; Niklas Altermark and Åsa Plesner, *Vi skär ner i välfärden för att rädda välfärden: det socialdemokratiska självbedrägeriet* (Stockholm: Katalys, 2021).

In the health sector, a significant number of publicly owned health centres have been taken over by private enterprises. There was complete freedom to establish private tax-financed health centres. The result has been a large concentration of health facilities in the city centres, where the consumption of public health services is much higher than in not-so-wealthy suburbs. The privatisation of health care has also led to a thriving market in private health insurance, which provides quick access to doctors, and sometimes even allows queue-jumping for surgery and other publicly financed services.[48] At the same time, pharmacies have also been privatised, producing much the same geographical imbalance.

The consequences of the privatisation of care for the elderly have attracted a lot of attention. A series of scandals have been exposed involving blatant neglect in profit-driven and understaffed facilities. During the Covid-19 epidemic there was a marked excess of deaths in private nursing homes.

But the most controversial developments have been in education. Sweden is perhaps the only country in the world where privately owned, for-profit schools are allowed to operate on the same terms, and with the same public funds, as their publicly run counterparts. Combined with the right of parents to choose freely which schools their children will attend, this has led to substantial segregation. Wealthy families tend to place their children in the same schools. These schools avoid accepting pupils with special needs, who are instead referred to municipal schools. The reform has also led to severe grade inflation. In order to attract more pupils, it has been shown that privately owned schools give significantly higher grades than municipal schools.[49] Segregation in education occurs in many other countries, but what makes Sweden unique is that both types of school are entitled to equal levels of state subsidy. One idea behind the school reform was that it would encourage the emergence of schools with a wide range of educational and pedagogical specialisations. Instead, the great potential for financial gain has led to a strong concentration of ownership within large commercial groups, which are often bought up by international venture-capital firms.

---

48   John Lapidus, *Social Democracy and the Swedish Welfare Model: Ideational Analyses of Attitudes towards Competition, Individualization, Privatization* (Gothenburg: Göteborgs universitet, 2015), pp. 141ff.

49   Per Kornhall et al., eds, *När skolan blev en marknad: trettio år med friskolor* (Stockholm: Natur & Kultur, 2022).

Public housing policy – one of the most successful elements of Social Democratic welfare policy – has also largely become market driven. Municipal housing companies may no longer benefit from state loans, but must now also operate at a profit. As a result, housing construction has declined sharply, and the housing shortage is more acute today than it has been for fifty years. The market economy has proved an ineffective tool for guaranteeing the right to housing. In addition, many municipalities have sought to sell off public housing as private units. Privatisation has been particularly widespread in the attractive inner cities, and the result has been severe housing segregation. The idea of a decent home as a human right has been replaced by that of housing as an individual investment and future asset, or a cash-cow for greedy land-grabbers.[50]

For half a century, increasing equality was one of the Social Democrats' top priorities. The social security system, unemployment policy, and a solidarity-based wage policy were all aimed at pursuing this aim. Class society was never abolished, but by 1980 social and economic disparities were smaller than ever before, and smaller than in most other industrialised countries. Since then, economic disparities have grown faster than in almost all countries in the Organisation for Economic Co-operation and Development. Since 1981, the share of total wealth held by the wealthiest 1 per cent has risen from 18 to 42 per cent. Measured using the Gini coefficient, Sweden is now the most unequal industrialised society, with a figure of 0.87 in 2020, while the US figure was 0.85 and Sweden's Nordic neighbours lay between 0.74 and 0.78. In the brackets higher than Sweden, we find countries like the Bahamas, Bahrain, and Brunei.[51]

Rapidly widening global inequality is now well documented. But the fact that Sweden is one of the most unequal countries is a sign that today's Swedish politicians have neither the ability nor the ambition to defend the solidarity-based welfare society.

One important vector of inequality in Sweden is its tax system. Since the turn of the century, a number of taxes on companies and the wealthy have been reduced or abolished. Social Democratic governments have

---

50 Markus Holdo, Emma Holmqvist, and Bo Bengtsson, eds, *Allas rätt till bostad: marknadens begränsningar och samhällets ansvar* (Gothenburg: Bokförlaget Daidalos, 2022).
51 Andreas Cervenka, *Girig-Sverige: så blev folkhemmet ett paradis för de superrika* (Stockholm: Natur & Kultur, 2022); Göran Therborn, 'Twilight of Swedish Social Democracy', *New Left Review* II/113 (2019).

abolished inheritance and gift taxes, while bourgeois governments have abolished wealth and property taxes. In 2020, the Social Democratic government abolished the special tax levied on those with higher incomes to help rebuild welfare. As a result, the overall tax ratio has been reduced. In the 1980s it was 50 per cent of GDP; today it is 43 per cent. Of course, this has also contributed to a reduction in the scope for social reform, and a further erosion of welfare.

At the same time, it is striking that the widespread privatisation has had very little public support. In a survey conducted by the prestigious SOM Institute at the University of Gothenburg, 67 per cent supported a proposal to abolish profits in the welfare sector. Social Democrats were even more supportive of the idea – but even among Moderates and members of the other bourgeois parties, a majority was critical of the profit system, and the proportion has increased in recent years. The maintenance of higher tax rates to guarantee the welfare system also enjoys strong support deep inside the core groups of the bourgeois parties.[52] This, in turn, can only be explained by the fact that the universal, publicly funded welfare state is perceived as a democratic achievement – as important as universal suffrage.

The Partial Implosion of the Labour Movement

Two main explanations for the unique position of Swedish Social Democracy in the political landscape of the twentieth century have emerged in this book. The first of these is the political alternative offered by the party to the citizens of Sweden: to provide protection against the inequalities created by the unregulated market.[53] Second is the party's organisational strength and hegemonic position within the Swedish working class. Both of these advantageous circumstances have now been eroded.

To borrow concepts from the sociologist Walter Korpi: the power resources that the Swedish labour movement was so successfully able to

---

52   Stefan Svallfors, ed., *Contested Welfare States: Welfare Attitudes in Europe and Beyond* (Stanford, CA: Stanford University Press, 2012); Johan Martinsson and Ulrika Andersson, eds, *Swedish Trends: 1986–2020* (SOM-institute, University of Gothenburg, 2021).

53   Ingo Schmidt, 'Limits to Social Democracy, Populist Movements and Left Alternatives', in *The Three Worlds of Social Democracy: A Global View* (London: Pluto, 2016), p. 251.

develop have been greatly weakened. The Social Democratic Party was originally a workers' party in both the political and sociological senses. The industrial working class was its main source of recruitment. Even when the party's electoral base broadened, most obviously after the ATP reform in the early 1960s, it was the LO-affiliated workers who constituted the party's base, in terms of both voters and affiliated members. In the wake of post-Fordism, this base has been eroded considerably. Since 1980, the share of the working class in the narrow sense – industrial workers and workers linked to the transport and storage of industrial production – has fallen from 27 per cent to 19 per cent.[54] According to Göran Therborn, a broader definition including workers in health care, low-level white-collar workers, and clerks shows a less dramatic decline, from 61 to 46 per cent. Meanwhile, the middle classes have increased from 31 to 46 per cent. The petty bourgeoisie (sole traders) and the bourgeoisie remain at roughly the same levels of 8 per cent and 1 per cent, respectively.

Almost half of all employed people are women, as was the case in 1980. At the same time, the gender division of labour in the Swedish labour market is high. The largest occupational groups among women are carers (in health care, care homes for the elderly, and so on), teachers, and staff in trade and sales. Women thus work to a large extent in the public sector – where wages are often lower. Around one-sixth of the workforce is foreign-born, and largely working class.[55]

For a long time, the class vote was very pronounced in Sweden, and was an important reason for the strength of Social Democracy. None of the bourgeois parties have had any anchorage to speak of within the working class, and their presence in the trade union movement has been negligible. In 1960, almost 80 per cent of LO members voted for the labour parties, most of them for the Social Democrats. With one exception, this figure remained between 65 and 70 per cent until 2002, since when it has steadily declined. In recent elections, it is mainly the right-wing populist Sweden Democrats who have mounted the most effective challenge for the labour vote. Within the group of workers as a whole – one-third of workers today do not belong to a trade union – support for the Social Democrats has fallen even more drastically: only 32 per cent

---

54   Göran Therborn, 'Klasserna idag', in Daniel Suhonen, Göran Therborn, and Jesper Weithz, eds, *Klass i Sverige: ojämlikheten, makten och politiken i det 21:a århundradet* (Lund: Arkiv, 2021).

55   Ibid.

vote for the Social Democrats. Almost as many, 29 per cent, vote for the Sweden Democrats. Among male workers, the Sweden Democrats have long been the largest party. Among white-collar workers, fluctuations have been more pronounced, but since 1964 roughly 30 to 40 per cent have voted for the Social Democratic Party. In 2022, 32 per cent of the middle classes voted for the party.[56]

Internationally, Sweden has for many decades had a very high level of unionisation. In 1980, 85 per cent of all workers and white-collar employees were unionised, though a degree of decline set in during the 1980s. The big downturn came after 2006, when the bourgeois government made it much more expensive to belong to a union unemployment fund. Today, overall union density is below 70 per cent; but, while white-collar workers' organisations have remained at a high level – above 70 per cent – only 60 per cent of those working in the areas organised by the LO are union members. Younger workers, in particular, are non-union.[57]

The fact that trade unions have long refrained from using their most powerful weapon – the strike – has of course further weakened the power resources of the trade union movement.

The Party

The decline in the Social Democratic Party's membership has been spectacular.[58] Until the early 1990s, most members were collectively affiliated through the LO. When this mechanism was abolished, membership fell overnight from 1.2 million to 250,000. Since then, membership has fallen by a further two-thirds. The party now has 75,000 members, most of whom are over sixty. In the 1970s, the Swedish Social Democratic Youth League (SSU) had 60,000 members, while today it generally fluctuates between 5,000 and 10,000 members. The Women's Union has lost 80 per cent of its members in the same period.

---

56   H. Ekengren Oscarsson et al., *VALU 2022: SVT:s vallokalsundersökning riks-dagsvalet 2022* (Sveriges Television AB, 2022), p. 21.

57   Anders Kjellberg, *The Membership Development of Swedish Trade Unions and Union Confederations since the End of the Nineteenth Century* (Lund: Lund University, Department of Sociology, 2017).

58   Kjell Östberg, 'The Decline of Nordic Social Democracy', in Anu Koivunen, Jari Ojala, and Janne Holmén, eds, *The Nordic Economic, Social and Political Model* (Abingdon: Routledge, 2021).

Significantly, the only organisation in the Social Democratic movement that has maintained its membership is the pensioners' association (PRO). The federation of consumer cooperatives has undergone repeated economic crises, which have led to restructuring and a resulting weakening of its ideological profile. Many People's Houses have suffered from financial problems. Several have been sold or closed, or taken over by municipalities.

A particular problem for Swedish Social Democracy is its weak press. Both at the national and local levels, Social Democratic newspapers have traditionally found it difficult to compete with the bourgeois newspapers, which have attracted much more of the advertising that is the life-blood of the press. Nonetheless, there were for a long time many Social Democratic newspapers, both in the big cities and in most counties. However, with the bankruptcy of the Social Democratic newspaper company A-pressen in 1992, most Social Democratic dailies have ceased publication. The situation in the big cities is particularly concerning. Among papers with national coverage, only the tabloid *Aftonbladet* survives. For a long time, it was owned by the LO, but a 90 per cent share was sold to the Norwegian Schibsted Media Group in 2003, on the condition that the LO continue to appoint the management of the opinion-forming pages.[59]

The success of Social Democracy must be understood historically in relation to its ability to interact with other social movements. These too have been weakened. The classic popular movements of the last century – the Free Church movement and the temperance movement – have dwindled in size and influence to an even greater extent than the labour movement, and their socially transformative ambitions have largely become irrelevant.[60] Meanwhile, most of the other political parties have lost members to at least the same extent as the Social Democrats.[61]

No widespread upsurges of social struggle have taken place in recent decades. The alterglobalisation movement of the turn of the century heralded a certain revitalisation of social movements in Sweden, especially among young people. The anti-racist movement has been

59   Ibid.
60   Lars Trägårdh, ed., *State and Civil Society in Northern Europe: The Swedish Model Reconsidered* (New York: Berghahn, 2007).
61   Kjell Östberg, *Folk i rörelse: vår demokratis historia* (Stockholm: Ordfront, 2021), pp. 311ff.

important, and has regularly resurged – particularly in connection with anti-immigration actions. Refugee solidarity has been the subject of long-term work, in which religious groups have also played a prominent role. The 'Greta effect' was of course evident in the Swedish climate struggle, but faded, at least temporarily, during the Covid-19 crisis.[62]

Some of the most influential movements have become institutionalised. Parts of the environmental movement formed a Green Party (Miljöpartiet) in the 1980s, and the party has been represented in the Riksdag since the 1980s. Certainly, there were also tensions between more radical *fundis* and more collaborative *realos* in Sweden.[63] Since 2000, however, the party has mainly functioned as a parliamentary entity, striking far-reaching agreements with the Social Democrats, and has been in government for seven years. The price of this cooperation has been severe compromises on refugee and defence policies – but also on environmental issues. The party has proved unable to profit from the growing salience of the climate crisis.

Parts of the women's movement came together in 2005 in a newly formed political party, Feminist Initiative. Behind the party was an eclectic mix of women with roots in second-wave feminism, gender researchers, and a new generation of young women's activists. For a time, the party was successful in local elections in the big cities, and had a representative in the European Parliament. But since the setback in the parliamentary elections in 2018, the party has lost influence.

The broader collective struggles that have sustained demands for more extensive political and social reforms during periods of deeper radicalisation remain largely absent. One important reason for this is the sharp decline in the trade union struggle: 2020 was the first year since official statistics began when the number of strikes recorded was zero.

Internal relations within the Social Democrats have been significantly influenced by the elitism and professionalisation that have generally characterised today's political parties.[64] The traditional mass

---

62 Abby Peterson, Håkan Thörn, and Mattias Wahlström, 'Sweden 1950–2015: Contentious Politics and Social Movements between Confrontation and Political Cooperation', in Flemming Mikkelsen, Knut Kjeldstadli, and Stefan Nyzell, eds, *Popular Struggle and Democracy in Scandinavia: 1700–Present* (London: Palgrave Macmillan, 2018).

63 Maggie Strömberg, *Vi blev som dom andra: miljöpartiets väg till makten* (Stockholm: Atlas, 2016).

64 Östberg, 'Decline of Nordic Social Democracy'.

parties of the Social Democratic type have evolved into professional 'catch-all' parties in which members and their activities play a much less prominent role. Most tellingly, the question of class, which was often an important part of the old mass parties, has receded from the foreground.

The tasks that members used to be essential for are no longer necessary. State party subsidies and sponsorship have led to membership fees now playing a negligible role in the party's budget. Opinion polls are replacing information from member organisations. The media and PR consultants are seen as more effective and carefully targeted bearers of the party's message than the membership. The Social Democratic Party today has a significant under-representation of workers in relation to its electoral base – and this is more evident in the higher reaches of the party. In Olof Palme's first government, in the early 1970s, half of his ministers had a background as LO-affiliated workers; today there are only a handful.[65]

Meanwhile, the party's leadership is increasingly recruited from a narrow social stratum, distinct from that of members and voters. The professionalisation of party leaderships and growing opportunities for careers outside the party, in business or lobbying organisations, have further reduced the need for feedback to the party from members.

The professionalisation of politics has also led to a sharp increase in the proportion of 'political broilers' – senior representatives with no professional experience outside politics. The term 'political aristocracy' has been used to illustrate the fact that many new leaders are the children of an older generation of Social Democratic politicians. When a new generation took over at the 2006 party leadership changeover, both main candidates, Mona Sahlin and Per Nuder, largely lacked professional experience outside politics – and both had fathers with prominent positions in the movement and the Social Democratic–dominated state administration.

For a long time, values based on the egalitarian ideals of the labour movement dominated even in the upper echelons of the Social Democratic Party. Leaders with roots in other classes also observed a strong loyalty to the values of the labour movement – Tage Erlander lived in an apartment building also as prime minister, and Olof Palme in an ordinary terraced house in a middle- and working-class suburb of Stockholm. These values have perished. Finance ministers such as

---

65   Ibid., pp. 131ff.

Kjell-Olof Feldt, Erik Åsbrink, and Per Nuder quickly moved on to lives as well-paid boardroom professionals. It is hard to imagine Wigforss or Sträng in that role.

Many other leading Social Democrats from the government and cabinet have also sought top positions in the business world, not least the so-called chancellery right. All the major commercial banks have had representatives from the chancellery right or Social Democratic Economic Association on their boards, and several have moved between assignments in the major banks and the central bank of Sweden.

In our day, top Social Democratic politicians, following their resignations, have mainly chosen putting their political capital at the disposal of big business through PR agencies and consultancies. Former prime minister Göran Persson is the clearest example. In other countries, these developments might not have attracted the same attention, but in Sweden, where the ideals of equality are still central to the labour movement, they have made a major contribution to the Social Democrats' loss of legitimacy.[66]

It is clear that the entire Social Democratic movement is disintegrating. The skeleton remains, but the powerful national hegemony that the Social Democratic movement long enjoyed, especially in communities with large industries, has weakened over time.

An example can be taken from one of the party's traditionally strongest areas, Ådalen, long dominated by forest industry. In the early 1970s, there were seventeen Social Democratic workers' communes in the municipality, twelve women's clubs, six SSU associations, the children's organisation Young Eagles, tenants' associations, the PRO, and a dozen trade unions – all of which were seen as part of the Social Democratic movement. There were also seven People's Houses and a large People's Park. The Workers' Educational Association (ABF) had a lively study programme and half a dozen employees. The consumers' cooperative built a large new department store. An annual meeting of the larger workers' communes might attract 200 to 300 participants.

Almost all parts of the movement remain today. But the activities have faded away, leading the organisations to ossify. There are only two workers' communes left. The larger of the two marshalled thirty participants at a recent annual meeting, which was considered a good turnout; the other has a couple of sparsely attended meetings per year. Almost all

---

66   Ibid., pp. 143ff.

the women's clubs have been closed; the SSU flourishes now and then, but withers away when young people leave the municipality to study elsewhere. Only the pensioners' association has increased its activities. The average age is high – and the difficulties in recruiting young people are obvious.

In the last elections, the party has lost its local majority for the first time since the democratic breakthrough. But the party is still the largest in local politics; a dwindling local elite still rules.

A couple of decades ago, it was obvious that the vast majority of union representatives were organised Social Democrats. That is no longer the case. At the central level, the Social Democrats still devote a great deal of effort to controlling who is elected to senior positions, and those without Social Democratic membership remain very rare. At the local level, this possibility is often lacking, and members of the right-wing populist Sweden Democrats are also elected to board positions.

With the partial collapse of the Youth League, the party has lost the reservoir from which it has traditionally recruited its leadership at various levels. In a majority of industrial towns, there is no Social Democratic youth activity at all – which, of course, further weakens the party's character as a class-based organisation.

The 2000s

The Social Democrats' turn to neoliberal policies has been poorly received, both by voters and within the party.

The change in policy was not the result of any pressure from below. On the contrary, as we have seen, protests against it were widespread in the 1980s. Voter support declined throughout the 1980s. In the 1991 elections, the party lost 5.5 percentage points of the popular vote, receiving its lowest share since the 1928 Cossack elections. The Social Democrats were able to bounce back in the election that followed, but continued the severe welfare cuts initiated by the right-wing government. The result was a new slump in voter opinion. The decline has continued in the current century. A party that had typically received 45 to 50 per cent of the vote since the 1930s now receives around 30 per cent.[67]

---

67   Kjell Östberg, 'Swedish Social Democracy after the Cold War: Whatever Happened to the Movement?', in Ingo Schmidt and Evans, *Social Democracy after the Cold War*.

The party retained government power between 1994 and 2006 through parliamentary cooperation with the Left Party and the Green Party. In 2006 four bourgeois parties were able to form a government, and they managed to maintain it until 2014. Between 2014 and 2022, Sweden was governed by minority governments headed by Social Democrats in coalition with or with organised support from Greens, Liberals, and the Centre Party.

Internal criticism of the Social Democratic Party's policies continued throughout the 1990s. It was expressed especially clearly in the 1998 elections, when a substantial proportion of the party's female voters voted for the Left Party instead. But the LO also strongly criticised austerity measures that had led to an unemployment rate of over 10 per cent – the highest since the 1930s. It went so far as to discourage its members from participating in the party's 1 May demonstrations.[68]

After the turn of the century, the LO leaders who were critical of the Social Democrats were replaced. The largest union, the Swedish Municipal Workers' Union, even became a driving force behind the privatisation of municipal services, and the second largest, the Metalworkers' Union (IF Metall), concluded an extremely pro-business agreement with employers, while demands for workplace democracy disappeared permanently from the trade union agenda.[69] IF Metall chair Stefan Löfven, who would later become prime minister, argued strongly for restoring 'the Swedish model' on a global scale through 'an international handshake between labour and capital'.

Support for neoliberal policies has remained fragile among party members. One sign of this was the outcome of the 2003 referendum on economic and monetary union (EMU) proposed by the European Union. Despite the active participation of all key party and LO leaders in the campaign for Swedish accession to EMU, a clear majority of Social Democrats voted 'No', and the proposal fell.[70] But criticism has been expressed most clearly in the membership's attitude to privatisation and profit-making in the welfare sector. As we have seen, opposition

---

68   Ibid., p. 215.

69   Lars Ekdahl, *Välfärdssamhällets spegel: Kommunal 1960–2010* (Stockholm: Premiss, 2010); Lars Ekdahl, 'Ett fackligt dilemma: Metall i politiken', in Lars Ekdahl et al., eds, *Svenska metallindustriarbetareförbundet. Vägval i motvind Bd 6 1982–2005* (Stockholm: Industrifacket Metall, 2017).

70   Henrik Oscarsson and Sören Holmberg, eds, *Kampen om euron* (Gothenburg: University of Gothenburg, 2004).

to the privatisation of welfare services has been strong even among bourgeois voters. Among Social Democrats it is much higher. At congress after congress, the issue of banning profits has dominated discussion – but the party leadership has refused to go beyond non-committal statements against 'profit hunting'.

An interesting sign of the mood among Social Democratic Party members was the election of Håkan Juholt as leader in 2011. The episode is in many ways reminiscent of the experience of the election of Jeremy Corbyn in 2015 as leader of the British Labour Party. The background was that the party leadership could not agree on which of the likely right-wing candidates would succeed Mona Sahlin, who had resigned after the 2010 election defeat. This opened the door to a relatively unknown backbencher with no ties to the Stockholm-based coterie that had long ruled the party.[71] Juholt was not a distinctly left-wing candidate, but he had travelled around the country and visited Social Democratic Party branches, and was very familiar with general feeling in the party. He began his leadership by putting into words the opinions he had encountered. He questioned welfare profits and called for an improved pension system – demands that the party leadership had so far rejected.

The immediate result was a sharp rise in the party's poll numbers. After a while, Juholt's popularity declined. This was partly due to personal shortcomings, but above all to the fact that he was subjected to an intense media onslaught from bourgeois newspapers, which were worried about a radicalised Social Democracy. Social Democratic newspapers followed suit. It is also clear that parts of the party apparatus openly sabotaged the work of the new party chair and engaged in internal campaigns to undermine Juholt's position. As a result, he was forced to resign after barely a year, and was replaced by Stefan Löfven.[72]

There was a right-wing shift in Swedish politics after 2015 that took several forms, and affected the policies of the Social Democrats in crucial areas. One reason for this has been the growth of right-wing populism, expressed particularly in the success of the Sweden Democrats. Unlike several other right-wing populist parties, the Sweden

---

71   Daniel Suhonen, *Partiledaren som klev in i kylan: berättelsen om Juholts fall och den nya politiken* (Stockholm: Leopard, 2014).

72   Ulf Bjereld, Cecilia Garme, and Jonas Hinnfors, *Att älska den man kan få: januariavtalet och svensk demokrati i förändring* (Stockholm: Atlas, 2022), pp. 94–7.

Democrats have their roots in the racist and neo-Nazi movements that grew strong in Sweden during the 1990s. The party's success was mainly a function of its criticism of immigration and immigrants.[73]

The debate on immigration culminated with the surge of refugees from Syria and Afghanistan in the autumn of 2015. Sweden was among the countries that received the most refugees. Large voluntary refugee reception centres were established, and the Social Democratic prime minister solemnly declared that Sweden would not close borders but build bridges. A month later, the borders were closed and the Social Democratic government declared that Sweden would henceforth implement the EU's most restrictive refugee policy.[74]

Historically, the Social Democrats' approach to immigration and the reception of refugees has not been without problems. Until the 1930s, Sweden was primarily a country of emigration. In the 1930s the Social Democratic government hesitated to accept Jewish refugees from Nazi Germany, only increasing its readiness sometime in the 1940s. During the postwar period, labour shortages were a growing problem for Swedish industry that was largely solved by importing a labour force. Most workers came from Finland, and initially West Germany and Italy. In the 1960s the Swedish public employment service set up special recruitment offices in Greece, Yugoslavia, and Turkey. But when the economy slowed in the 1970s, the borders were closed to labour immigration from outside the Nordic countries.[75]

Refugee migration has at times been numerically significant. In the 1970s many refugees arrived from Latin America, in the 1990s from the Balkans, and more recently from non-European countries including Syria, Afghanistan, Ethiopia, and Somalia. On several occasions in the past, a Social Democratic government has imposed drastic halts on refugee admissions – but never using such extreme means as in 2015. Overnight, the rhetoric also changed, now portraying the wave of refugees as an uncontrollable invasion that flooded Swedish municipalities and threatened Swedish welfare.

---

73 Gellert Tamas, *Den avgörande striden: tre decennier i Sverigedemokraternas värld* (Stockholm: Polaris, 2022).

74 For an insightful interpretation of the changes in attitude during these years, see Erik Hansson, *The Begging Question: Sweden's Social Responses to the Roma Destitute* (Lincoln: University of Nebraska Press, 2023), Chapters 7–9.

75 Ingvar Svanberg and Mattias Tydén, *Tusen år av invandring: en svensk kulturhistoria* (Stockholm: Gidlund, 1992).

The Social Democratic government implemented a series of measures to bring Swedish refugee policy closer to the EU's minimum standards. Border controls have been tightened, family reunification has been made more difficult, and refugees can no longer count on receiving permanent residency permits. But these measures did nothing to dampen the rhetoric of anti-immigrant currents. The Sweden Democrats continued to grow, while the Social Democrats' 2018 and 2022 election results marked a new low for the party since 1911.

The Social Democratic Party managed to retain power in 2018 only through far-reaching compromises with two bourgeois parties, the Liberals and the market-liberal Centre Party.[76] The Social Democrats made sweeping concessions in the agreement, including tax cuts for high earners and the introduction of market-oriented rents. Most notable was the party's decision to weaken the Employment Protection Act, one of the trade union movement's most important achievements. Meanwhile, the restrictive immigration policy continued. The party also promised not to oppose further privatisation of the public sector. The price for the party's inability to develop a policy to defend welfare was paid in the 2022 elections.

While the most important issue for voters was health care, and while the impending climate disaster was increasingly clear, an aggressive right wing, with the help of a passive and unimaginative Social Democratic Party, focused the election campaign around crime, tougher prison sentences, and immigration. Instead of discussing measures to combat climate change, the election campaign was limited to discussing how quickly nuclear power could be expanded.

The Social Democrats' tactic was essentially to align their programme with that of the right.[77] The government entered the bidding for longer prison sentences, proudly declaring that it has tightened around seventy criminal laws. Likewise, it has emphasised the link between crime and immigration. Leading representatives have argued for special legislation for 'non-Nordic' residents, while the prime minister has spoken condescendingly about 'Somalitowns'.

The government's most high-profile capitulation, however, was the decision to abandon 200 years of formal Swedish neutrality policy and

---

76 Bjereld, Garme, and Hinnfors, *Att älska den man kan få.*

77 Jonas Hinnfors, 'Socialdemokraterna: högervridning och hot utifrån', in Niklas Bolin et al., eds, *Snabbtänkt 2.0 22: Reflektioner från valet 2022 av ledande forskare* (Sundsvall: Mittuniversitetet, 2022).

apply for NATO membership. Following the invasion of Ukraine by Russia on 24 February 2022, the initial Social Democratic reaction was that Sweden joining NATO would contribute to the further destabilisation of the security situation in northern Europe. After an intense campaign by the right-wing parties, however, the party leadership bowed to the pressure without consulting the party membership. The most compelling reason for this was to remove the issue from the election campaign, which it succeeded in doing.[78] Accession to NATO and the war in Ukraine were completely absent, along with the climate crisis, from the campaign leading up to the September 2022 election.

Nevertheless, the Social Democrats lost government power to a right-wing coalition of four parties. The right-wing bias that was evident throughout the election campaign was particularly prominent among the right-wing parties. The three traditional bourgeois parties – the Moderates, the Christian Democrats, and the Liberals – all lost vote share compared to 2018. At the same time, votes for the populist Sweden Democrats rose sharply, making it the largest party in the right-wing bloc.[79]

Up to the 2018 elections, there was a demarcation line of decency within the Swedish bourgeoisie against cooperation with a xenophobic extremist party.[80] That line is now fully erased.

On the contrary, on immigration or crime the programme of the Sweden Democrats became predominantly that of the incoming bourgeois government. The Sweden Democrats are now the dominant right-wing party. Outside the big cities, they often receive 25 to 30 per cent of the vote, winning contests more or less equally with the left and the right. Clearly, a significant proportion of those votes have come from workers who previously voted for the Social Democrats. Today, the Sweden Democrats are successfully challenging the Social Democrats in the working-class vote, each party taking around 30 per cent. Among men, the Sweden Democrats are already in the lead.

The Social Democrats have continued to lose voters in areas where they previously had a strong showing, including the traditional industrial towns and in northern Sweden. In addition, the party made spectacular

---

78   Jonas Harvard, 'Ett historiskt val. Om neutraliteten som en ickefråga i valrörelsen 2022', in Niklas Bolin et al., *Snabbtänkt*.

79   Niklas Bolin and Kajsa Falasca, 'Valet som delade Sverige', in Niklas Bolin et al., *Snabbtänkt*.

80   Anders Backlund, *Isolating the Radical Right: Coalition Formation and Policy Adaptation in Sweden* (Huddinge: Södertörn University, 2020).

losses in some areas with large numbers of immigrants, traditionally Social Democratic strongholds. This was due to protests against the party leadership's contemptuous statements about these areas, and against the party's repeated claims about links between immigration and crime. By contrast, the party made progress in the big cities, which contained large parts of a middle class that found it difficult to accept the traditional bourgeois parties' close collaboration with the Sweden Democrats.[81]

Although the party increased its share of the vote by 2 percentage points, achieving 30.3 per cent, this was the second-worst result in 110 years.

The autumn 2022 elections thus represented the completion of the Social Democrats' transition from a socialist workers' party with the ambition to build a robust welfare state and fundamentally transform society to a party without ideas, led by a professional leadership with increasingly fragile working-class roots.

---

81   Ekengren Oscarsson et al., *VALU 2022*.

Conclusion

What, Then, Are the Strengths and Weaknesses of Swedish Social Democracy?

The Movement

The unique position of Swedish Social Democracy, internationally as well as domestically, cannot be explained without understanding its organisational strength.

From the beginning, the trade unions were the base of the Social Democratic labour movement. Their strength rose with the rapid growth of Swedish industrial capitalism around the turn of the twentieth century, and by the beginning of that century large parts of the industrial working class were unionised. The emergence of the LO gave blue-collar workers a unified trade union structure linking them closely to the Social Democratic Party. Sweden was ethnically and religiously a relatively homogeneous country, and there were no successful attempts to organise on a different basis than class.

But Swedish Social Democracy had a much broader social and organisational base. Alongside the party's workers' communes, youth associations, women's clubs, cooperatives, educational associations, high schools run by the workers' movements, and temperance societies constituted important points of support. Close relations with other popular movements, especially the temperance movement, further contributed to party members' high levels of education, both culturally and in organisational work.

The Social Democratic movement thus became the natural organisational platform and social agent of the Swedish working class, dominating the mill towns and working-class districts of the big cities politically, socially, and culturally. The movement's programme challenged existing society in several areas. It called for the empowerment of its class, and articulated the idea of a society not based on exploitation. In this way, the movement helped to shape the working class as such. The movement became a collective intellectual entity. Its representatives were products of the social movements from which they came. And the leadership of the party, including newspapermen and parliamentary representatives, would for several decades be recruited predominantly from the working class.

The view that the Swedish labour movement was from the outset geared to resolving differences by peaceful means – an idea often promoted by the Social Democrats themselves – has little support in reality. Sweden was at the top of the international statistics for strike action in the early twentieth century, during the 1930s crisis, and in the 1970s. At the same time, leadership of the party was transferred early on to a tightly knit professional stratum based in the parliamentary caucus and among trade union officials. This bureaucracy also came to be the base of the class-collaborationist, reformist current that systematically outmanoeuvred the left, with its more class-struggle-focused perspective. The contradictions caused the party to split in 1917. The left of the party joined the world communist movement, but failed decisively to break the hegemony of the old party within the working class. Instead, most of the left's leaders gradually returned to the mother party – a process facilitated by the Communist Party's increasingly Stalinist alignment.

During the interwar period, the dominance of Social Democracy was strengthened, and the 'people's movement's party' developed deep roots in industrial towns and urban working-class neighbourhoods. The party's local activists increasingly dominated municipal politics. A local welfare bureaucracy gave organisational strength, but also increased the party's focus on parliamentary work. Although the revitalised social movements that characterised the period, particularly through the women's movement and a surge in trade union organisation, had a much broader base, the party often succeeded in linking them to its project.

The Social Democratic Party's successful takeover of government power in 1932 meant that, from then on, it was also seen at the national level as a competent party that was eminently suitable for government. Its advanced reform programme and ability to recruit the radical intellectuals of the time gave the party a hallmark of modernism. The postwar period further strengthened the party's power resources.

Fordism was the era of the mass parties, and in Sweden the Social Democrats' position remained unchallenged.

The various elements of the movement – the LO, the youth federation (SSU), the Women's League, the education branch (ABF), and the cooperative sector – were larger than ever. The party's position within the working class was unchallenged, while the Communists were languishing in the shadow of the Cold War. Gradually, the party's support began to grow among the growing white-collar stratum, which helped maintain the party's image of representing modernity. A new generation of intellectuals, often with working-class roots, applied for jobs in ministries and governmental agencies, and the Social Democrats dominated the welfare bureaucracy at all levels.

Confronted with the demands for social reform that characterised the radicalisation of the 1960s and '70s, the Social Democratic movement itself became radicalised. In national and local government, the party's competent and experienced representatives were to a large extent able to deliver the reforms that were being asked for. However, the party also had to pay the price for its long hold on power, with its gradual shift from movement work to parliamentary work, and from member democracy to bureaucratic decision-making. The election loss in 1976 can be seen partly as a reaction to this change in the party's character.

The Social Democratic government's accommodation to neoliberal policies in the 1980s was also the beginning of the party's organisational decline. The fact that the party was no longer the obvious guarantor for the working class against the consequences of the crises of capitalism led parts of the working class to seek alternatives. The hefty loss in the 1991 elections – which also put New Democracy, a xenophobic party, in parliament for the first time – was a first indication of what was to come.

There are also structural explanations for the weakening of the movement. The deep economic crises of the late 1970s, early 1990s, and around 2010 led to a sharp decline in the industrial working class and, crucially, a weakening of the industrial centres that constituted the main social base of Social Democracy. At the same time, the party failed to build a strong presence in the new residential areas around the big cities, where the Social Democrats' new potential voters, not least among the immigrant population, were largely located. The most important guarantee of cohesion in maintaining the Social Democrats' identity, and the environments in which the party's policies could be anchored, communicated, and to some extent created, had vanished.

The party's membership base was gradually eroded. One million members disappeared when collective affiliation to the LO ended in 1991; a further two-thirds have been lost since then. Unionisation among workers, which for a long time stood at 80 to 90 per cent, has fallen sharply; among younger workers, fewer than 40 percent are organised. Youth and women's unions have lost most of their members.

The Social Democrats have lost their special status among the working class, and their share of the vote is now on a par with that of the right-wing populist Sweden Democrats. In the Social Democratic Party, leaders are recruited from an increasingly narrow social circle that is distinct from those of the party's members and voters. Party leadership has become professionalised, and the career paths of those in all parties have become increasingly similar. The loyalties of those leaders increasingly lie with their political class. The Social Democratic Party has largely developed into a professional 'catch-all' party.

Towards a Different Society? Ideology and Politics

The Swedish Social Democratic Party has a reputation for coherent ideological continuity. It is true that the party has had several prominent thinkers who have made important ideological contributions to the party's programmatic development, and there has been a tendency to try to construct a narrative of a party with deep ideological roots retrospectively. But the impact of these ideas on the formulation of practical policy has been limited.

Socialism was, of course, on the horizon from the outset as a lofty goal; in this respect, Swedish Social Democracy was no different from its European counterparts. Even Branting clung until the end to the dream of state-owned, large-scale production as the 'backbone' of a future socialist society. But socialism would come anyway because of the growth of the working class and the inherent contradictions of capitalism. In the meantime, the task of the labour movement was to expand political democracy and use its growing influence to improve the social situation of the class – although there were those who, unlike Branting, believed that the process could be accelerated by mobilising the labour movement in strikes and other mass struggles.

The revolutionary situation at the end of the First World War profoundly transformed this perspective. The left of the party gave its full support to the revolutionary currents, and was forced to leave. In a few years, the possibility of socialist development suddenly became an urgent question for large parts of the party. Universal suffrage and the formation of a Social Democratic government brought into focus the question of what the party should use its influence for. The experience of the council movement and the struggle for democracy in the workplace pointed to the possibility of extending the boundaries of politics into the economic sphere, and attempts were made to formulate a strategy combining the demands of industrial democracy with a programme of radical social reform that would point the way towards a different society.

The decline in labour radicalisation, the postwar depression, and the fragile parliamentary situation drove the radical wing of the party into retreat. Parliamentarism came to be fully accepted. The question of economic and industrial democracy as the basis for socialist social transformation disappeared from the agenda, and along with it the question of socialism. Instead, a political objective was formulated which, with an elegant ideological superstructure borrowed from Nils Karleby, became the guiding principle of Social Democracy for years to come: the goal was nothing; reforms were everything.

Two issues sat at the top of the Social Democratic reform agenda: the fight against unemployment and the development of a basic social safety net for the working class. But reforms required resources – and here socialist dreams were of little help. The new generation of Social Democratic leaders knew no other way to create the necessary resources than to boost industrial production. Thus, the central task of every Social Democratic government from then on was to create the conditions for as much growth as possible, and to facilitate this by encouraging enterprises – albeit still capitalist-owned and -operated – to rationalise and make production more efficient.

The party has taken this task very seriously. One aim of the active crisis policy of the 1930s was to help industry function at maximum efficiency. The government's aim was to take overall planning responsibility for the long-term growth of capitalist production. With this in mind, after the Second World War the government initiated a large number of investigations within the framework of the Postwar Programme. The practical outcome was insignificant: the business community was grateful for the tax cuts and the possibility of pooling profits offered by Social Democratic governments, but was not interested in allowing politics to interfere in industrial planning or – above all – in investment.

It was only with the tripartite corporate system that emerged in the postwar period that the Social Democrats and Swedish capitalists were able to find forms of institutionalised cooperation and mutual trust that could unite them in driving forward the growth of Swedish industry, while at the same time minimising social conflict. The trade union movement – singing the praises of growth in all keys – played a crucial role in this. Through the Saltsjöbaden Agreement, the LO had committed to avoiding strike action by any means necessary. Meanwhile, through the Rehn–Meidner model, the trade union movement adopted a wage policy that actively contributed to the rationalisation of the economy. At the same time, the government took responsibility for restructuring the labour market through active policies tailored to that purpose. But the model was a class compromise that required strong trade unions. Together with economic growth, it granted conditions for social reforms, even though the Swedish welfare system remained on a modest level well into the 1960s.

The widespread radicalisation that culminated in the 1970s, which deeply affected both Swedish Social Democracy and the trade union movement, challenged the model of corporate consensus in some crucial areas. The government announced an intensified state industrial policy, in which the activities of already state-owned enterprises would be coordinated and expanded. The proposal for wage-earner funds even threatened the right of capital to decide over production. But the Social Democrats withdrew from any proposals that interfered with the effective monopoly of capital over production. That was the line drawn by capital – and again accepted by Social Democracy.

From the neoliberal turn of the 1980s to the present day, the party has unreservedly endorsed the view that economic growth must be left to the market. Historical references to ideologues like Ernst Wigforss and Karleby, or to Olof Palme's defence of the solidarity-based welfare state, ring hollow as the public sector is sold off and the Nordic welfare model eroded. And Swedish Social Democracy has not produced any relevant new ideas – or political innovation – in the last forty years.

Tim Tilton and many others argue for the socially transformative power of Social Democratic ideas, but they have difficulty showing how and when those ideas can be translated into social reality. Instead, there are often significant gaps between ideas and action. Wigforss, for example, formulated some of Social Democracy's most radical programmes and most beautiful dreams. At the same time, it was he who closed the door on any form of radical industrial democracy in the early 1920s, imposing reform freezes and trustful cooperation with employers that cooled off the radical currents of the late 1930s and '40s.

The Limits of Democracy

The Swedish labour movement was the leading actor in the struggle for expanded democratic rights. Early on, the struggle for freedoms of speech, assembly, association, and the press were at the centre of this effort – which was both an obvious component of the party's programme and a means of surviving the repression of the ruling classes. The Social Democrats were also the only political party to stand unreservedly for universal and equal suffrage for all citizens. They did not develop their own idea of what democracy should look like; the party, and especially its leadership, simply accepted the Liberals' and the popular movements' positive view of parliamentary democracy.

In the dramatic years surrounding the First World War, the democratic perspective suddenly broadened. The international debate on the council movement raised the question of workers' power in the workplace, as well as that of economic democracy. The leaders of the new generation of Social Democrats participated in this discussion with great commitment. As radicalisation faded and the split in the international labour movement rendered council democracy controversial for Social Democracy, the debate on workers' power over work was reduced to the idea of creating various toothless bodies to oversee cooperation between employers and trade unions.

Social Democracy ultimately chose to accept liberal democracy, with all its limitations. At the same time, representatives of the labour movement made great efforts to democratise political structures, not least at the local level. The traditional elites were gradually replaced by workers. The broad labour movement, with the workers' communes at its centre, functioned as a network of local counter-hegemonic bodies in which programmes and dreams of a more decent life for the working class could be formulated – and increasingly implemented. Members were at the same time activists, movement builders and local politicians. A similar development took place at the national level, in the wake of the party's rise to power.

A new goal was now formulated – that of expanding the boundaries of democracy: political democracy was to be followed by Social Democracy. By gaining social rights, citizens would be able to live a safer and richer life, and to realise more fully their hopes and aspirations. The third phase, that of economic democracy, could then be realised. To a large extent, the creation of a welfare state based on solidarity could be said to have fulfilled the aspirations of social citizenship.

In the 1970s, the question of economic democracy reappeared after half a century in the wilderness. The trade union movement called for the abolition of the unilateral power of employers to manage and distribute work. The Social Democratic government quickly implemented the Employment Protection Act and the Co-determination Act, as well as a new Work Environment Act – all of which aimed to restrict employers' rights. But the issue of extending the boundaries of democracy was given real momentum by the LO's proposal for wage-earner funds, which challenged the ownership of capital and aimed to give trade unions real opportunities to decide on the direction of production. All of these proposals were met with great enthusiasm in the labour movement, and in youth and women's unions advanced discussions were held on extending economic democracy in a socialist direction, with power coming from below.

None of these hopes were fulfilled. The party leadership worked actively to deprive the proposal for wage-earner funds of any socially transformative elements, and ultimately succeeded. Instead, it advocated a 'functional socialist' solution in which the question of workers' empowerment would be resolved through legislation and institutional reform. The question of ownership was taken off the agenda. However, the main result – the Co-determination Act – did not include any power in the form of decision-making or veto rights for the unions, and the employers successfully blocked any attempt to introduce them. The Social Democrats also abstained from using the Co-determination Act, in their capacity as a public-sector employer, to give the unions such tools.

In the 1980s, the issue of workplace democracy disappeared from the labour movement's agenda, and it has not reappeared. Instead, the neoliberal counter-revolution entailed an increasing shift of power from politics to the market, reinforced by the weakening of the welfare state and the partial sell-off of the public sector. Meanwhile, economic austerity has greatly reduced the scope for political decisions to be made in the interests of the working class. A series of institutional reforms have worked in this same direction. EU membership transferred power to a variety of extra-parliamentary bodies, such as the European Central Bank and the European Court of Justice. Supported by the Maastricht and Lisbon treaties, for example, the EU has pushed member-states to accelerate liberalisation and market adjustment.

Finally, the dissolution of a party built on popular movements has eroded the local power bodies that have traditionally provided the democratic foundations of the Social Democratic movement.

The Liberating Welfare State

More than anything else, the success of Swedish Social Democracy is linked to the creation of a solidarity-based welfare policy.

The demand for a social safety net was an obvious part of the Social Democratic programme from the outset. Until the First World War, emphasis was placed on work-related reforms, such as worker protection and the eight-hour day, supplemented by a general formulation of society's obligation to provide for citizens in a humane manner in the event of illness and accident and in old age. Much of the concrete reform work was initially performed in cooperation with liberal forces, and the results were often modest. In the 1920s, the fight against unemployment, the demand for unemployment insurance and pensions, had few results.

In the 1930s, social policy became a central area for the Social Democrats. The minister of social affairs, Gustav Möller, was deeply committed to the fight against poverty and unemployment. But the more radical demands came from elsewhere – from the social engineers in the wake of the debate on the population crisis, or from women who at the local and central levels began to formulate demands on family policy and the right to work that were central to the future welfare society.

Only after the Second World War were the conditions in place for a broad social policy offensive on issues such as pensions, health insurance, housing policy, and child benefit. There was no general Social Democratic plan for how policy should be shaped. Möller's attempt to implement a system inspired by Beveridge's ideas of basic security complemented by voluntary supplementary insurance was rejected. Instead, under pressure from the LO, a system gradually emerged that relied on general and universal rights based on the principle of income compensation in case of illness and unemployment. The level of social insurance did not differ from that implemented in many of the other Fordist welfare societies in the 1950s and '60s. But the fact that the entire welfare system – education, health care, childcare, care for the elderly – was also financed, owned, and operated publicly gave it a special potential for social transformation.

However, it is not so easy to see, as Gøsta Esping-Andersen does, the solidarity-based welfare state consciously created by Social Democracy as a tool for a more comprehensive social transformation. The growth of the welfare state was largely the result of temporary political power relations involving much broader strata than Social Democracy alone.

The solidarity-based welfare state reached its peak in the 1970s. The reforms implemented then were possibly the most comprehensive ever undertaken anywhere. The reforms had a pronounced gender-equality bias; without in any way abolishing class differences, they helped to make Sweden more socially equal than it had ever been. At the same time, support for this welfare model was strong even within the core of the bourgeois parties.

The entire expanding welfare sector stood beyond the reach of capitalist exploitation, and it was seen as an important tool in a continued offensive to increase the space for politics at the expense of the market. The welfare state was also seen as an important precondition for growth – not least in its creation of hundreds of thousands of jobs for women, who were increasingly seeking to enter the labour market.

The neoliberal revolution changed this perspective fundamentally. Welfare spending was increasingly seen as a cost that hindered growth. Social Democrats themselves came to consider the welfare sector to be a problem. It had become too hypertrophied and burdensome, and therefore had to be cut back. It also needed to be made more efficient – and the solution offered was an increased market orientation. The Social Democrats also accepted deregulation, competition, and the privatisation of public services. The justification was that introducing these measures, among others, was the only way to save welfare.

The result has been a gradual erosion of the social safety net, and no one today sees the public sector as a possible battering ram to reduce the power of the market. Moreover, market-inspired welfare reforms have mainly benefited the middle class, not the working class.

The Bourgeoisie

The political bourgeoisie

A key reason for the Social Democrats' long tenure in government was that, for much of the twentieth century, the political parties of the Swedish bourgeoisie were relatively weak and divided. This partly reflects the political weakness and backwardness of the bourgeoisie, compared to economically dominant big business and the long-growing influence of the Social Democrats over the middle class.

The Conservative Party, now the Moderates, with its traditional base among landlords, the bureaucracy, and parts of big business, accepted the democratic breakthrough only with hesitation, and for a long time actively opposed social reforms. The Liberals, with a traditional base in the popular movements, had a much more positive attitude to modern welfare policy, and their economic policy after the Second World War was influenced by Keynesian ideas. The Farmers' Union, from 1957 the Centre Party, was relatively independent of the dominant political ideologies. It supported protective tariffs and accepted extensive state measures in support of agriculture.

The antagonism between the bourgeois parties was so great that it prevented closer cooperation. Even when the bourgeois parties gained a majority in parliament at the end of the 1950s, agreement remained impossible. One reason for this was suspicion of the other two parties of the conservative opposition to social reforms. Only when the conservatives accepted an expansion of the welfare state could the first steps be taken towards a joint challenge to the Social Democrats. The government formed in 1976 was still politically fragile. The bourgeois governments that have taken office since then have been considerably more united and determined. This has been facilitated by a shared commitment to a neo-liberal agenda, including public-sector liberalisation and tax cuts as key elements, primarily targeting the middle class. From 1979 until 2022, the Moderates were the dominant party on the right, while today they are outflanked by the right-populist Sweden Democrats.

The economic bourgeoisie

Swedish capital, on the other hand, has from the start been well organised and determined, and has often acted in unison and effectively, not least towards the labour movement. In party politics, it has moved freely

between the conservatives and the Liberals. There have been few prominent capitalists in leading positions in the bourgeois parties or in
bourgeois governments. They have, however, given the bourgeois parties
frequent ideological support and generous financial contributions
through foundations and think tanks.

Swedish capital is characterised by a strong concentration of ownership, dominated from the outset by finance capital based in the large
commercial banks. It is sometimes referred to as 'the fifteen families', but
its concentration has been greater than that. The Wallenberg group has
at times controlled through its bank, now the Skandinaviska Enskilda
Banken, around half of the leading Swedish companies.

Big business has also been extremely well organised through associations, today most importantly the Svenskt Näringsliv (Confederation
of Swedish Enterprise). It has been represented above all by spokes-
men of the Swedish export industry. Keeping the working class in its
place has been a central task from the outset. Section 32 and the general
strike it provoked in 1909 were important elements in this strategy. At
the same time, it developed good contacts at an early stage with the
parliamentary leadership of Social Democracy through the Liberal
Party. As we have seen, Wallenberg had great direct influence on the
Liberal and Social Democratic government that was formed in 1917.

Suspicion arose when a new generation wielding more radical language took over the leadership of Social Democracy at the same time as
social contradictions were increasing during the interwar economic
crises. The successful counter-offensive of the Right in the 1928 Cossack
elections can be seen as an expression of this.

When the Social Democrats after the war showed a tendency to
interfere in the internal affairs of industry, the powers behind capital put
their collective foot down by pumping huge resources into a counter-
campaign against any attempt at state-planned management in the
run-up to the 1948 elections. The Social Democrats escaped defeat
with a mere scare, quickly returning to a much more pro-business
policy. The result was the 'Swedish model' – the most coherent of the
many corporate systems that emerged under Fordism. With the Saltsjöbaden Agreement as a platform and the trade union movement as a
transmission belt, labour relations were regulated in a way that particularly benefited Swedish export industry.

After twenty-five years, this model was challenged – first of all from
the left. A radicalised trade union movement did not want to pay for

the heavy profits of big business with the solidaric wage policy. Employers' unrestricted right to manage and distribute work was deemed unacceptable, and the unions advocated ownership of business through wage-earner funds. The response was a gigantic counter-offensive from the Swedish business community. Hundreds of millions of kronors were pumped into the campaign. And they did not hesitate to take to the streets. At the same time, capital withdrew from most of the corporate bodies that still existed.

The Swedish economy has of course been affected by the increased globalisation and liberalisation of the international economy. Foreign influence on the Swedish stock market is now significant. Several classic Swedish companies, not least the car industry, are now under foreign ownership. At the same time, the major Swedish companies have long had most of their operations in other countries. Owners of relatively new companies, such as IKEA, H&M, and Tetrapak, and of high-tech companies such as Spotify have rapidly climbed the wealth ladder.

But economic power still lies with the traditional ownership groups based in the big banks, led by the Wallenbergs. The Confederation of Swedish Enterprise has continued to inject large sums into think tanks – not least to ensure the continued sell-off of what remains of public welfare provision.

Social Movements and Class Struggle

Göran Therborn has argued that a major reason for the Social Democrats' success is luck.[1] It is obvious that the party has been able to take advantage of the successive economic upturns that characterised parts of the twentieth century. The crisis during the 1930s turned into an international boom towards the end of the decade. The party's postwar rule coincided with the long postwar boom, which created the material basis for the Social Democratic welfare state. The temporary success of the Third Way around the turn of the twenty-first century coincided with international economic recovery.

---

1   Göran Therborn, 'A Unique Chapter in the History of Democracy: The Social Democrats in Sweden', in Klaus Misgeld, Karl Molin, and Klas Åmark, eds, *Creating Social Democracy: A Century of the Social Democratic Labor Party in Sweden* (University Park, PA: Pennsylvania State University Press, 1992), pp. 29ff.

But the conquests of the Swedish working class are also linked to waves of radicalisation, recurrent periods of strikes, increased social struggles, and the emergence of new social movements and revitalisation of existing ones. Virtually all important democratic and social reforms can be linked to such periods of intensified class struggle.

The democratic reforms after the First World War were a direct consequence of the massive hunger demonstrations initiated by working women, who were largely unorganised either politically or as labourers. The social reforms initiated in the 1930s came about amid the threat of widespread strike movements, a surge in trade union organisation, and women's struggle for the right to work and for basic social security. The spectacular peak of the solidarity-based welfare state in the 1960s and '70s coincided with the emergence of a series of new social movements with transformative ambitions, in which the women's movement played a decisive role, and with a strong radicalisation of the traditional labour movement, mainly expressed in a wave of spontaneous strikes.

Certainly, parts of the Social Democratic Party have often played a central role in these processes. The party has harboured dreams of a society free from injustice and class oppression; it has not been a monolithic organisation. Conflicting views have constantly been pitted against one another. The party and the LO have often had different views and interests. Women have had to fight against prejudice and patriarchal structures. This complicates Walter Korpi's argument about the power resources of the labour movement. As Jonas Pontusson has noted, Korpi sees the labour movement as a unified and rational actor with an inherent ambition of system-transformation.[2] But within Social Democracy there are different layers and interests that are sometimes at odds with each other, as well as subject to external pressures.

Swedish Social Democracy has been represented by skilled leaders at all levels, who have been able to translate many of the movement's demands and dreams into practical policies. But they have at the same time imposed constraints, particularly in not challenging capitalism and respecting the established parameters of political intervention.

As a result, the party leadership has often found itself at odds with the dynamics of social mobilisations. After the First World War, great

---

2   Jonas Pontusson, *The Limits of Social Democracy: Investment Politics in Sweden* (Ithaca, NY: Cornell University Press, 1992), p. 17.

efforts were made to persuade workers to abandon the struggle in the streets and squares, and to concentrate their efforts instead on the parliamentary assemblies at local and central levels – in other words, to give up the fight for a deeper democracy. In the 1930s, the party intensified its attempts to isolate the communists and socialists of various shades who had played an important role in the revitalisation of the social movements, so as to ensure that their efforts did not interfere with the rapprochement with the business world. When the force of 1970s radicalisation challenged the right of capitalism to decide over work conditions, and raised the question of workers' power over their jobs, the party leadership retreated, choosing to replace demands for wage-earner funds with the toothless Co-determination Act. Wildcat strikes were fought against, and social movement activists were monitored. When opposition to the neoliberal turn led to widespread trade union protests, the party leadership went on the counter-offensive.

In short, the Swedish welfare state is the result of a class struggle enacted by currents and movements whose base extended way beyond the confines of the Social Democratic Party.

The Limits of Reformism

All the elements that were once the strength of Social Democracy have today been eroded: the class base; organisational strength; a programme that aimed to provide broad sections of society with protection against the crises of capitalism; the decommodified, solidarity-based welfare state as the basis of a society built on equality and reduced social inequality; the idea of a democracy that also embraces work and the economy.

The reasons for the failure of Social Democracy are manifold. The years of ceaseless economic growth are gone. Social movements and social struggles have suffered serious setbacks. Most importantly, capitalism has proved a formidable adversary. But it is also clear that the strategy of reformism has been inadequate – in fact, a central cause of Social Democratic defeat.

The conquests of Social Democracy have been extensive. When we are faced with the brutality of our time, some measures in the old toolbox can seem almost boldly revolutionary, wrote the French Marxist and philosopher Daniel Bensaïd in one of his later texts. But what is missing in the box is a conscious strategy that transcends current boundaries in the direction of a more sensible order, opposing solidaristic welfare and social ownership to privatisations and the competition of all against all.[3] Reformism's faith in the possibilities of politics was so great that it refrained from challenging economic power. Swedish Social Democrats abstained from using the potential of the public sector for transcending the limits of capitalism. In withdrawing from the idea of wage-earners' funds, they ultimately abandoned the possibility of challenging private ownership. They were thus powerless when the neoliberal counter-revolution swept across the world. Stopping halfway, without attacking these basic power relations, is the defining weakness of reformism.

What reformism lacks is a strategy for intervening so deeply in the fabric of society that a different way of organising the world reveals itself. Every single demand is important in such a programme: the defence of social rights; the reduction of working hours and provision of decent working conditions; the fight against racism; the right to abortion; and, above all, drastic measures to stop the climate catastrophe.

At the same time, such a programme increasingly presupposes actions that challenge the market and capital. The re-creation of the solidary welfare state requires deep interventions in private ownership. Fair working conditions and the right to work require extensive restrictions on employers' rights. The climate crisis demands fundamental social change. Capitalist society's power and property relations based on exploitation, capital accumulation, and profit must be replaced.

There is no fixed, predetermined path towards such a socialist society. But it must be built from below, based on the exercise of democratic rule in which power is exercised collectively. Instead of building alternative power structures and harnessing the strength of the working class to challenge the economic power of capitalism, Swedish Social Democracy continued to link its future to the growth of capitalist industrial production.

The price for this error, and for being a part of the neoliberal turn, has been high. As Gerassimos Moschonas has pointed out, this is not a pragmatic correction of traditional reformist politics, but a redefinition

---

3   Daniel Bensaïd, 'Keynes, et après?', *Contretemps*, 11 August 2009.

of the party's entire structure and profile. When Social Democracy has lost its role as the representative of the interests of the working class, and broken with the political and programmatic roots that constitute its heritage, all that remains is a party of power without an ideological compass.[4]

---

4   Gerassimos Moschonas, *In the Name of Social Democracy: The Great Transformation, 1945 to the Present* (London: Verso, 2002), p. 150.

Index

production and productivity 3, 86,
139–40, 169, 192, 224
proletarian writers 108
pro-Nazi currents 101, 126
protectionism 100
Przeworski, Adam 42–3
public administration 119

racial biology 124–5
racism 46, 101, 124–5, 281
radicalisation 144, 177–8, 221–2, 224,
268, 270, 271, 277–8, 280
1960s 3, 6–7, 179–81, 237
environmental movement 191–4
international solidarity 195–202
international solidarity groups 180–1
the New Left 182–3
popular movements 104–8
retreat of 70
role of intellectuals 181
waves of 6–7, 279
women 178, 189–91
workers 183–9
youth 180
radicalism 1, 142, 146, 157
railways 12, 16
rationalisation and the rationalisation
movement 78–81, 141
rearmament 134
rebellion threat, 1918 60
recession, 1974–75 223
reform, and economic growth 78–81
reformism 78–81
limits of 280–2
reforms 152, 237, 270, 279
1860s 12–13, 13
1917 57
1918 60–1
1930s 128–9
1970s 177, 178, 215
bureaucracy 57
deceleration, 1938 130
education 170, 204–5
equilibrium parliament 215
gender equality 202
health care system 203–4
importance 104
labour-law 188–9
pensions 154–6

programme, 1920 67–71
welfare policy, 1950s 152–6
welfare state 202–7, 274, 275
refugees and refugee policy 127, 256,
262–3
Rehn, Gösta 148–9, 230–1
Rehn–Meidner Model 148–9, 152, 171,
173
religion, freedom of 14, 20
rent disputes 106–7
representation, increase in 36, 36
restructuring crisis 223
retreat 224–9
revolution 36–7
right to strike 85–6
right-wing tendency 38
Riksförbundet landsbygdens folk (RLF)
101–2
Rothstein, Bo 152
royal dictatorships 73
rural areas, early democratic development 10–11
rural flight 23–4, 173
Russia, invasion of Ukraine 264
Russian Civil War 64
Russian Revolution, 1905 23, 62
Russian Revolution, 1917 52–4, 58, 67,
72, 73
Russo-Japanese War 23
Ryner, Magnus 5

Sahlin, Mona 234, 257, 261
St Petersburg 51
Saltsjöbaden Agreement 131–3, 150,
186–7, 228, 271, 277
Samordnad näringspolitik (Coordinated
industrial policy) (LO) 171, 175
Sandel, Maria 26
Sanders, Bernie 1
Sandler, Rickard 25, 30, 65, 76, 90, 127,
166
Sassoon, Donald 133
Savings and Construction Association of
Tenants 107
sawmills 11, 15–16
Schmidt, Helmut 245
Schröder, Gerhard 246, 247
Schüllerqvist, Bengt 96
Schumpeter, Joseph 73